PUSH COMES TO SHOVE

TWYLA THARP

PUSH COMES TO SHOVE

LINDA GREY
BANTAM
B O O K S

NEW YORK • TORONTO • LONDON • SYDNEY • AUCKLAND

PUSH COMES TO SHOVE
A Bantam Book / December 1992

BOOK DESIGN BY YOLANDA CUOMO

Library of Congress Cataloging-in-Publication Data
Tharp, Twyla.
  Push comes to shove : an autobiography / Twyla Tharp.
    p.   cm.
  Includes index.
  ISBN 0-553-07306-0
  1. Tharp, Twyla.   2. Choreographers—United States—Biography.   3. Dancers—United States—Biography.   I. Title.
GV1785.T43A3   1992
792.8'2'092—dc20
[B]   92-17977
                                                                         CIP

Published simultaneously in the United States and Canada

Bantam Books are published by Bantam Books, a division of Bantam Doubleday Dell Publishing Group, Inc. Its trademark, consisting of the words "Bantam Books" and the portrayal of a rooster, is Registered in U.S. Patent and Trademark Office and in other countries. Marca Registrada. Bantam Books, 666 Fifth Avenue, New York, New York 10103.

PRINTED IN THE UNITED STATES OF AMERICA

FFG   0   9   8   7   6   5   4   3   2   1

AN AUTOBIOGRAPHY

1

People ask,
"How do you make a dance?"
My answer is simple.
"Put yourself in motion."

Cora and Jesse Tharp, 1905   Bertha and Raymond Confer, 1913

As a very small child I spent several months a year living with my Quaker grandparents in the nineteenth century. They worked their Indiana farms using no machinery whatsoever, so things were both very hard and very simple. I could put a seed into the ground and watch it grow; learn that everything from the hogs' steaming guts to scraps of cloth would find a use; or come out of the cellar, the tornado gone by, to see the huge weeping willow with its roots sticking straight up and not feel my world was threatened. Chaos was addressed in the Quaker meetings on Sundays and on Wednesday nights, when the community of Friends set about reconciling all life's events through love. Perhaps I would never fully understand all the whys and wherefores of the upside-down tree, but I could learn to feel comfortable with it in its new state and get on with things. Working the farms, we were all very pragmatic. The crops had to be in the ground, tended, harvested. Elegance was efficiency. Everything, including me, mattered.

Then, when I was eight, we moved from the Indiana farmland our Quaker families had tended for more than five generations to live on the edge of the California desert. The uprooting completely

John and Mary Tharp family, 1870 (above); my mother, 1928 (below)

destroyed my sense of home and place, leaving me with a restlessness ever since and marking the start of my attempts to understand life through motion. I always believed this relocation was my mother's idea, just as everything, when I was growing up, seemed to come from her. Mother is a strange combination of pragmatist and dreamer, capable of combining a hardheaded practicality with a willful self-delusion that can blind her to the devastating effects

her plans sometimes have on those she loves. Without being political, she was a feminist. She believed she could get anything done if she worked hard enough, and I began to see life in terms of Mother pushing the family into pursuing her vision of what it should be. Mother's name is Lecile, and by the time I was a teenager we children had dubbed her Lethal.

My mother's mother, Bertha, was at the center of my farm child's world. She was very beautiful and sharp-witted and the only woman in Jay County with a college education. In her quiet way she never allowed any of her children to forget that she had married beneath herself and that well-loved Pap, her handsome and kind husband, was still a farmer, labored when he read the Bible, and had lousy penmanship. She was austere and demanding, and even though there were breeding animals on the farm, her Quaker life reeked of prudery. All of Bertha's children were married for at least a year before they could bring themselves to tell her, and when I started dancing lessons Mother had to swear my scrawny little legs would be covered by pink tights.

My father's side of the family was a bit more liberal—vacationing in Florida, spending some time and money on themselves. When I was twelve, my father's mother, Cora, was the only one in the family who could bring herself to explain I wasn't dying with my first period. Cora liked to snuggle, even on warm summer evenings, and was very artistic, making paintings with seashells she collected. She also managed, amid a stark and barren landscape, to encourage my father, William Albert, to create three small ponds for goldfish and lily pads and to develop his own eye with paintings and drawings. All of my grandparents saw all of their children through college degrees, and so I suppose what I saw as wondrous places, these farms where I could feel self-contained and intact, were a harsh reality for the adults. All of them, including my father and mother, worked very hard to ensure that some of them would escape; no one who had to earn a living wanted to be tied to the vagaries of the earth. But I have always felt that anyone

Cora, 1906

My father, age two, in front of his
family's farmhouse, 1910

who is looking for absolutes could at least find consolation in nature's mysteries. This bottom line has helped me through thousands of studio hours when I am lost and searching for a way out.

Sweethearts as children, my parents eloped upon college graduation and shortly after moved into town. With his meager savings, my father bought a Ford dealership and started a construction firm, remodeled the car agency, and began leasing out tricky farm equipment that only he seemed able to repair. At the same time he

Tharp barn and stock, 1910

Lecile and William Tharp, 1932

encouraged my mother, whose degree was in music, to sign up students of a local piano teacher who had just died. Working hard for the next nine years, my parents saved the money necessary to start a family, and in 1941 my mother entered this new venture with characteristic efficiency: she delivered five babies in the next four years.

I was the first.

"She'll grow up to be famous," Mother wrote on a stork-filled birth announcement designed by my father, "of that we've no doubt." Changing a mundane "i" to a sexy "y," she turned the pedestrian Twila—borrowed from one Twila Thornburg, the reigning Pig Princess at the Eighty-ninth Annual Muncie Fair—into the infinitely more promotable Twyla. This spelling, she always said, would look better on a marquee.

During my childhood, Mother continued her own music studies. Her constant companion, I spent my first years listening to piano practice, a stream of out-of-context bits and pieces that trained me in music fundamentals. Music seemed as much a part of my mother as her voice or her touch. To this day, whenever I hear Mozart or Bach—and Gershwin, Fats Waller, and Cole Porter too,

Mother and me, 1942

for my mother practiced Tin Pan Alley as well as the classics—I feel loved.

Mother's second baby died shortly after birth. The tragedy caused her a deep, still-present pain, and, partly to ease her suffering, she began to give me ear training. I was a year and a half. Setting me on her lap, she showed me "the milk route of the fifths," and taught me to distinguish between major and minor, diminished and augmented triads. As we worked, she found I had absolute pitch, a natural ability to pick out on the piano whatever she sang. So, when I was four, she took me to an expert in children's piano.

Miss Remington approached teaching creatively, color coding the keys. C was yellow, D was red, E green, F brown, G purple, A was black, and B was blue. To this day, tones suggest both color and emotion to me: C is brightness and clarity, D is fire, E is cool, F is dense, G complex, a hybrid red and blue; A is dark, opaque, B rich and vibrant. "Miss Rem" recorded my progress in a dog-eared blue notebook, grading my weekly assignments with stars and decorating them with cheerful picture stamps—Santas, robins, butterflies, chicks, and flowers. From some lessons written in

Miss Rem's notebook, 1945

that book, it's clear her approach was physical as well as aural. Many of her instructions could easily become dance: "Hands flat on the table, pull yourself up and drop yourself down (don't use knees), this is the way to play." "Seven little keys are we: ABCDEFG. Backward let me hear you say: GFEDCBA." "From key to key is half a step which I must take. But when I leave a key between, a whole step I shall make."

With my mother and the twins, 1944

As Mother's other babies arrived—twin boys when I was three, followed by a sister eleven months later—my musical excellence became a private conspiracy between her and me. At seven I was entered into the National Federation of Music Clubs' piano competition in Indianapolis and came out at the top of the junior division against kids twice my age. When Mother announced my triumph in the *Dunkirk Star*, I realized it would be through performing that I could connect with her.

My father was another matter; I never found a way to connect with him. He always congratulated me on my accomplishments, but my performances did not bring forth the troubling warmth and darkness, the absolute bonding that working to excel forged between my mother and me.

In first grade, I threw a tantrum when my straight A's were marred by one A minus. Certainly both my parents had a hand in creating my early perfectionism. My father's own sternness and insistence on distinction helped set an impossible standard for me to follow. "I don't care if you dig ditches, as long as you dig the best ditches," he liked to say, and to this day I cannot sing "Happy Birthday" out loud without extreme self-consciousness or tears, my perfect pitch telling me how poor my voice is. On the job eighteen hours a day, he was a local legend of energy, speed, and honesty. During the war, he worked several farms in addition to his other businesses. He would plow with two tractors simultaneously, tying off the steering wheel of the front one and then running back to drive the second until he had to turn the front wheel again. One day he slipped between the two machines and the second ran over him. Only his leather hunting jacket—shredded by the tractor— saved his life.

All these exploits made him intimidating and distant to me. If it were not for blurry baby photographs proving the contrary, I would swear he never touched me—except once for a beating he gave me for lying, and a second time, by way of good-bye, just before he died.

· · ·

With my parents, 1942

In 1947, when I was six, my parents made four trips to California to oversee the drive-in movie theatre they were building in a California desert town named Rialto. I sensed my world was about to change and I didn't understand. I became very uneasy. Suddenly I needed to pee a dozen times a night. At the same time, the twins and my sister, Twanette, became totally unmanageable. The twins, Stanley and Stanford, were both called Stan because my father couldn't tell them apart, a responsibility I often took on for him. My brothers and sister lived in a world of perpetual confusion and energy, functioning as a team—"the three little ones." In the nursery they developed their own language—a not unheard-of occurrence among twins. By the time Mother realized her children weren't speaking English, they had evolved an entire vocabulary which only I could understand and interpret: the word for Father, for instance, was a bass babble that sounded exactly like a tractor, a word coined from Daddy's constantly being near large motors. Many of their words weren't sounds, but gestures, slaps, claps, and hand signals, and translating their private dialect into English helped me realize movement could mean many things.

When the twins were three, Mother tried a new strategy: thinking separation would break their solidarity and force them to speak English, she kept one at home and sent her other children off to

Left, Stanley Wayne and Stanford Vaughn; right, the twins with Twanette, 1948

different relatives for several months. I went to my Grandma Bertha's farm, and while I was there Sarah Margaret Cherry Confer, Pap's mother, died. I remember her all in black, laid out on the bed in the downstairs north bedroom, where she had borne her four children. Her husband had died around the time of the delivery of their last child, and she then managed to work off the mortgage even though the house burned down and her oldest son, Homer, died all in the same year. She plowed the fields, tended the animals, got in the harvest, and on retirement traveled throughout Jay County as a paramedic. My mother was proud to have been given Margaret for her middle name after this tough and dearly loved small woman.

Mother's plan to teach her children English failed. Whenever the family was reunited, the twins simply swapped places, baffling and exhausting the adults. Mother gave up, and with our parents in California to oversee the drive-in's construction, the kids' madcap play became extreme. Posting Twanette on an ottoman to warn them of approaching adults, they would set about stacking snow in the living room, run downstairs to unplug the freezer, smash the piano bench through an antique cherry chair, kill small mice in the hallways, make mixtures out of Tide detergent and Mother's best perfume. Once they found three thousand dollars she had stashed behind a loose brick in the basement, and flushed it down the toilet. Another time, one twin tried jumping out the second-floor window while the other climbed up the chimney. They loved to answer the door naked, diapers wrapped around their heads.

One day, after my parents returned, we were in the kitchen. Mother was stuffing a spoonful of some gunk into one twin's mouth, then moving the food assembly-line fashion down to the other kids —she had given up on separate spoons when she found them sucking each other's thumbs.

"Won't it be grand," she began, "when you get through high school and start your own life in college. . . ."

Her ruse of a rosy future didn't fool me.

"I like it just fine right here with all my friends and in this house," I replied. I was the best piano-playing kid in town and the smartest in school. Why would I want to go off and have to start all over again? So what if my parents were gone so much they were no longer dependable? I could live with my grandparents on the farms. Through all my parents' absences, my grandparents were always there for me and I knew they really loved me.

But protest was useless. We were going. Mother had it all fig-

First-grade class, 1947

Daddy and Grampa Jesse, 1930

ured out. First the Ford Motor Company was sabotaging my father, giving him only four cars a month to sell. He could do much better in California with its growing population, where he would sell Chryslers. Obviously, it was impossible to run the drive-in from Indiana. Besides, there was an impending polio epidemic in Indiana and only clean dry desert air in California, and of course there was Hollywood, where I would have a much better shot at being a star than stuck in Jay County. Rialto, California—where we were going—was less than a hundred miles away from the City of Dreams.

So on a morning early in August 1949, we piled into the car, both sets of grandparents there to see us off. My father was particularly close to his family. He and his father, Jesse, often hunted rabbit in the pockets of wildness still on the farmland and went together on extended trips to Michigan for larger game. All the grandparents were bitterly saddened at the thought of losing children and grandchildren, and the four of us clung to the old folks. Grampa Jesse used his familiar ploy to spring all us kids loose: he tossed a handful of change from his pocket like seed to birds. The trick worked every time, and now the three little ones went for it. I didn't. My parents had to pry me loose from my Grandma Cora. We started driving, and I remember the flat landscape disappearing into a nothingness, an emptiness of which I'm reminded every time I enter a studio and am enclosed by its blank walls.

Traveling west, I mainly threw up. Mother claimed my upset stomach was from bad chocolate milk or greasy french fries, but I knew it was two thousand miles of being lost. The three little ones punched each other the whole way, cried about toys we had left behind, tried to tickle my father's neck with a Japanese wind-up butterfly that kept tangling in his hair, and rattled off the make and model of every passing car.

Father drove over the speed limit because Mother insisted we had to do eight hundred miles a day and check into a motel before dark, when all the No Vacancy signs went up. I looked out, imagining myself holding a long, huge blade from the window, leveling everything in the car's path to the height of my chin. I was really homesick, missing my grandparents and the growing things on their farms, and as I saw cars passing with extra water bags hanging from their radiators—which we didn't have—I was pretty sure we were never going to make it across these flat, empty, ugly, dried-out, scary mud beds from which the heat rose in curly lines. We were just going to die right there, runaways from home.

The worst part, however, was stopping for the night. I wanted to stay at the interesting-looking motels—the ones shaped like wigwams, spaceships, huge pickles and hamburgers, or places featuring gigantic, garishly painted plastic cows, tires, fat children, or dinosaurs. But we always seemed to reach these places too early in the day to stop, and anyway, our parents would never have let us stay in a motel that proclaimed itself a petrified log, a giant sequoia, or a meteor crater. Since it was "only for the night," they went for the cheapest, most rundown choice available, and we would pull into a cardboard-thin, regular-shaped joint with an absolutely boring dinner menu that definitely favored hamburgers over steak.

Coming in the door to the diner, an adorable two boys–two girls family, we presented a standard American picture. However, the three little ones—deeply engaged in their continued fantasy games of warriors, diplomats, kings, and subjects—soon put a stop to that. I prayed for two booths and for my parents to let me sit with them, separate from the little ones, allowing me to pretend my mother, my father, and I were a regular family, and this horrid appendage over there, another. But no, we all sat at one table, and my mother ordered for everyone, hamburgers and french fries all around. By the time the food was set on the table, one of the Stans would have negotiated or pried away whatever shiny thing—nut, bolt, or dime—the other Stan might have spied between the car and the restaurant; Twanette would be playing whichever side looked as though it might keep her from getting hit; my father would have his eyes closed and be nodding his head from "pushing" the car its six or so hundred miles for the day; and I would have retreated behind the cover of my book, my attempt at proving that someone at this table was a rational human being. Only my mother looked as though she belonged—august, fully in control.

Mornings we were up and in the car before the crack of dawn, making our practically comatose way from the motel-room cots into our clothes, then out into the bracing air, my mother's paranoia reminding us, as we threaded our way through the parking lot, to "keep it down," for she was always afraid we would disturb someone, someplace, every moment of our lives. Once in the car, we huddled asleep again, until everyone needed to pee and we had to stop for breakfast anyway.

Late in the fourth day, we finally made it into Rialto, a community stuck along Route 66, somewhere between Fontana and San Bernardino, California, a one-story, pastel-colored, standard Old West town with a single main street, a stand of eucalyptus trees, three civic buildings—the bank, the library, and the police station —and a few stores. There was no ocean—we had been promised waves—only orange groves, their filthy smudge pots burning to keep the trees from freezing on cold nights. The groves were tended by Mexicans who had settled here hoping to find jobs at the Kaiser steel mill in Fontana or with the forestry division rangers who specialized in fighting Southwestern brush fires. This was the high-flying community to whom my father would sell glitzy DeSotos and Plymouths and for whom my mother would exhibit the finest Hollywood features.

We headed immediately for Mother's outdoor movie palace. She had commissioned the QRS Sign Company to construct the drive-in marquee before our arrival. Daddy had designed the neon welcome mat, a seventy-foot vertical support for "FOOTHILL" and a ninety-foot horizontal section for "DRIVE-IN THEATRE," with lots of space for all those glorious stars and film titles. Cantilevering the whole thing was a huge musical scroll, the F clef a mad study in Miami Beach deco. Mother couldn't wait to see this spectacular manifesto of the cultural standards she was going to bring to an artistic wasteland.

Foothill marquee, 1955

But what greeted us at the theatre grounds was a mess. Over the weekend a seventy-five-mile-an-hour wind had swept through Rialto, flattening the marquee; the huge sign lay strewn all over the highway. Although bone-tired like the rest of us, Mother always had reserves for anger, and she was furious. The sign should have withstood hundred-and-twenty-mile winds! Those QRS people were going to pay! Nobody would take advantage of us again. She would see to that!

I wasn't so sure. To me, cowering in the back seat of the '47 Ford, it seemed we were stranded in the only home we had left.

2

When I go into a studio I know exactly what I want, but never quite how I'll get it. Each dance is a mystery story.

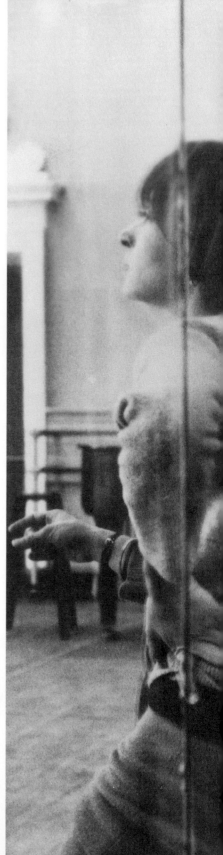

We fit perfectly into Rialto. The town was made for the homeless. You didn't live there, setting down roots, but used it up and drifted on, leaving the place to become one more ghost town. My parents built their new home in Quail Canyon, a wild, unsettled area directly over the San Andreas Fault and so near the foothills that my mother remained perpetually terrified of the brush fires that singed the dry mountains every fall. She kept all her important papers packed in boxes, ready to be moved at a moment's notice. California encouraged impermanence.

The house itself was built by hand—my father's, that is, and those of his infrequently appearing Mexican helper. I remember seeing this helper balanced on a high stepladder, using a long board to brace the huge timbers my father was hammering twenty feet overhead into the living-room ceiling. Building the house cost my father a year of backbreaking labor, often in temperatures that reached one hundred and twenty degrees in the shade: a modern

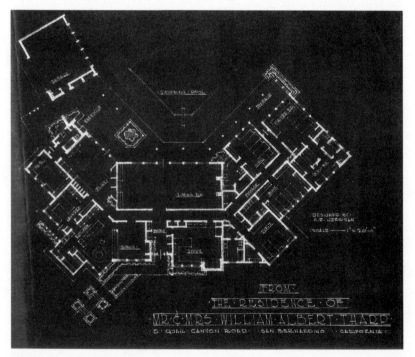

Blueprint: Quail Canyon house

mansion, six thousand square feet, U-shaped, ultra-equipped; Mother's dream house. My father did everything himself—plumbing, wiring, masonry for the patio, barbecue pit, and three brick fireplaces, all the built-in furnishings, finished in my mother's personally selected designer turquoise. Then he moved on to his next project and left us to try to convert this construction into a home.

It wasn't easy. The place was cavernous and empty, a sprawling, three-quarter-acre study in excess that featured, among other

Quail Canyon living room under construction, 1949

things, a laundry room with a sewing surface large enough to lay out patterns plus an industrial-sized washer and drier; a formal dining room (never used); a forty-by-twenty-foot living room complete with Steinway grand refinished in the motif turquoise my mother had picked for the place; a phone booth; a guest wing; separate suites for the boys and girls; and a playroom that included a "practice section" featuring a built-in tap floor, ballet barres, and closets filled with acrobatics mats, batons, ballet slippers, pointe shoes, castanets, tutus, and even capes for matador routines.

Most excessive of all was the kitchen. With forty-five running feet of counter space, it contained the latest appliances and design features, including a full freezer, refrigerator, two sinks, desk area, and marble candy block, all conveniences that, because my mother never cooked, were never used. At our house you opened the icebox at your own risk: more often than not the food was moldy. Mostly we ate out at the drive-in. Often my dinner consisted of Coke syrup, straight from the tin, and mountains of candy corn, red hots, ice cream bonbons, and—my favorite—the salt and kernels that fell through the grating as the fully opened popcorn was scooped into bags. By some miracle of nature, I still have perfect teeth.

It was in this kitchen that my mother and father held their only fight—at least, the only one that I ever witnessed. Occurring shortly after we had moved in, the flare-up centered around the eating alcove's seven-foot-wide, frying pan-shaped, red Formica and turquoise-painted table, an enormous piece of work that my father had constructed after first building a prototype of my mother's design for her approval. Now, having completed the final version, with its built-in lazy Susan, he invited my mother to sit down and try the table for height.

"Too high," she promptly said. "I have to raise my arms. See, if I were cutting something on a plate—"

"Move your chair closer," said Father.

"No, this is a comfortable distance. It should be like playing a piano; the hands should rest easily."

"But it's not a piano," Father observed. "We can get different-height chairs."

"I like this chair," said Mother. "Besides, it shouldn't be that hard to make a table properly."

Conversations were rare in our family, arguments never heard. Practicing in the playroom, I was drawn by my parents' voices to spy on them.

"Goddamn it!" he yelled. Cursing was a major transgression in an ex-Quaker family, and whenever my father did I always felt a chill run down my spine: if my Grandma Bertha was correct, he would now go straight to hell. "Why did you say it was O.K. before?"

"It wasn't O.K. before. I said it was a little high."

"And then I cut it down!"

"Get your measure. See if it's thirty-six inches from the floor. That's what I said I wanted."

Spying from the playroom, I was frightened. I had never heard him scream at my mother before.

He measured the table; thirty-six inches exactly.

"It doesn't matter what the numbers say," said Mother. "It's still too high."

Then it happened: my father picked up a hatchet from the floor and hurled the weapon at my mother's head. I went cold. My mind could not take in what I had seen. What was he doing?

He missed only by a couple of inches and promptly left home— probably forever, I figured. But after two days of no communication, he returned. In my better moments, I think of the alienation in my family as theatre, one-acters by John Guare: the loony triplets ripping from one end of the place to the other, frantically gibbering, babbling, and gesturing; the mother, her sand-castle life built equally of determination and whimsical hyperbole, blithely sacrificing lives to build her empire; the father, returning from the forest hunt with an elk or wildebeest or both slung over his shoulder, sending hatchets flying above everyone's heads. But on my sad days there seems no humor in the situation, only pain. I can still feel the terror of those forty-eight hours when my father was gone.

Mother's approach to education was even more determined than her approach to housing. She gauged the quality of my education by my grades, and if I received less than an A minus, the teacher was considered "possibly inept" and would be closely watched. If I continued to slip, Mother pulled the plug, once actually marching into class, pronouncing the mathematics instruction inadequate, and yanking me—to use her word—out of the class then and there.

Her diligence had two consequences. First, I attended seven different schools between third grade and my freshman year at college. Second, I was a nervous wreck because of the constant pressure of knowing that anything less than perfection meant failure and could get me transferred—which meant starting over yet again.

Monitoring my academic progress was only the beginning. Wanting me to be prepared for any and everything, Mother's real tour de force was her extracurricular agenda: a selection of teachers from a one-hundred-mile radius to provide me with "the very, very finest training" in baton, ballet, toe, flamenco, drums, elocution, painting, viola, violin, acrobatics, shorthand, German, and French.

Dance started at the Vera Lynn School of Dance in San Bernardino—offering the usual neighborhood dance class staples of tap, toe, and acrobatics, as well as occasional specialties like Hawaiian dance, rope twirling with tapping, or the inevitable combination, toe tap—and proceeded to the Mraz sisters, two French girls who had married dentists and moved to Fontana, where they taught in a garage. Always big on credentials, my mother, like many Americans, believed the best recommendation was being foreign—preferably French, but failing that, at least English. There on the concrete floor I was first presented with the concept of "port de

My teacher, 1953; Right, me at nine

bras," "de la finesse," and "avec grâce"—all of which made me miss the hard-hitting tap routines at the old Vera Lynn studio.

Mr. Windoes in San Bernardino taught violin; piano was Edythe Wagner, a Juilliard graduate who lived in Redlands. Drums were Mr. Parsons, a former percussionist with the Boston Symphony, who gave private lessons in Bloomington. Flamenco, castanets, and cymbals were taught by Enrico Cansino, an uncle of Rita Hayworth's—enough said on the credentials front. I always liked the heavily accented heel work of the masculine flamenco much more than the ornate skirt-flashing and castanet-clicking of Enrico's very young third wife. Baton twirling was Ted Otis, an ex-world champion at the University of Southern California, who taught in Pomona. All told, Mother once estimated, she drove me thirty thousand miles a year to one lesson or another.

I never questioned this mad schedule. As we drove from town to town, I prepared homework by the glove compartment's light, or replayed lessons in my head, recalling where and why in a combination I had dropped a baton, or visualizing the fingering in the opening bars of MacDowell's "To a Wild Rose." I never stopped to ask, "Why am I doing this?" I just went along, trusting that my mother had some grand master plan we were accomplishing together.

When I was twelve, I entered a new world. Mother yanked me from the Mrazes and began a twice-weekly, two-hundred-mile

round trip to Beatrice Collenette, Mother's ultimate credential coup. "Herbert Hoover's descendants went there," she often said. "Everybody was somebody except us."

As a child, Beatrice Collenette had been selected by Anna Pavlova to be taken into her home—London's Ivy House—with six other young ballerinas. Trained by Pavlova and her master, Enrico Cecchetti, Collenette later toured with Pavlova, accompanying the great ballerina on her last tour in 1931, when she contracted pneumonia. "Pavlova traveled democratically with the corps. That was how she caught the draft," the now plump Collenette told us in her aristocratic voice. She still literally worshiped at the feet of the great dancer: over her desk stood a huge blowup of Pavlova poised delicately in razor-sharp toe shoes. Much later I learned the negative had been altered. But at that time I thought, What wondrous control. Balanced on an area smaller than a dime, Pavlova showed no tension whatever in her shoulders, arms, or legs.

Anna Pavlova with students. Collenette is fourth
from left, back row

Students in Collenette's class, dressed uniformly in cotton leotards and stiff tutus, were divided into five color-coded classes. After working very hard, I was admitted to the upper class and allowed to wear deep blue. And toe shoes. This last was a fantastic accomplishment. Since we arrived in Rialto I had worn toe shoes to show off, running downtown on pointe, pulling behind me a little red wagon loaded with comic books to exchange in the downtown drugstore. But now the shoes were for real, legitimate. I applied myself to the endless lifting and lowering of the body's weight through the toes. I seemed out of the pull of gravity as, using the barre on the wall for support, I told myself that if I worked hard enough at these fundamentals, I would develop the ease and comfortable grace that made life in toe shoes a natural thing.

With her sense of proprieties and right form, Collenette stressed the basics rather than the show-off aspects of ballet. She also provided live music, not just records, played by a blind pianist whose melodies filled my body with a desire to express rhythms and emotions. The pianist played with her Seeing Eye dog still in the harness at her feet. I am so nearsighted that as a child, before I had glasses, I could not see into the mirror. So, of course, I understood that you play and dance by feel, not sight.

Collenette followed the traditional series of exercises ballet dancers have pursued for several centuries. The form begins at the barre with pliés, demi- and grand, warming and stretching the knees and the large muscle groups of the legs. Then work begins more specifically, starting with battements tendus for the ankles and feet, and progressing by degrees, rond de jambe, to frappé to grands battements, each exercise using the whole anatomy but inching the focus higher and higher up the leg until finally the critical and fragile groin muscles are fully stretched. (Since all ballet nomenclature is in French—because of its seventeenth-century codification under Louis XIV—Mother paid special attention to my tutoring in the language. My French is still best described as *amusant*, and my flat, twangy accent will break the ice at any rehearsal.)

Away from the barre, the center exercises begin with tendu, once again emphasizing the feet—but this time without the barre's support. Class then moves on to petite allegro, for speed and final warming of the muscles, so that the adagio, the very slow controlled movements, can be executed. These are the most difficult. Some exercises have a bit of leeway, but the adagio does not. The slightest tensing or quivering is always immediately and painfully evident.

Then comes the petite batterie, lifting the body into the air, giving special attention to the articulation in the feet. These exercises set up the big jumps, the traveling exercises that climax with jetés and combinations of various movements on the diagonal, where one covers the most distance in a rectangular space.

Any time left in the ninety-minute class—and often even if there was not, because Collenette knew we loved the treat—was devoted to the pointe shoes. Everyone rushed to get the shoes from her dance bag, the heels neatly folded back, the ribbons wound about and tucked in. We stuffed in the "bunny pads"—nowadays dancers use nothing or wads of paper towels, but we had the real fuzzy skins of rabbits shaped for our toes. Actually, we were eager to suffer; everyone knew that Pavlova's feet were very sensitive—one of Collenette's jobs had been to break in shoes for "La Maîtresse" before a performance—and we thrilled to hear of the ballet macho of Pavlova exiting as the Dragonfly in a trail of bloody footprints.

We ran to the barre for the relevés, stretching the ligaments. Then we took our places in the center. Everyone was assigned a place according to her level of accomplishment: best in front. While I found this competitive arrangement proper, I became "guinchy"—tight, nervous, and drawn in—at the thought of not making it to the front. I held back, not wanting to expose myself, afraid that I might fall out of a pirouette or lose my spot, building barricades of fear inside myself at the thought that I might not be excellent. Many years later I would have to work hard to overcome this fearfulness in order to reach any real accomplishment.

Class always ended with a gesture of révérence. Collenette pushed herself up from her chair with difficulty, responding to our deep curtsies with a dignified nod. I felt a sense of connection as I acknowledged the gift of her past, the past of Pavlova and the ballerinas before her, an unbroken line of dancers, a family of greatness and beauty and dignity, which, through the hard work of

In costume for Collenette's recital, 1956

my body, I might join. I felt humbled to have so much entrusted to my keeping.

Of course, all these lessons required endless hours of preparation at home. I became my own jailer early on, meticulously drafting time-efficient schedules. The following dates from 1953, when I was twelve:

Winter Schedule

Monday
6:00 - 6:15 : put practice clothes on
6:15 - 7:15 : Ballet
7:15 - 8:00 : Violin
8:00 - 8:30 : get dressed, clean room, breakfast
8:30 - 9:00 : go to school
9:00 - 3:00 (P.M.) : school
3:00 - 3:15 : go to Mr. Windsors
3:15 - 4:00 : Violin lesson
4:00 - 4:30 : come home, snack, practice clothes
4:30 - 5:00 : Baton
5:00 - 5:30 : Tap
5:30 - 6:00 : Baton
6:00 - 7:00 : kids Ballet (go to show once a month)
7:00 - 7:30 : kids Baton
7:30 - 8:00 : kids Tap
8:00 - 9:00 : homework, shorthand
9:00 - 9:30 : eat supper, get ready for bed

My sense that one had to be in control every moment of every day was reinforced by my mother's rigid self-discipline: I never saw her with empty time on her hands. By the time I was eight, leisure, if it ever came, produced only dread. Recreation was completely foreign; it mystified me how kids could play together, simply inventing their days as they went along, not knowing each morning exactly how the day would unfold.

I was especially threatened by Twanette and the twins. They thought of life as a game. Terrified by this unknown concept, I distanced myself even more from them. In the big house Mother had planned to put girls in the pink room, boys in the maroon. However, we found that my parents' children didn't naturally divide by gender but by age: them and me. They were a tight-knit society, I was an outsider. They were rebels, I was a collaborator. They were creative, I was a grind. The end came quickly. One day, Twanette carefully littered just her side of our room with wads of newspaper. Unable to live with such clutter, I soon after moved into the guest wing. Serving as a buffer zone, I sopped up most of my mother's attention; the three little ones banded together, thwarting her ambitions on their behalf. Once Mother decided we should be a string quartet, but after only a few sessions the three little ones took their instruments to school and bashed them up in an assembly skit. Eventually they would manage to have cars, run for school office, go out on dates, make it to the beach parties the night after the prom. All of this would remain a mystery to me, because my schedule allowed no room for extracurricular social activities.

Once I had moved into the guest wing, I considered myself an only child. Lonely, isolated, missing my grandparents terribly, I made the guest bedroom a memorial to my Indiana past, complete with Currier & Ives prints, an antique spinning wheel and yarn winder, a cherry-wood doctor's secretary holding all my cat's-eye and block-pattern nineteenth-century pressed-glass pieces. I also had an old set of doctor's implements complete with a folding saw for amputations. In my early teens I decided to become a doctor— medicine and dancing seemed the only professions in which you could legitimately look at naked bodies.

Alienated and restless, I identified with my father. He too went stir crazy much of the time. Whenever he couldn't get along with my mother, or when he wasn't building for a long stretch of time, he went hunting, using bows he designed to compensate for his small size. He fished in Baja, bagged elk and caribou in Alaska,

KUDU AND CONQUERORS — W. A. Tharp of San Bernardino (right) poses with native gun bear- er and tracker who helped bag kudu during safari in Bechuanaland, Africa, early this month.

Sitatunga Brought Down on Safari

Rare Trophy Bagged in Only 30 Minutes by S.B. Hunter

went on safari in Africa. He seemed intent on conquering one of every kind of creature on the face of the earth.

My sister became a vegetarian at a young age to protest the bear and venison that appeared at family barbecues, but I ate mine singed, as close to raw as possible. I felt there was honor in my father's solitary treks into the wilds; he was confronting the basics of living. Hunting with him in Utah, just the two of us, I wandered one afternoon into a meadow not far from our camp. Suddenly an elk appeared at the edge of the clearing and paused. I quietly lifted my bow, drew, released. The elk snorted and twisted his body—I could see the arrow lodged in his shoulder. In that moment I too recoiled, sensing his hurt. But while I felt disgust at my own power

My father (second from left), 1962

of destruction, in the moment of impact I imagined I had become a member of my father's lodge.

In the little free time available to me as an adolescent, I fought my anxiety and isolation by reading. Seemingly miles and miles of books crowded and stacked the cupboards that ran the length of the house. When my restlessness grew intolerable, I prowled the halls, selecting indiscriminately from the accumulated Book-of-the-Month-Club novels, issues of *Reader's Digest, National Geo-*

graphic, and *Popular Mechanics*, the *Encyclopaedia Britannica*, classics—Plato, Shakespeare, Milton—medical books, biographies, and Grove's *Complete Dictionary of Music*. By the time I was ten I had read the Bible twice—once in a child's abbreviated version—and I picked up *Anthony Adverse*, learning God knows what, though my mother always seemed a little ashamed that I had found it. Within a short time, I began to skim all the popular novels that my mother ordered, hoping a historical novel with some sex would slip through. Those that did generally offered romances with clear, strong men pursuing coquettish women who, teasing at first, soon became enticingly passive, an attitude I wished to adopt but couldn't, since everything in my life pushed me in the opposite direction: disciplining myself to gain control over my life, my future, and by extension, over any who would share it with me.

By the time I entered tenth grade at Pacific High School, I was known as a bookworm. I wore short pixie haircuts and glasses —sharp-cornered pink metal affairs to poke the eye out of any venturesome boy—and prim, expensive Lanz dresses, the Fifties approximation of Victorian England. I made sure to keep a book under my arm so that I could pop my nose into it if anyone, especially a boy, might head my way to say hi: I wanted to make it absolutely obvious to everyone that I had much more important things to deal with than anything they might have to say. No one ever stopped me, but had some friendly, brave boy said, "Nice weather, isn't it?" I would have known, even though I'd never heard his last name and probably wasn't sure of his first, that what he really meant was, "Want to screw?" and my answer would have been, "We have to get married first." (I had not read *Peyton Place*, by flashlight under the covers late at night, for nothing.) My reservations were exactly what my mother intended. As she once told an interviewer, "Twyla just didn't like most of those kids. And she didn't have time to squander with them after school because we had places to go. The boys were afraid of her—they knew she could mop them up in math and science. And dating and proms would have gotten in her way."

Senior class photo, 1958

Mike Mellon, 1956

Nonetheless, I did have two defiantly outside-the-mainstream friends. Donna Becker, wealthy, overweight, and the only Jew in school, and Mike Mellon, a piano prodigy who, several years after high school graduation, hanged himself in the State Institution for the Insane at Patton. Mike was my best friend, gentle but with an evil sense of humor. We talked a lot about the meaning of life.

The one break from my studies and bookwormishness was the drive-in. From our arrival in Rialto until my departure for college, I worked nightly at the theatre in the summer and every weekend during the school year. I "put up" hot dogs (prestuffing the meat into rolls and rationing mustard and relish into little paper cups), popped and bagged corn, stacked candy on the shelves and ice-cream bonbons in the freezer, waited on customers, and worked the box office. When business at the box office or snack bar was slow, I watched the movies and cartoons, learning in the process what an audience likes or doesn't, because when they were bored we'd have a rush at the snack bar and I was expected to be in there.

The drive-in was strictly my mother's baby. She decided how much the hot dogs cost and picked the dates for the "all-you-can-bring-in-your-car-for-a-buck" nights. She hired the help, counted and banded the paper money, and rolled all the coins, keeping a sharp lookout for any valuable collectors' items; she selected the projection, snack bar, and office equipment, took the money to the bank, and kept all the books—eventually she became a certified public accountant at Valley Junior College, where she also studied marketing techniques. Of course she selected all the movies, screening only pictures that wouldn't offend the community: Westerns—Roy Rogers and Dale Evans sent her a card, personally thanking her for her loyalty through the years; Doris Day and Rock Hudson comedies; Astaire-Rogers and Gene Kelly musicals. Once, after showing a borderline picture—*The Moon Is Blue*, in 1953— she received admonishing calls from the local Catholic priest, who objected to the use of the word "virgin" and to a character who happened to be illegitimate.

To me, this sort of repression was disappointing. Early on I disagreed with my mother's choices of films. Unsure about a lot of things and mostly willing to take her opinions, I was nonetheless certain she was fooling herself about the drive-in. From the movies to the couples in the cars, the drive-in was about one thing and one thing only: sex. Everything there was illicit to me; that was the place's overpowering attraction. Walking the ramps, flashlight in hand, I counted heads in those cars Mother suspected of gate-crashing. Breathing the balmy air, heavy with the smell of orange blossoms, I experienced the drive-in as one large piece of pop art, a three-dimensional enactment of the world's great erotic traditions. Scouring the cars for extra heads, I strained to get a closer look at the bodies tangled together on the floor, or pushed into back seat corners, and saw couples in every wanton position and stage of undress.

Looking away a moment, gasping for breath from the sudden heat warming my stomach, I would see the screen, and that too was to die. There, four stories high, was a close-up, a man reaching out for a woman's throat, taking her gently, easily, one of his hands at the nape of her neck and the other—off-screen—close to the base of her spine, reaching ever closer to the openings of her body, until their lips brushed and settled onto one another. My God, what did Mother think she was showing people? The sighs and studied cries, the carefully coached embraces, the limbs first demurely revealed, then gradually stripped, the seductive and delicate kisses, the men's direct, deep gazes—these were the masterpieces of the greatest love experts of all time, created for one purpose and one purpose alone: to make people want to make love. The art of these Fifties movies was in sustaining forever the moment before sex. They were a great big come-on, arousing without satisfying, and I sensed early that this perpetually suspended condition could be translated into art.

On those rare occasions when I brought my mother to a violating car (which I did as infrequently as possible, just enough to keep my job), her outrage at the sexual shenanigans seemed out of place. To me it was unthinkable for these couples not to respond to the passion pouring from the giant masters. "Come along," Ava and Lana and Marlon and Clark sang. To me the sex was quite pure; it was my mother who was prurient. Mother even tried to stop my father from kissing or holding her in front of her children, and physical life in my Quaker family was neither easy nor casual. Touching was definitely something you thought twice about, almost an invasion of privacy. Limbs were to be kept covered, and my father often protested that my mother's cap sleeves were too short. All the same, as I grew into adolescence, I started wearing the tightest and shortest possible short shorts, cut just below the butt, with little sandals or ballerina slippers, because even then I knew my legs were good for quite a lot. Late at the drive-in after rehearsals for Collenette's recitals, I'd prop myself into some distorted and hopelessly uncomfortable position, my legs poised against gravity, replicating a cheesecake pose from one of the projectionist's Vargas calendars, my nude mesh stockings rendering me irresistible (even though my improvised garter of pennies and string bulged ludicrously at the hips) to any passersby who might look in the window. Some nights, going between the box office and snack bar,

I'd jeté from ramp to ramp, showing off in the hope that someone would discover me, and I suspect even then I was a little confused as to where I wanted my legs to take me—to Hollywood or into the back seat of a Cadillac. Probably both at the same time.

By my junior year, jetés were not enough. Going to "sleepovers" at my friend Donna Becker's house, I snuck out to date an older boy. Everything about this relationship was forbidden: not only was he older, but he had a job (and was therefore independent of his parents), smoked Camels, drank beer, and played heavy poker every Friday night. He had also killed a man—some said on purpose—a coach who crossed the track when the boy threw his shot put. He had revamped a Model A with a rumble seat, and I can still feel the heat between us, "Teach Me Tonight" blasting from the car radio, as we struggled with the wires, buttons, and hooks to all the garments that hindered our pursuits. Our lust was all the more irresistible because we never went "all the way." Our feverish investigations on tuck and roll leather car seats stopped short because we both knew my father would shoot him if my virginity were lost. How my parents would know beats me, but I knew they would.

Having to sneak around with my first sexual explorations, I felt guilty before anything had really happened. From a Quaker grandmother whose children kept marriages secret, from a mother who did not want to be seen touching her husband or being touched, from Hollywood censorship, I got the idea that physical behavior was best taken up in great secrecy. All body parts had to be kept hidden—except legs. Ever since Betty Grable, legs had been allowed out in the open, and they became a powerful metaphor for me. Fortunately, mine were well formed and capable of doing almost anything I asked of them. Furthermore, they were my only constant companion: day in, day out, they were there—to try out games, to play, to create adventure.

In my teens this play took a particular form. As a young child, being obedient and anxious for love, I had stuck to the exercises my teachers assigned, but in my teens I began to improvise, an endeavor that would end up absorbing thousands and thousands of hours of my life. My curiosity began to emerge. What would it feel like to twist the torso to the left and extend the leg to the right? Would it work at all? Or is it possible then to go around? Try. See how close you can come. Is this particular endeavor worth the work it takes to accomplish, or is it better to go on and try something else? Sometimes when my body was empty of ideas, I searched the playroom cupboards for discarded garments. How would the legs operate if you wore this sweatshirt as sweatpants? What could the tension produce? This patch of the floor is very slippery—how can I move differently here than over there where the floor is not so fast? I searched physical and emotional and musical motivations— all different, all valid.

I pushed myself hard in my training regimens. I used my technique studies athletically, to strengthen my body, forcing my ballet —never easily or gracefully executed—to be bigger, harder, faster. I never understood the routines Collenette had us learn to perform just as she had performed them in Pavlova's company. Why be a snowflake or a butterfly? I thought. I wasn't Collenette, and she wasn't Pavlova. Collenette's recitals lacked authenticity for me.

Sixth-grade square dancing with Rickie Trenary, 1952

My sixth-grade square dance club's performances at local hospitals and old folks' homes made more sense: "Pick out one person and look them straight in the eye," my teacher had said. These team efforts left our audiences feeling better and grateful for our attention. What we did was natural and honest. Pretty was never an issue. What was pretty, anyway? The lying ease of a retouched photograph over Collenette's desk? If a movement felt good, that was pretty, and to this day those moments when my mind surrenders and my body takes over and moves of its own accord, governed only by muscles and reflexes—falling where it wants, stopping as it can, building the momentum to speed—are the only instances when I recognize true order. The body, outside the mind's control, moves intuitively as though in a barroom brawl.

The time I first experienced this sense of liberation is still vivid. When we moved into the Quail Canyon house, I used to build prefab ruins from mud, bricks, and wires, blobs of hardened concrete and chunks of dried, rubbery paint left over from my father's building. I was in the habit of going into these secret places—they looked like miniature Mayan cities—created away from the house in the surrounding desert.

One morning, hidden away, reading in my private place and accompanied only by my cat, I heard the sound of a rattler very close by. I looked up, startled, but not too frightened because I knew of a bird that could make a similar sound. But then I saw it about fifteen feet away: a rattlesnake, and a big one. There were seven rattles on his tail, which meant he was at least seven years old—and smart. I let my cat down gently, hoping the animal would not charge. Next to me was a hoe I had used the day before to mix mud for my bricks. I eased toward the hoe, moving as little as possible, never taking my eye off the snake's head. Then I charged, bashing him. My attack worked; the snake was out cold.

I draped my trophy over a branch of an olive tree and began whooping it up around the tree. The three little ones heard the commotion and came out to take a look. I was pleased by the audience. Now and again the rattler shivered, making his tail sound; one of the kids had the good sense to realize the creature was only stunned, and went to get my father. By the time Daddy arrived, the snake was regaining consciousness. My father grabbed the hoe, pushed me back, then quickly knocked the snake to the ground and chopped its head off from behind. I was scolded but not spanked—my father probably applauded my nerve. But whatever he said didn't matter because I remained high from the physical exhilaration; the fright, the battle, the victory, all made my adrenaline surge. I had tapped directly into the primitive drive that celebrates brave physical conquest, good over evil, through ceremonial performances. I had created my first dance.

3

Warming up, I begin
in the smallest possible
position. Then I
move out, entering my
body until it is ready
to begin new work.

Mother drove me to college directly from the beauty parlor. She wanted me—her product—perfect in every way for the premiere outside Rialto.

Only I didn't feel perfect. To my mother's way of thinking I had been thoroughly prepared, yet I still couldn't drive, swim, cook, talk to most people, think reasonably about what someone else might want or need, imagine the reality of wars, understand that politicians ran things, or know the cost of a quart of milk. The knowledge she had given me was like the luggage she made me cart to school: stuff I would be discarding for years to come. I began to feel my mother's training had prepared me for everything except the one thing that mattered most: practical life itself, especially the practice of living with others.

At Pomona College there was a tradition, banned a few years after I arrived, that allowed each sophomore man to pick a freshman woman for weighing and measuring as she arrived on campus. The results were entered in a large book. As I walked onto the dorm porch, I was already self-conscious about my belongings, hair, and nonexistent bust. It was just my luck to be picked by the renegade of the class, a handsome beatnik who wore leather thongs and a rough Mexican vest and carried a black sketchbook under his arm. From reading *Life* magazine I knew this made Peter Ford

Peter Young, 1962

Young a "bohemian," a "leftist," and an immediate menace who, of course, would be attracted to the out-of-place.

In the following weeks, Peter Young always seemed in the way as I made the rounds of my all-purpose liberal arts courses, and every day I found hidden for me a note, picture, or small poems embellished with his vaguely Aztecan drawings. In short, Peter was impossible to turn down, and I found myself going—though not sleeping—with him.

Through him, I was introduced to a larger world—artists, including a couple who lived out of wedlock, my first foreign films, museum shows, the writings of T. S. Eliot, William Carlos Williams, and William Burroughs, coffeehouses, where the jazz and ranting poetry seemed indulgent and so disconnected from common sense as to be un-American. I refused to do drugs or drink and I hated staying up after midnight—not much good as a beatnik girlfriend. Peter persisted. When he took me home to meet his mother—an intellectual Santa Monica potter—he told me that she would find our sleeping apart unnatural. A virgin at twenty, I insisted that I did not: I was surely one of my generation's last holdouts for love and marriage.

Similarly disquieting were the "Tower Girls." These were the Simone de Beauvoirs of Pomona, two juniors and four seniors who roomed in a quaint tower attached to the dorm and smoked cigarettes and pot, used diaphragms, and talked about abortion. Sophisticated, arrogant artistic types—painters, drama majors, writers—they questioned women's role in society and seemed bent on breaking all the rules. Terrifying and challenging me, they still had no right, I felt, to comment on art. They were dilettantes—the Tower Girls, Peter, and all his friends. They aped the bohemian life, reveling in the easy California life-style. I knew the truth: becoming an artist required enormous discipline, years of struggle. I engaged in endless discussions about art with my high school friend Mike Mellon, also a freshman at Pomona. Why did this note, this color, this word follow that one? Why were we here? Where did we come from? What did it all mean? Determined not to take anything for granted, my roommate, Virginia Borsen—a philosophy major—and I wore only angel shifts made from bed sheets, under which, it was rumored, we were naked. Donning them as our daily uniform, we freed ourselves from the trap of fashion; now we were in alliance with real workers everywhere. We even stopped shaving our legs and armpits.

That summer I moved to Los Angeles to continue my dance studies. Mother located and paid for a studio apartment high over Hollywood on Ivar Boulevard (at the opening of *Sunset Boulevard*, William Holden looks out my window). My heart raced every morning as I walked down the steep hill to Hollywood and Ivar, just four blocks from Schwab's, where Lana Turner was discovered. Now I was at the center of it all.

Using the rudimentary L.A. bus system—which meant I had to allow an extra forty-five minutes to get anywhere on time—I crammed in as many classes as possible: Wilson Morelli, with whom I'd begun studying ballet after graduating Collenette; John Butler, who taught a repertory class with his assistants, Carmen de Lavallade and Bella Lewitzky; and at the old Lester Horton studio, where Alvin Ailey had begun, the remaining faculty taught a technique that practiced the isolation of each toe of each foot!

Peter drove up often from Santa Monica. After a year of putting him off I began to feel very guilty about sending him home when we had made out almost to the point of no return. Finally I slept with him. I didn't know if I wanted the sex or just to be released from my feelings of inadequacy, and my first completed sexual encounter left me feeling duplicitous and confused. Without the commitment of marriage, I felt as I had with my first high school beau: sex was becoming synonymous with guilt. After all, my parents were paying the bills, and by their rules I had acted dishonorably. Later that fall, back at Pomona, where of course all dorms were strictly segregated then, a custodian caught me making out with Peter in the chapel during a rainstorm. The dean threatened an expulsion. Apparently all authority—not just my parents—

found sexual behavior best forbidden. Mother got the sentence commuted by arranging a mid-term transfer to New York's Barnard College—a Seven Sisters college, good on the credentials front. Jumping at the chance to part me and my "good-for-nothing," she didn't know that Peter was already in New York, enrolled in the Art Students League.

Gram Cora, commandeered by Mother as my chaperone, lived off-campus with me in a sunny apartment on Riverside Drive. I was enrolled in the Barnard dance division, but after a morning spent portraying sunrises, I decided the Barnard dance classes were—to use my mother's phrase—"simply a joke." To its credit, the college allowed me to set up my own dance curriculum, using all the resources of New York City, in order to fulfill the physical education requirement. My academic major would be art history.

I began studying ballet with Igor Schwezoff, a choreographer and dancer from the Kirov and the Ballets Russes de Monte Carlo, and my Los Angeles teacher Wilson Morelli's master. Morelli had encouraged me to move on to Schwezoff, who taught at American Ballet Theatre along with Olga Pereyaslavec. At first I liked the Old World feel of both these teachers, but eventually their classes —taught primarily to maintain professional dancers, both those at American Ballet Theatre and Rockettes from Radio City Music Hall, who came to class between shows still in full makeup—began to feel staid and impersonal. I had heard about Balanchine's classes from several New York City Ballet dancers—Violette Verdy and Mimi Paul—who sometimes came to Pereyaslavec's class to get in an additional barre, and given my choice I would have studied at the American School of Ballet, which prepared dancers for Balanchine's company. I clearly saw Balanchine's dancers were the quickest and the most elegant, working with a commitment to dancing that was purer than ABT's dancers', who talked much of the time about their careers—casting, tours, and overtime. Balanchine's dancers talked about the excitement of new ballets. But fortunately his school was closed to the general public;

had I been allowed access to Balanchine, I probably would have signed up for life and never developed my own idiom.

Instead I began to study with Richard Thomas and his wife Barbara Fallis, alumni of both American Ballet Theatre and New York City Ballet, who taught in a tiny studio across from City Center's stage door on Fifty-sixth Street. Barbara had taken the full syllabus of the Royal Ballet (then called the Vic-Wells) in London and gave a beautifully balanced and consistent class. Richard, who had studied with Bronislava Nijinska, was occasionally erratic but a brilliant teacher. Astute in his observations and corrections, inventive in his combinations, he was particularly strong with petite allegro work, the very fast, intricate combinations designed to develop a dancer's agility, expecting us to execute these phrases not only forward, going toward the audience, but also inverted, going away from them. Though frequently awkward to perform, the inversions expanded the dimensions of dancing for me.

Packed with fifty dancers in a forty-by-thirty-foot room, Richard's classes afforded a valuable opportunity to work with great professional dancers. Two of these were Toni Lander and Cynthia Gregory. Cynthia was just beginning to develop the strength and confidence that would become her trademark. Toni was already in her prime, exercising a technique of such beauty that one could not even begin to decipher the seamless coordination of her torso, head, arms, and legs—a perfection that some claimed represented the most precise and perfect expression of classicism. The movements I struggled to make sense of—head inclined to the right, left arm across, right leg going forward—Toni performed effortlessly. My movements were rational decisions, choices made among thousands; hers were so natural they seemed like instincts.

Watching Toni and Cynthia, I realized I was suffering from my eclectic training: with all my various approaches I had not received the firm grounding required for a classical technique. With each new teacher I had started from scratch, realigning my placement and reexamining my line. I had been given too many options. A classical artist must learn things at a very young age and then absorb the lessons through practice so that the fiendishly difficult maneuvers that come later will look as natural as walking. This ideal is impossible to achieve if the mind questions "How?" or "Why?" To fly straight into an arabesque with no hesitation or to hold the body serenely in balance for eight pirouettes demands a solid, unquestioned technique. The fact that my homespun, painfully gathered training allowed me to keep up at all with the extraordinary dancers around me testified to my determination and raw physical ability. But the comparisons I made between myself and dancers such as Lupe Serrano—who always took the full barre in the center of the room, unsupported on pointe—were painful. Over and over I wondered, "Will I ever be a dancer? Do I have any business dancing?" And the most destructive of all questions for the professional dancer: "What is dancing, anyway?" How could one become a classical dancer while at the same time asking what it means to move outside the regulation forms?

Determined to expose myself to all the forms of dance, I attended every concert I could find, stalking dance systematically through the listings of *The New York Times*, *The Village Voice*, and *Dance* magazine, like my father hunting every creature on earth. Over the next several years, I saw the companies of Martha Graham, Merce Cunningham, Jerome Robbins, José Greco, Erick Hawkins, Lenny Dale, Paul Sanasardo, Paul Taylor, Jean Erdman, Shirley Broughton, Pearl Lang, Joyce Trisler, Midi Garth, Anna Sokolow, Daniel Nagrin, Murray Louis, Gladys Bailin, Alvin Ailey, my former teacher Carmen de Lavallade, Robert Cohan, Robert Joffrey, Sazushi Hanayagi, James Waring, Donald McKayle, Pauline Koner, and Glen Tetley. Watching each, I asked myself one question over and over: "Is this how I should be dancing?"

To address this question I studied with over half these choreographers. Two have stayed with me particularly: Martha Graham and Merce Cunningham.

When I began, in June 1961, Graham was sixty-seven and about to stop teaching regularly. The decision was a matter of practicality and style. After more than forty years of dancing, Martha's body wasn't strong enough to lead daily lessons, and her physical infirmities—the arthritis in her hands, for instance—betrayed her profound sense of propriety. To Martha, making a good public appearance was not a question of others' expectations, but an obligation to herself. She extended this sense to her company as well. Of all the modern-dance pioneers, she alone insisted that things be properly done. For fifty years she bore the standard of modern dance, demanding that it be showcased in the very best fashion to wide audiences, not just in out-of-the-way auditoriums and church basements for the exclusive pleasure of the avant-garde. She was a woman of intense pride, propriety, dignity, and I loved her for it.

The Graham studio was a three-story house, rumored to be a gift of some Rothschild or other, on the Upper East Side, near Bloomingdale's. In the front on the ground floor were two small studios, and in the back, a large, beautifully proportioned studio where Martha held forth. In this sanctuary we bounced on the floor before class, stretching in one yoga position or another. Later, I asked Martha if she had studied yoga, because so many of its positions were at the center of her technique. All she wished to acknowledge was that she used to see "Miss St. Denis doing a lot of it in the corner."

When Martha entered the studio to begin class, we sprang to our feet and stood respectfully for a moment as she slipped out of her ballet slippers. This symbolic routine had much meaning. Modern dancers, of course, were defined by their bare feet. At the Graham studio, ballet shoes, with the heel crushed in the back like loose bedroom scuffs, were worn only to go from studio to studio to keep the feet clean: you protected your feet outside the studio but exposed yourself once you got down to work. By stepping out of her slippers—she did so without touching them—Martha signaled the transition. And as she motioned for the pianist to begin, you could see that even her vanity, which was enormous, bowed to the pragmatic needs of her art. With huge bunions on both sides of her metatarsal, and others on the insides of her feet like fists attached to the bone, her feet were the only ones I have ever seen more enlarged, more conventionally ugly, than my own.

Then Graham's pianist, Cameron McCosh—one of the very best accompanists I've ever heard—began to play, his intense music filling my body with its passion. Members of Graham's company who were not teaching also took her class, and their dedication pulled me even deeper into the movements. Helen McGehee, Ethel Winter, Linda Hodes, Bertram Ross, Richard Kuch, Richard Gain, Robert Powell—these dancers had spent so many hours in this studio that they were able to move within its parameters as within a stage set, almost clipping the edges of the low benches as they swirled with mighty releases into full revolutions on the floor, pouncing out of deep contractions within inches of the piano and walls. I felt honored to be in these classes, to be allowed to watch the commitment these people had to one another and their work, and to share in the intensely sensual experience of sweeping across the floor in triplets executed so swiftly that your ears whistled. The falls to the ground, faster and faster, first on five, then four, then three, then two, and finally a death pitch on one, were for the foolhardy. That was me—in my mind that was all the mortals who, through Graham's training, raised themselves to the mythic level of Greek heroes and Christian martyrs.

Of course, there was always much gossip about Martha. One heard she had practically destroyed her performing career in her forties and fifties with drinking; that her vanity extended to her sitting hour after hour, patiently burning her own image with a lit cigarette from any frames of archival material that displeased her; that she wept at her dressing table as early, cherished pieces such as *Primitive Mysteries* were reconstructed, because she could not bear to detach herself from her memories and see another dancer replace her; that her relationships with men were always chaotic; that her marriage to Erick Hawkins, fifteen years her junior, had failed because he had proven less driven than she was. There were rumors that she was unhappily linked to her musical director, Louis Horst, throughout much of her life and that she lusted after the monumentally gorgeous men in her company—many of whom were homosexual—as Balanchine did for his ballerinas, who were often young enough to be his granddaughters. But who could expect things to be any different? I could believe all the rumors, or not, and not care a bit either way. Martha was prodigious in her art, and the rest was superfluous. I aspired to join her, never judge her, and years later, when a reporter asked her about my devotion, Martha generously replied, "Well, we're alike. We're both rebels." That was always what I felt counted.

Yet at that time I hesitated committing myself to Martha. Her dances were narratives, requiring her dancers to play roles. This involved an element of pretend with which I was uncomfortable. I could not begin imagining myself a Fury or, for that matter, even the star of the piece herself, Clytemnestra. I could not picture myself other than what I was—an Indiana farm girl to whom seeds meant plants, not metaphors.

Merce Cunningham must have had similar feelings when he left Martha's company in the late Forties. Martha's dancers approached ideals in their roles, portraying gods and goddesses, but Merce's company became a blend of individuals who stamped their dancing with their own personal characteristics; no one in the Cunningham company danced in roles with names other than their own.

Teaching in a building he shared with Julian Beck and Judith Malina's Living Theatre on Sixth Avenue and Fourteenth Street, Merce was unconcerned with the great mythologies and dedicated to more mundane concerns—how we walk and run. He employed a technique poised between ballet and Graham. Class began with the classical exercises, but done unsupported in the center, utilizing parallel and turned-out positions interchangeably. He focused especially on the back, dividing it into three areas—upper, middle, lower. This concentration helped him to create an idiom offering much greater rhythmic sophistication than Martha's; compared to Merce's light, fast dance, Graham's movement was chunky.

Merce was smaller than many of Martha's men. Lacking the perfectly lean, classically proportioned ideal of Erick Hawkins, Bertram Ross, or Paul Taylor, he had a little pudginess which connected him with Everyman, and he seemed to look on everything with a wry smile. A Puck, he was a marvelous dancer. His enormously developed practical knowledge of dance, his coordinations of unlikely body parts, and his bursts into space on any front —not just the proscenium front—offered him a richness of choice that explained his need to sometimes use the *I Ching* to make decisions for him. Although I never deeply sympathized with an aesthetic grounded in chance, and never responded to the open plains of no beginnings, middles, and endings in Merce's dance or in the music of his great collaborator, John Cage, I nonetheless respected the two of them for extending Dada thought. Their rebellion, at the time, was clean and strong enough to inspire others, and Merce's classes spawned a whole generation of American choreographers. Steve Paxton, Barbara Lloyd, Judith Dunn, Viola Farber—all of whom became choreographers—worked together in the Cunningham company. With Carolyn Brown and Merce himself, still in his prime, they formed one of the greatest ensembles modern dance has ever known. I always regarded this troupe and the classic Graham company of the Fifties and Sixties as the standard when I began to build my own several years later.

I rounded out my dance education with jazz, adding the life and bounce (albeit forced) of show biz to the graceful elegance of classical ballet and the self-righteous rigor of modern dance. I luxuriated in the lush movements Eugene "Luigi" Lewis taught on Broadway between Fifty-fourth and Fifty-fifth streets. Everything there was shamelessly seductive—the pelvic thrust, the syncopated rhythms, the girls in their high boots and their leotards cut in what I thought of as "the Fosse line," so high on the sides that the leotard crawled into the crack of the buttocks. I disliked the sleazy part of Fosse's work—the appropriate term, "male chauvinist pig," had not yet surfaced in American culture; nonetheless I loved the women's heat and sensuality. And while I applied myself as seriously to the jazz classes as I did to those in ballet and modern, there was no avoiding the fact that jazz was the most fun. The dancing felt great, and the mile-wide smiles on everyone's faces projected the essence of health, exuberance, and good times.

Years later I learned this delight was mostly artificial, part of the famous Broadway flash, the razzmatazz, the insincere "sell." But at the time you could have fooled me. I felt the pleasure, believed the zest. Jazz dancing exploded with vitality, the same energy that propelled the best of Martha and Merce's work, the best of ballet too, when the movement had nothing to do with theories or steps but simply burst into space. At these moments I felt a juiciness in moving—whether jazz, modern, or ballet—that gradually would unite all dance for me.

My feel for a unifying factor in dance was supported by another trend just beginning in New York. Studying ballet with Margaret Craske was an eclectic group of modern and ballet dancers—Paul Taylor, Carolyn Brown of Merce's company, Sallie Wilson, Antony Tudor's protégée at American Ballet Theatre, and Helen McGehee, the small fireball from Graham's company whose presence had to be kept secret because everyone feared Martha would feel betrayed. These dancers were the beginning of a hybrid form, one I came to think of as the crossover dancer, the one capable of any technique. Gradually I too was developing an encyclopedic sense of the different weights of the body emphasized by ballet, modern dance, and jazz, of the various speeds, stances, and shifts of center that could be explored. And I was coming to understand that each of these demands could work together to combine, ultimately, into something more than a patois of isolated techniques, become a new language, capable of saying new things—or old things in new ways. I was beginning to imagine a special niche for myself, a place in this swirling kaleidoscope of choices that no one else could fill, a kind of dance no one else could do.

I was coming to define myself as a dancer, much as I fought off the discovery. From the tattered practice clothes to the talk of ruthless competition for the few paying jobs available, there was clearly no financial security in a dance career. In 1963 a corps member of a professional company earned one hundred and ten dollars a week. Also, as a near graduate of an Ivy League school I harbored the intellectual snobbery with which so much of our culture looks at both the dancer and the athlete, pronouncing them dumb. Still, I proceeded to dance, because of all the things I could do, dancing was the thing I could do best and enjoyed most.

Each morning I awoke, I went deeper into the habits and routine of a dancer. Still on course from the night before, I slid into the new day by pulling on yesterday's pair of tights, rinsed before I went to bed. I hurried to "overdress," putting practice clothes on under my street clothes so that as little time as possible was wasted; all dancers are obsessed with time.

Climbing the studio stairs, I began to stretch and mentally focus on the day's challenges. Perhaps I could get a little higher on my legs, making that elusive fourth pirouette a bit smoother. Unpeeling in the dressing room, there was no time for gossip—I was already anticipating what the fourth pirouette might feel like, beginning to believe it was possible as I walked into the studio.

I always warmed up early, long before class officially began. The studio itself did not matter, although wood floors and natural light brought back warm feelings of being with Collenette because the real terrain I occupied was my body. I wanted to be in total control of it, for that is much of dancing: a lifelong commitment to the discipline of the body. I admired it in the mirror: the instep curved as I sat spread-eagled on the floor, my legs open pliantly in one perfect straight line, my torso reaching upward as I stretched the length of the rib cage from the pelvis. For a moment I felt completely right about being in the studio; this was where I belonged, at home, fully contained in this time and space.

But I also looked into the mirror with a touch of ruthlessness, for the body cannot lie. Either I execute four pirouettes—clean, without fudging or wavering—or I don't. There is no need for discussion, only performance. I insisted on progress every day and when I saw it I felt virtuous, rewarded by improvement, confident in my unquestioned daily routine of classes, study, and dinner. And possibly an argument with Peter, for who but another dancer could appreciate such a regimen? Evening movies were for others: ten o'clock was bedtime, and I still had tights to rinse. During the day I could think of little other than dance; at night I fell asleep quickly.

A workaholic of the highest order, I struggled through the unstructured wasteland of Sundays. I knew my calling was a jealous one and permitted no other idols. Many in my profession radiate a certain godliness, a purity of purpose. Unlike almost all others, dancers are allowed, indeed encouraged, to remain children forever; Balanchine often said that no one over twenty-one could dance anymore. When dancers work we are silent, seen and not heard, and we do what we are told by the choreographer or rehearsal director, with little or no discussion about what or how we will dance. I knew that if ever I had an opportunity to join a professional company, I would be one of the "boys and girls" until I left.

I was also free to be totally self-involved. My whole life revolved around physical conditioning and the satisfaction of my body's simplest needs. There was little time for intellectual curiosity or emotional investments outside the studio. Like a child, I felt my body to be invincible—no aging or death as long as I continued to refine my instrument. People envied me, seeing only how clear my course was, and how easy that made all decisions. What few could understand was that dancers are hooked, that their bodies are so chemically dependent on work that even when limbs and joints can no longer tolerate the labor, their bodies will cry out for it. I have seen dancers struggle in the face of sudden withdrawal and I have seen some continue as anonymous "lifers" into their fifties and sixties, grotesque sights at the barre.

When I thought about becoming a dancer, I worried that I might not be good enough, that I too would become one of the lifers, desperately obedient to the rounds of professional dancing, possibly into the grave. I worried that I might have no real talent, no special gift, that I was just a dance junkie. Every dancer must face this question, and ultimately it is the mirror and the dancer who must answer it. My reflection told me I had legs that were stronger and could carry me higher than my classmates'. And I also had a will that let me eliminate everything that stood in the way of my becoming the best dancer I could be. By a gradual process, begun long before my move to New York, I had invested every bit of my dreams, my hopes, my energies in defining myself as a dancer. It had been dance—my connection to Collenette and Morelli and Igor Schwezoff—that brought me to New York City, not my mother's selection of an Ivy League school or my attachment to a college beau. There was no choice: I was becoming a dancer.

4 Starting from scratch in the studio—no rules, no references—success can be measured by only one thing: the hairs on the back of your neck.

When she wasn't cooking, cleaning, shopping, and hooking her rugs, Gram Cora attended to her main chore: keeping Peter Young out of my bed. When she failed, Mother flew me back to California, insisting I have my wisdom teeth pulled (they were not giving me any trouble, but she feared they might) and announcing, while I was still groggy from the anesthesia, that Gram Cora, the rest of the family, and soon *everybody*—meaning all her neighbors— would know I had slept with this Peter Young, and so I had to marry him whether I wanted to or not.

I didn't. I remained unsettled by his liberalism. Besides, I knew he was still dallying with a young woman he had met in Mexico, and by then I had evidence of more than one pass he'd made at Twanette. But when Mother, Father, and I reconvened the next day in the turquoise living room and she repeated her demand, I was furious at being threatened but more frightened of finding myself on the street, penniless and without any means of support to defy her. My parents, after all, were paying for the groceries, so I came back to New York and talked Peter, my leftist bohemian, into marriage.

We were wed out of town by a country preacher in the presence of the church cleaning woman and another unknown witness. After

After my wedding, 1962

wandering in the parish graveyard, we mailed off the marriage certificate that proved the deed to my mother, and without it were refused rooms in several charming inns on the way back to the city. We wound up spending our honeymoon on a friend's sofa.

Then Gram Cora headed back to Indiana, and Peter and I were left to confront each other for the first time in peace. Without having to struggle against all odds to sleep together, without the tension of "us against them"—parents, establishment, conven-

Mother's choice of wedding
announcement photo in the local paper

tional morality—our marriage eroded from the first day; only our opposition to others had held us together.

In New York, Peter continued living on the fringe of the art world. He knew William Burroughs slightly, we attended jazz clubs and poetry readings by Paul Blackburn, Gilbert Sorrentino, and Louis Zukofsky. For a while we were adopted by George Oppen, the poet, and his wife Mary, a potter. An older couple, politically

active in the Thirties, George and Mary lived over the docks in
Brooklyn Heights. Dinner with them was always a special treat,
but to me, this circle reflected a truth about Peter: he was a con-
noisseur, able to recognize quality but lacking the chutzpah to
create anything himself.

Living off-campus, first with Gram Cora, then with Peter, I had
participated very little in college life; just like the teenager who
had walked through high school hallways in silence, I still felt I had
so much to do that was more important than talking to people. I
jammed my Barnard curriculum between my ballet, modern, and
jazz classes, and crammed course work into the weekends, memorizing thousands of illustrations on the subway trips I took to my
two and sometimes three daily dance lessons. All this work was
exhilarating because so much of my life was yet to come. I knew
and accepted that I was completely unformed, but I felt I was
beginning to have the tools with which to shape my future, a future
that centered around dancing. But because I still didn't know how
that might work, I never told anyone I was going to be a dancer.

Although I was working very hard, I had no idea if I was good
enough to make it professionally. And even if I did, what was a
dancer to this culture? There were the June Taylor Dancers on the
Jackie Gleason show, and there were nightclub and Broadway
show dancers, but all these gypsy dancers seemed tainted by ques-
tionable morals, hustlers who had to exploit people and opportunities just to survive. There were ballet dancers, but they were from
a tradition in which they were spoiled and subsidized, pampered
and petted mistresses to czars. What did saying you were going to
be a dancer mean to the guy on the street, to the American middle
class earning its living in the real world? How could I explain that
there were things that are important in all our lives that could only
be expressed in dance, that there were not only physical truths but
behavioral values and emotional reservoirs that could only be investigated and demonstrated by bodies in motion? That there were
times and situations where words could not be trusted to do the

job? That there was a genuine and specific need for dance, not just in me, but in us all? I could perhaps have used the word "artist," said that was what I was going to be. People would have assumed I said that because I was studying painting. It too is a visual art, but unlike dancing, painting makes its truths into a product you can hold. And that can be sold. Painting has a solid market and therefore is respected in an entrepreneurial society. However, I never intended to be a painter, not seriously, and certainly had no intention of teaching or curating. Nonetheless I had continued my art history major. But what, as a dancer, would I do with the history of art, other than get a sheepskin to send home to Mother as I had my marriage certificate? At the time I could not see any use to the major, but I had begun to use the discipline of art history to reinforce my own sense of what is classic in art. I was locating that strain that survives generation after generation—graphic, simple, bold, fundamental, whether in Cycladic women, Shaker furniture, or Celtic manuscripts. I was getting my proportions right, finding the line beyond which, on one side, is a refinement that bleeds life and on the other, a condition where things are so rough, expressionistic, or vague that all you can see is indulgence. As I came to believe in my own artistic cravings, I became ever more self-righteous, thinking I was coming to know the difference between good art and bad art, and I had even less patience for the experimentation Peter saw as being the center of art, tolerating what I saw as confusion. I liked work that looked as though the artist clearly knew what he was doing and believed in it.

And that was another thing. Why was it always "he" to denote the artist, a pronoun I unconsciously use even now? Where were the women? In pre-classic, Greek, Romanesque, medieval, Renaissance, baroque, rococo, and Romantic art, where was one woman's name we all knew? Where in the history of art—music, architecture, painting, sculpture, most centuries of literature—had a woman made a difference? Sometimes I stole time from memorizing the required art history and looked through the meager dance sections in the stacks. There in the dance collection of the public library, I found my answer: images of Isadora Duncan, Mary Wigman, Doris Humphrey, Ruth St. Denis, and Martha Graham. These women were the pioneers of a new art form. In creating modern dance, they had struck out on their own, and running my fingers over the plates, I literally tried to absorb their power and authority. In their art form, they were genuinely potent—not relegated to second-class status, not dilettantes, dabblers, Sunday painters. They could only have done this in America, where women were gaining equality earlier, and this too mattered to me. I was not interested in entering a profession where I was handicapped by second-class status. Now I knew both what I was doing in art history and in dance, and when graduation day came I skipped the ceremonies. Working toward becoming an artist in a way that I could understand, I chose to go to a rehearsal instead.

The rehearsal was with Paul Taylor. Paul had a fledgling group and I just walked in. That's the best way to describe our union: as Paul has said on more than one occasion, I chose him, he certainly didn't choose me. I just started hanging out at his studio, more or less refusing to leave, my legs pulled up under my chin, trying to take up as little room as possible, unclothing Paul in my mind, X-raying his body, absorbing his movement.

Paul Taylor, Tharp, Liz Walton, Danny Grossman, Dan Wagoner, 1963

In my senior year at Barnard, I had seen him perform as a soloist with the Graham company on Broadway. My judgment was instantaneous: he was simply the most gorgeous creature imaginable. It may be that I decided to become a professional dancer just to be near him. He had a background in fine art, attending college on a painting scholarship, and was friendly with Robert Rauschenberg and Jasper Johns. At six feet one, Paul seemed enormous; his muscles were sharply cut, honed by years of swimming. Beautifully proportioned, his body could spring into movement with almost no preparation. His dancing prowled—critics regularly used animal phrases to describe him, referring to his "feline grace." I felt his movement stemmed from a special comprehension of the beast inside him, a fearlessness that came from his mind's refusal to question his body's abilities. A late starter, he danced in a way that could honestly be called natural—I never could see the how of his movement. The length of his limbs allowed me to observe each bit of movement as it flowed organically into the next, giving a marvelous grace to all his transitions. His solos in, say, *Aureole* (1962) or *Junction* (1961) were always designed to indulge the deep coil of his body: standing on one leg, he curled everything precisely toward his center, then allowed his body to reach farther out into space than I would ever have thought possible. The completeness of his movement swept me up and I imagined myself carried through space on this grand creature. Still, when he chose to move quickly, he always seemed to have a jump on the other dancers.

Paul was tenuously perched on the cusp of reality: he never appeared completely at ease with the human world. He studied animals in the zoo for hours, possessing an uncanny knack for animal mimicry. His dancers were his family; he had little human contact besides us, his deaf-mute live-in friend George (nicknamed Babe), and the company's manager, Charles Reinhart, who also booked the company and functioned as the stage manager on the road. Though virtually a recluse, Paul never acted pettily. Generosity was the hallmark of his dancing and his personal life, whether as a company director or a friend. He had little to give—Charlie's ambition was to clear enough money from performance fees to be able finally to afford a shower stall in the cubbyhole behind the studio Paul called home. Still, he shared his few treasures easily. Once—after just a little pestering on my part—he gave me what we all believed was an ancient human skull from Israel into which he had poured many hours of cleaning and reassembly.

My very first dance role came via the same route of perseverance. Thinking that I should learn a little humility, Paul put me into *Scudorama* (1963), but limited my part to one unlit upstage crossover, a crablike crawl, legs opening in a split, torso and head following after, performed underneath a huge striped beach towel. Even though I was completely invisible, I was committed to my role. I figured everyone would notice me, even if they couldn't see me, and if my passion couldn't reach through a towel. . . . The piece, however, was jinxed. Paul wanted to cancel the performance at its Connecticut College premiere because the music didn't arrive and—owing to an injury—he was going to have to cover both male roles. But I refused to let him fink out, saying he owed the piece to his audience and, more, to me, because this was my debut and we could certainly do the piece in silence.

With no music, all the dancers were out of sync, but I was happy: I had made it onstage for my first professional engagement. By the end of the piece, however, Paul was exhausted and rested out an entrance. As I made my crawl upstage, head between my legs, I hissed, "Paul, get back out there!" Paul claims he only followed my command because there was a tear of disappointment in my eye—the towel must have slipped—but whatever the reason, he made the final entrance.

My arrogance—I made no bones about claiming I was the company's best dancer next to Paul—won me no friends. Shortly after the *Scudorama* premiere, the company went on tour. Paul put the question to the troupe: "Well, shall we keep her?" Everyone but Dan Wagoner voted no. Still, when the company returned to New

York, Paul went against the vote, his only caveat being that I change my name—he thought Twyla Tharp too flamboyant. I proposed Twyla One. He said what about my married name, Twyla Young? That seemed common somehow, but I agreed, and appeared in sixteen Taylor company performances that year billed as Twyla Young. The other dancers, because of Paul, eventually accepted me in spite of myself. "I just dreaded telling the others that she was going to be in the dances," Paul has said. "She was trying to give the impression of great savoir faire, trying to look foxy and tough. Which she wasn't. She wasn't tough at all. She was very vulnerable. She was little, and she kept saying, 'I'm big.' I'd say,

Tharp, Dan Wagoner, Danny Grossman, Liz Walton, Sharon Kinney, Bettie de Jong, Paul, Renée Wadleigh, 1963

'You're cute,' and she'd say, 'I'm big.' I can hear her now, walking around the studio, saying, 'Gimme, gimme, gimme.' And she'd get it."

After my Barnard graduation, Peter and I bought into a loft in downtown Manhattan on Franklin Street where he could paint and I had a twenty-by-seventeen-foot practice area. For seventy-five

TWYLA THARP

dollars a month we got raw space: no elevator or sprinklers, just exposed wooden beams, brick walls, and wooden floors, big windows at either end, a toilet, and a sink. That was it. Plus the feeling that we had escaped the middle class. We were working artists, living in lofts zoned for light manufacturing in the center of the raw fabric district, bounded by produce and meat-packing warehouses, with carcasses hanging from their canopies. The neighborhood was a residential desert. The nearest laundries and supermarket, the Pioneer Market at Bleecker and Sixth, were fifteen blocks away. Since all loft living in what would later become Tribeca was still illegal and the city inspected frequently for building code violations, all beds had to be quickly convertible to couches. You weren't permitted more kitchen space than a painter's studio might require, but what mattered was that there were no restrictive walls. We slept (on a mattress on the floor), bathed (in an antique tub that eventually got installed), and cooked (on a hot plate kept on the bathtub cover), all in the same area in which we worked. There were no subdivisions in our life. We did not leave to go to work; that would have been bourgeois. It felt good to be persecuted; everyone knew real artists had to pay dearly for their freedom. When we moved in, our downstairs neighbor, Bob Huot, a painter, told us to tear up our envelopes so no one could trace our address and to distribute our garbage in *all* the neighborhood trash baskets, not just the one on our own corner, lest we draw attention to the fact that someone was living in the building.

In the fall of 1963, Paul started to work on a new piece, *Party Mix*, and I watched him closely as he made up dance phrases in the tiny studio. Paul was a midwife, pulling movement out of thin air. He worked close to the intuition, not judging, but accepting.

I realized that in making a new work there is no use for language. In these moments, those who dance must watch and learn silently. It was surely no accident that Paul's friend Babe was deaf and mute and that they communicated by sign language. Watching this new piece take form, I began to think I could do better. I certainly felt, with the earnestness that belongs to the untried, that my commitment was to higher goals than Paul's. I felt he was dallying, that his dance was becoming entertainment. When the costume designer proposed wigs as part of the costuming for *Party Mix*, my misgivings were confirmed—Paul was entering the realm of theatrics and make-believe. I felt abandoned and embarrassed.

That same fall, Peter was drafted and left for Fort Dix in New Jersey. Alone in the loft, I found myself listening for Bob Huot, our downstairs neighbor, to stir in the mornings, and I often managed to be downstairs to pick up my mail at the same time he went out. Several late afternoons, as I dragged my way up the ninety-three stairs to our loft, with my twelve-pound dancer's bag on one shoulder and the groceries or laundry on the other, Bob—big and burly, with his full coppery beard and huge laugh—came out while I rested on his landing and offered to take the bags the rest of the way up. I was ever so grateful. Several tea dates were exchanged.

Bob's loft was as different from my empty, rigorously sparse space as possible. His home contained a cupboard for dishes and tinned food, an icebox—one of those beautiful ancient affairs with the coils on top for recirculating the coolant—a convertible sofa, a big desk, and a few heavy chairs as well, all of them found on the street and carried upstairs by Bob, as well as an enormous collection of music, including wonderful old American records—early, raunchy blues—and his favorite big guns: Bach, Bruckner, Brahms, Beethoven. The overwhelming impression was one of mass and substance.

He was also a painter, a real artist. He had several work tables on wheels, covered with rags and brushes, glue for priming, and gallons of acrylic paint. Large canvases were everywhere. One whole wall was occupied by a stretcher rack packed with finished paintings. Several pieces in various stages were always being worked on. I couldn't judge the quality of Bob's art, but I was sure

Bob Huot and *Rassmussen*, 1965

he worked very hard, probably as hard as I did, since he held a full-time day job in addition to being a painter. There was no bullshit about Bob Huot; he didn't have the time or language for it. He was always about his business.

One day late in winter, Bob knocked at my door. I figured the visit was about milk or sugar. Instead he asked, shyly, if he could use my tub; his water heater was out and he had to attend an opening that night. I told him sure, and we chatted for a few minutes before I unfolded the bathtub screen for him. As he ran the water I got into a hammock I had hung near a window so you could see all the way to Canal Street. As I looked out the window I glanced into an old mirror I'd found on the street and hung between the windows. From this angle, Bob's large, naked form was reflected. I liked his body: it was strong, very muscular, and he had more hair everywhere—back, sides, and front—than I'd ever seen before. Mind you, I was twenty-two and this was only the second nude man I'd seen in my life (third if you counted my father). I got out of the hammock to drape a towel over the screen for him. I waited for him, watching out the window as he dried himself. I turned to offer him some tea as he folded the screen and set it against the wall, but he had to leave. On the way out he invited me down to a party Friday night.

I waited anxiously. I was attracted to Bob and I was attracted to his circle. They were the real deal, neither dilettantes nor performers, for by now I differentiated between those who rendered the work of others, e.g., me doing Paul's dances, and those who did their own work. I knew that until I took on the full responsibility for my art I was only a tool, not a serious artist. Friday evening came and I went downstairs knowing I had dues to pay before I could really join the New York art scene.

Doug Ohlson, Bob's best friend, and his girlfriend Jane were already there. We were soon joined by sculptor Carl Andre and his friend Rose Marie Castoro. All of the women at the gathering were active painters or sculptors or performance artists, all working at their own careers. Even so, the women remained at the living end of the loft while the men drifted back into the studio to look at Bob's latest work, talking about a new color he had invented, "a new, really hot pink, dynamite lipstick color." Bob was a pigment chemist, and he and Doug worked together at Neti's paint factory. There was a buzz, an undeniable sexuality one felt with the men and women pulled apart, but as the women's group cursed and swore like men, fuming about the difficulty of getting gallery shows and the attendant press, I clearly sensed there was an enormous amount of resentment toward the essentially macho world of painting and sculpture that existed in New York. Perhaps this explained why some prominent women artists—such as Georgia O'Keeffe and Agnes Martin—preferred the isolation of the Southwestern desert to the New York art scene. The party heated up as George Sugarman and Al Held came by with Ronnie Bladen; all three were having woman problems that evening. The loft began to fill, and Bob exchanged light bulbs painted red for the clear ones as the Beatles' early music played. Larry Poons arrived with the Judson dancer Lucinda Childs, LaMonte Young with Marian Zazeela, who inscribed the elaborately curlicued announcements for his minimalist, Eastern-influenced concerts that were chanted and intoned and could take all day. And all night. Maybe all week (this really was slow music).

LaMonte passed around a joint. I abstained. Soon LaMonte and Marian, the filmmaker Hollis Frampton, Carl, and Rose Marie were sitting cross-legged in a corner, toking up. Bob asked me to dance, and although I was flattered by his attention—I knew he was un-attached at the moment—I was much too shy, too inhibited by the seriousness of my commitment to dancing to treat movement so cavalierly. I did ballet, modern, tap, or Spanish, *not* free-form. That was disrespectful, and furthermore, terrifying. Besides, I was a married woman. Touching meant business in my family. I couldn't casually enter the arms of a stranger.

Yvonne Rainer floated by, a high priestess of the Judson Dance Theatre. She cut a striking figure with her jet-black hair styled in a replica of Louise Brooks' stern bob. She went off with the sculp-tor and performance artist Robert Morris, leaving Diane Wakoski on the edge of the dance floor, watching them move closer to-gether. Diane wrote poetry, but her life seemed a mess. As she talked with me she sounded bitterly unhappy about moving out of Morris's loft and into her own apartment. I worried about the pain and insecurity of bohemian life that I might be letting myself in for, being attracted to Bob Huot.

By the end of the party, Bob Huot, Bob Morris, and LaMonte reminisced about *War*, a performance piece they had presented at the Judson Church in January.

"Whose idea was the pigeons anyhow?" asked LaMonte, very stoned.

"Doves," corrected Bob Morris.

"My favorite part," LaMonte continued, "was the voodoo dolls and the taunts. You should have seen yourselves baiting each other before the charge."

The next morning, I went down to help Bob clean up. As I picked up the last of the paper cups, I stopped to look at the painting that had been the evening's center of attention. I saw now that the masking tape the hard-edge painters used to assure a

Bob Huot in war costume, 1963

razor-sharp line between color areas was still in place. Bob explained it hadn't been quite dry enough to strip off last night. He asked if I would like to pull the tape. I was a little nervous about ruining the painting, but Bob showed me that a steady, even pull would keep the paint from "chipping"—adhering as the masking tape came up. As I gently lifted the tape, Bob took my hand, guiding my motion. My body heated instantly. I loved his strength and size. I loved feeling his authority, feeling I could trust him with my body, feeling he knew what he was doing. We kissed gently. Then he lifted me off the ground and swung me round and round, ending the moment but increasing the desire. And my guilt about Peter.

That weekend, as I made a perfunctory, obligatory bus trip to visit Peter at Fort Dix, my innards churned. I thought how real Bob was—his dedication, concentration; I admired the respect he commanded from his peers, even from older, established artists. Talking with him about art challenged me: he didn't waste time trying to make brilliant observations like Peter, but pressed me to figure out how art applied to me and encouraged me to see how I could use ideas in my art. Bob was going somewhere, starting to make an income and support himself with his art, while pushing himself to stay at the forefront of painting, sculpture, even live performance. In short, he was a practicing artist, and I found him irresistible—strong, a mature man. Compared to Bob, Peter seemed to me stringy, pale, smaller, a boy in my mind; he didn't stand a chance. As the bus pulled into the station, I decided I would have to tell him about my attraction to our downstairs neighbor. Instead, I accused him—justly—of making another pass at Twanette, told him he was flabby and ugly, and informed him we were through.

Bob and I started going out regularly.

We went to Happenings: the curtain rose on Claes Oldenburg's weather balloon, which slowly began to inflate. Then the curtain went down.

To early Warhol films: the kiss began and continued and continued and continued and continued until the film ran out.

To concerts at the Judson: Alex Hay hugged pillows as a prerecorded tape asked, "*Are* you comfortable? Are *you* comfortable? Are you *com*fortable?" Steve Paxton and Yvonne Rainer walked slowly toward each other, taking an eternity in their frontal nearnudity.

To bars: the Cedar Street Tavern, where the abstract expressionists—de Kooning, Smith, Rothko, Kline—used to hang out, then Max's Kansas City, north of Union Square, where chick-peas were the featured hash and Leo Castelli's front booth was where everyone wanted to be.

As we discussed the work we grew closer, although our opinions were not necessarily the same. My mother's well-trained snob, I didn't really like any of the performance art. Most of it seemed cute and coy, and it made me angry: almost everyone appeared glib, smug, self-satisfied, and unskilled. Just about anybody seemed to think they could do just about anything. My sense of humor in those days didn't extend to art or probably, for that matter, to much else.

Bob was a bit more generous, although in the New York art

scene there was not a lot of tolerance among the various camps. Bob and Doug Ohlson were rigorous hard-edged painters, holders of the flame being passed down from Tony Smith, Ad Reinhardt, and Barnett Newman. It seemed to me they could find borderline minimalists like Ellsworth Kelly or the Washington painters Ken Noland and Morris Lewis soft and romantic. Certainly the Pop artists—the Warhol group and Larry Rivers—were considered whimsical and commercial, and Oldenburg and Rosenquist, two great technicians, were on the line because they rendered recognizable objects. Still, through Bob I was exposed to all these artists, visiting their studios, and I always sensed, looking at their works in progress, that even the ones who were not the purest by the Huot/Ohlson/Frampton/Andre scale nonetheless had the passion to make it through a lifetime of questioning.

There was an expression, "in the air," and that meant there was a current lots of people were plugged into. Each artist raced to find answers in his or her own way. There was a community downtown and both its supportiveness and its competitiveness were positive forces in getting work done. Well-educated and very arrogant, friends since they were students together at Andover, Hollis Frampton and Carl Andre had lofts in the same building on the fringe of Chinatown. Bob and I often spent evenings and Sunday afternoons with them, drinking beer and discussing the ancient questions: "How do we see?" "How do we know?" The point of their work wasn't to create beautiful objects. Scientifically and mathematically inclined, their art concerned perception. Hollis's film *Zorn's Dilemma* investigated the number of cuts it was possible to register in a second, predating the speed of music video cuts by nearly twenty-five years.

I, for the most part, didn't know how to fit in. Everyone was older, and I hadn't done anything yet. But Bob's acceptance of me seemed an endorsement, and I intended to work to become a peer. Our relationship deepened as these events, conversations, and studio visits increased my capacity for adventure. Passion is passion, and the love and excitement for work I felt in all these artists brought me closer to Bob. It also helped make me impatient with myself.

For the moment, I had no credentials as an artist, seeing myself as only a performer. I'm sure this is part of what goaded me toward becoming absolutely and intolerably obnoxious in Paul's studio. One of Paul's very first dances, *Epic*, in 1957, had been a cause célèbre. Accompanied only by the phone recording "At the tone, the time will be . . . ," and dressed in conservative businessmen's clothes, Paul performed everyday gestures—walking, sitting, waiting. The performance's audacity was matched by the late Louis Horst's review in *Dance Observer*—a column of blank space.

To my young way of thinking, it was this rebellious strain in Paul, the one that challenged the established definitions of dance, that made him an artist. But as he started to work more and more within the sphere of pure dance, making dances like *Aureole* and *Party Mix*, I, like most of the theoretically oriented avant-garde, began to think he had sold out. I was critical then of what I now prize most in him—a menschlike dedication, sense of humor, and ultimate modesty; he never was one to insist on the eternal importance of what he did. But at the time, whenever Paul's instinctual sense came through in the form of occasional wildness and physical abandon, the cool, cerebral 1960s avant-garde was embarrassed by it, threatened by his raw heat and power. I was too, and questioning him constantly, I began to break the cardinal rule of studio workers, which is to accept unjudgmentally, for new work is vulnerable. Later you can judge, but at the moment of creation, my saying to Paul about a given dance phrase, "You're kidding," snarling a little as I tried the movement on, was certainly not supportive. During the first phase of new work, no artist can or should tolerate "You can do better." Better than what?

Of course what I was really saying was "*I* can do better than that." As Paul worked I would look at his choices—the movement he selected, the way he set it into phrases, how those phrases were put together in a larger context—and while I understood his choices I thought I could feel alternatives that might be more interesting. Subconsciously I was promoting a break with Paul because I wanted to make dance that could have a greater integrity and vision, work that would be tougher and more relevant. I took dance, its possibilities and its traditions, very seriously, and I began to question Paul's desire and ability to make anything more than easy, pleasant, decorative work. I also felt he was not using me well, that I could make more of my dancing talents. But I didn't have the confidence to leave. I needed to get fired.

My final falling-out with Paul came over money. I didn't want more; I wanted less. The company paid us for twenty performance weeks so that we could then collect unemployment during rehearsal weeks. This strategy—still being used by many professional dance companies—instituted the federal government's first, if unintended, arts subsidy program. Paul believed that after doing this for two or three years we could create a large enough audience to sustain us and we could then go back to making serious dance. But I kept telling him that his crowd-pleasing tactics and cheap pieces like *Party Mix* would make him forget how to work seriously. He would become confused, lose his artistic integrity, and get locked in a vicious circle, always having to generate a larger and larger income. In the performing arts, the more you work, the more it costs to work, as the support staff, per diem, and travel costs eat up any margin. I kept warning Paul over and over about the dangers of selling out, and it was just a matter of time before the end came.

At a party hosted by Clive Barnes—then dance critic for *The Times* of London—Clive asked me how I liked performing in *Scudorama*. I responded defensively. Embarrassed by the small size of my role, I said the piece was dicey, totally commercial, and rather like being in "a cowboy-melodrama soap opera." Paul overheard me. On the way out, he asked, "Whose side are you on, anyway?" Blinking innocently, I replied, "Are there sides to be taken?" The next day he called me into his room and suggested I be given some time off to go out on my own: a "trial by fire" he called it.

It was November 1964. Bob and I had shied away from living together after my breakup with Peter because we wanted to be certain that if we got together, it would not be from convenience and I would not be on the rebound. Unable to afford the upstairs loft alone and being frequently on the road with Paul, I slept on Diane Wakoski's floor in Chelsea when I was in New York. But now, no longer a student or a member of a professional dance troupe, and in the middle of a divorce, I didn't quite know what to call myself, what I should be doing, or where I should be living. But I wisely allowed myself to act intuitively. On New Year's Eve, Bob and I were at a party, went into the bathroom, took off our clothes, got into the shower, and started seven very good years together.

The other aspect of my desire that went unquestioned was my passion to dance. It was only how I was going to do it that wasn't clear. I had continued taking classes with Merce and I thought of dancing with the Cunningham company, but his work was ultimately too cerebral for me. I was obviously unsuited for ballet, even if my pirouette or pointe work had been up to it—which they were not. Nor did I like trying to look anything like, let alone *exactly* like, every other dancer in the chorus. All the same I auditioned for commercials and industrials, even for the Radio City Rockettes, who loved my kicking and fifty-two fouettés on pointe, but couldn't I please *smile*? I was much too small in every direction to work as a Latin Quarter show girl, but still I tried. Finally, between rounds of auditions, interviews, and unemployment lines, I could stall no longer. If I was going to dance, I was going to have to learn the lesson Ruth St. Denis had taught Martha Graham and which Martha had once shared with me: "I went in and Miss Ruth said, 'Show me your dance.' " "I don't have one," Martha replied. Miss Ruth responded, "Well, dear, go out and *get* one."

. . .

Trying to find a toehold in dance-making, I shuttled back and forth between my desire to dance and my fear that not only would I embarrass myself as a choreographer but the critics and the audience would say I wasn't even good enough to be a real dancer. However, as I started to assemble the pieces—finding a space to work in, locating performers willing to work for free with a first-time choreographer—my curiosity about people's reactions preoccupied me more than my fear of ridicule. For the first time, I began to discriminate between fear and excitement. The two, though very close, are completely different. Fear is negative excitement, choking your imagination. Real excitement produces an energy that overcomes apprehension and makes you want to close in on your goal. In the future I found that whenever I pursued situations that prompted the discomfort I know as excitement, I came out of the experience intact. But fear always existed for a good reason, and those situations invariably would leave me damaged and diminished.

I started to work on my first concert, anguishing over the question "What is dancing?" I allowed myself only one assumption: dance is movement in space and time. The space was a small Bauhaus auditorium, Room 1604, belonging to the Hunter College art department, where Bob worked as an instructor. The structure of my work utilized the curvy walls, balcony, and small stage of the place. The entire evening—April 29, 1965—lasted seven minutes. Any stragglers missed the whole thing. Seven minutes was all I could handle and about all I had to say. It would be enough to test the waters.

Having accounted for time and space, all I needed was a beginning, a middle, and an end. I began in the dark with almost nothing, "a radio beginning" as I like to think of it, entering upstage of the audience. The ending was face down, in a blackout, an homage to death: how else to end definitively? Then all I needed was the middle, a way of getting from the beginning to death as directly and economically as possible. But how could I select from the infinite number of choices to make a middle? The solution was to decide what couldn't be eliminated.

My answer was the right angle, the diagonal, the spiral, and the circle. These are the basis of all movement; everything else moves in patterns through a combination of these four. Fine, but how to make this dramatic? I figured I'd better couch my diagonals and spirals in sex and surprise if I wanted to reach an audience.

Sex was—when the lights came on—myself in a backless leotard cut high on the sides with red pants, slightly bell-bottomed but tight at the hip, stopping short to reveal ankles in velvet high-heeled bedroom slippers.

The surprise was a real shocker: circling my right arm one time, a full three hundred and sixty degrees in a plane parallel to my body, I snapped a yo-yo down to sleep, then brought it up. Perfecting this move required hours of practice. I think I left it in because I needed something real to worry about, distracting me from the inevitable opening-night nerves.

O.K., what next? I stepped out of the bedroom slippers and into a pair of large, skilike wooden shoes. I stretched my back first into a right angle, then reached farther out onto the diagonal—like a skier soaring off a slope, free, out into space. Then I left these shoes, went onto the stage, and held a relevé in second position, the arms reaching diagonally out from the shoulders, spread-eagled. The double diagonal, the X, Leonardo's Vitruvian man. All three minutes of Petula Clark's song "Downtown" played and I did not move, except to rotate the X once, ninety degrees in space, to reveal the form in profile. Blackout.

Part Two extended the diagonal farther out in space. Two couples (one including Bob Huot) came together onstage, rushed down a set of stairs in the middle of the apron, then spread out and exited diagonally, the same side they'd come from. The X of my vertical relevé moved into horizontal space. Blackout.

Part Three was spirals and curves. Changing costumes during Part Two to a white cap, fencing jacket, and tights, I raced down

hANk Di·re

A SHORT EVENING OF DANCE BY TWYLA THARP

8:30 PM APR 29,30 HUNTER COLLEGE

LEXINGTON AND 68TH ROOM 1604

hANk Di·re

PERFORMERS- CHRIS CONSTANCE, ROBERT HUOT

ANN MCFARLAND, ANNE SEVERSON AND TWYLA THARP

LIGHTING- JENNIFER TIPTON - COSTUMES PROPERTIES- R. HUOT

RESERVATIONS ONLY WO64396 1-5PM

hANk Di·re

the stage steps, caught hold of a subway pole, spun around it,
executed a baseball slide just above the ground, then hit the deck
—splat!—sprawling forward on my face, taking the weight through
the backs of my wrists, spread-eagled once more, though now face
down, an homage to dance icons after a long apprenticeship, and a
reference to the bows that end all well-taught ballet classes, a
moment of reverence as the students both acknowledge the instructor and begin to practice an action they will need to make as
performers before an audience. The curtain call was embedded in
the dance. I wanted to connect my first choreographic effort
with the end of my classwork, to show my dance as an extension of
my lessons, not a departure from them. This content was prompted
by both loyalty and pragmatism: it has always seemed to me
that there's a better chance for a future where there has been a
past. Blackout and clear. There was no acknowledgment of the
audience.

Tank Dive: the title referred to my sense that my chances of
succeeding as a choreographer like Graham, Balanchine, or Cunningham were the same as someone diving off a forty-foot platform
into a teacup of water or, better yet, from a very high platform,
about nine hundred thousand feet up, into a thimbleful of water. It
was not a solo concert but a full-fledged event, a complete production. Bob Huot designed the fliers, props, and wardrobe; my friend
Jennifer Tipton lit the piece. I did the necessaries: sewed, got
mailing lists, took announcements to the printer, addressed and
stamped, tried to get press coverage—everything to assure that my
efforts would not go unnoticed. I didn't promote myself as a star. I
had always seen myself as a star: I wanted to be a galaxy.

The next morning, I raced from the Franklin Street loft to West
Fourth Street for the early editions of the *Times* and the *Post.*
Waiting for the newsstand attendant to give me my change, I felt
as though I were holding my breath for final grades. Not thinking it
classy to paw through the papers on a street corner, I went into the
nearest Chock Full O'Nuts. I ordered a coffee and a powdered-
sugar doughnut. Then I looked for the reviews. Nothing. In either

paper. *Nothing.* Did I have the right papers—May 1, 1965? I couldn't believe the critics didn't realize what we had here was history created last night.

The moment was a real crisis of confidence and taught me an important lesson: if you want to create art, you'd best have a deep belief in yourself and no ulterior motives. Today I'm grateful for the relative obscurity of my first five years as a choreographer. I had time to develop my own backbone, to find what I deemed important without having to cater to public taste, so that when reaction finally came—both negative and positive (for they can be equally misleading)—I was well grounded. There was no financial remuneration and little attention paid me those first five years; so I simply went on asking myself, "Do you want to do this or don't you?" Today I try to keep both money and celebrity from standing in the way of asking this same question every day.

I took the weekend off, then got on with the next dance. In the rest of 1965, I choreographed a second, longer, full evening of work, made one sixteen-minute film (including the splicing), and completed a six-week commercial gig, a sort of furry hootchy-kootchy (I had chopped the paws off one of my father's bearskin rugs) which I performed for pay to lure tourists into the Alaskan exhibit at the 1964 World's Fair. All the time my attention and energy were solely devoted to dancing. I was in the studio by myself three hours a day, while continuing to take classes with Richard Thomas and at the Cunningham studio and working part-time as a Kelly Girl temp to pay bills. Even when I wasn't in the studio, an intensive and obsessive inner dialogue continued: what's important? Why? How do I show that through movement? I looked at the ocean, at Bob playing cards or tossing a football with a friend, and thought: what does this tell me about dancing? Is there anything in their movement I can respond to or can use? Living had little use for me other than how it could be funneled into dance.

This intense concentration was thrilling, but it was also costly. At first Bob was very supportive of my work, but as the year went on our home life became more difficult. Bob wanted us to marry—perhaps he thought that would change my focus—while I liked things as they were: no wedding rings, change of name, confusion of identities or roles. I had just been married and it had not come to much. Bob and I were both intact as individuals and were together when we chose; that seemed a good relationship to me.

Our differences came to a head when I accidentally became pregnant. Bob wanted the baby. For me, mothering was out of the question. I knew I could not be a parent and dance and choreograph. Not yet. Maybe one day I would have the experience to orchestrate all that, but for now I felt a baby would so severely curtail my momentum that I would never recoup.

Finally Bob agreed. We scraped together the seven hundred and fifty dollars for an illegal abortion and went to an ice-cream parlor in Orange, New Jersey. There I was put into a car, blindfolded, and driven around the block for a few minutes to shake my sense of direction. Then I was taken to an empty room on the second floor of a shanty. I had the abortion with no anesthesia, "Hot Time . . . Summer in the City" blasting from a radio the whole time to cover my cries. Bleeding a lot, I was driven back to the ice-cream parlor almost immediately. The experience remains intensely painful, one of the few that make me wonder whether my professional and artistic aspirations were really worth the price.

As I began to work on the next concert, I felt the need for another dancer. I had already asked Margaret Jenkins, a large woman with a resourceful mind who came from Merce's studio, to dance with me for no pay, a difficult request which Margie graciously made easy. But two dancers—Margie and I—seemed too intimate. Three would be closer to cosmic. Margie had the answer for this problem. She lived next door to a young dancer named Sara Rudner in a Broome Street tenement. Sara, as it turned out, was also a Barnard alumna, graduating the year after me. ("I'd never seen a name like that," Sara says about coming upon me in the 1963 yearbook. "That was my first introduction to the concept of

'Twyla Tharp' and I just got hysterical.") Margie had invited Sara to see the second concert I had given at Hunter, after *Tank Dive*, and knew Sara was interested in working with us. "I walked into that room," Sara says, "and I saw this dancing and I was knocked over. I had never seen a dancer like Twyla. The body was totally functioning, the physicality of it was tremendous. But the face was just impassive. It was an expression I had never seen before."

Now all that remained was for Margie to get me to see Sara, who was performing in a Paul Sanasardo concert. It wasn't an easy task. I had stopped attending concerts by 1964, figuring I had pretty much seen it all. Having started my own work, I did not want my eye to become biased by other dance. Besides, in working with Margie I had learned that developing dance means developing dancers—the two are inseparable, and anyone who attempts to bypass this step is kidding himself—and I figured that this Sara would already have been spoiled. But Margie finally got around my defenses and convinced me Sara was worth the sacrifice. I stayed for maybe two minutes and muttered to Margie on my way out, "She'll do."

But first, so she would know we were serious, we had an audition for Sara at the Franklin Street loft. Because the floor was unfinished and treacherously splintery, we warned her to bring shoes. She did—saddle shoes. (To this day, Sara dresses in a funky assortment of odds and ends.) According to Sara, the audition consisted of my making movement on her (which I intended to use in the next dance), watching her execute it, rubbing my hands together and saying, "Oh, you've got a lot of energy." And then she heard my mind going "Tick, tick, tick." That was it. We began to work.

We didn't stop for the next twenty years. Sara made an inestimable contribution to my art. She developed major roles in all the dances from *Re-Moves* (1966) through *The Fugue* (1970), *Eight Jelly Rolls* (1971), *Baker's Dozen* (1979), *The Catherine Wheel* (1981), *Nine Sinatra Songs* (1982), and *Fait Accompli* (1983), which was the beginning of *In the Upper Room* (1986). Critics have written thousands of words attempting to describe Sara's beauty as a woman and dancer. A gorgeous creature, with wonderful curly hair and a full but perfectly proportioned body, she combines an abundance of expression with a unique control. (Reportedly fans bought front-row seats and binoculars to watch in detail the incredibly refined complexity of her solo in *Deuce Coupe*.) Yet to me, all the critical praise of Sara has missed her most extraordinary quality: the modesty with which she has lived her life and done her work. Never selfish, never considering anything hers, Sara exists in a free world. Her quicksilver quality, so often noted, is a feature of her generous spirit. Lacking vanity, she has no style or image to maintain. To me as a choreographer, she offered the perfect instrument, a deeply intelligent dancer, superbly trained, who was willing to try anything, to move with me into the "white zone," the open, scary void you occupy as you create a new piece. She embodies a kind of rare courage. In 1985, toward the end of our career together, I, and every dancer in the studio, was moved daily when rehearsal ended and Sara simply melted into the ground, collapsing in pain from the arthritis developing in one hip. But never did she "mark" the movement, withholding anything she might contribute to me or the younger dancers.

For the next seven months, four hours a day, six days a week, we rehearsed. This time I was determined to take the necessary time to make a piece that, whenever it came, would have its own identity and be reminiscent of nothing. Unlike my first two concerts, which I had prepared in the relative anonymity of Hunter, now we rehearsed at the Judson Church gym.

Our presence represented a challenge to the established avant-garde on their home turf. Passing the stars—Trisha Brown, Yvonne Rainer, and Steve Paxton—in the hallways, we were uneasy. We were younger than they and had issued no manifestos— members of the Judson crowd loved making overriding statements on the nature and purpose of art. Most importantly, we had the gall to *dance*. This was definitely not chic. At the Judson you could only

Sara Rudner, The Raggedy Dances, 1972

walk and run—if you danced, you had sold out. Ostensibly, the dogged insistence on minimally inventive movement was based on the Judson group's desire that dance be "inclusive"—not limited to dancers, but something anyone could do, even, say, painters. Declaring the ballet shoe verboten, and bare feet old-fashioned, the Judson dancers used Keds in order to identify with the common man and to separate themselves from Martha, Merce, and Paul. While the Keds gave up something in movement—the thin leather sole of a ballet shoe frees the foot to use all its strength to propel the body up or out, while the bare foot grounds the body with its traction—at least the Judson's Keds made a statement.

I thought inclusiveness fine, but why shouldn't dance include dancers? Painters certainly didn't think everyone could paint. In fact, most painters didn't think any other painters could paint. I understood the idea that dance should be of, by, and for the common person, but just because you could run didn't mean glissade was wrong. Although several Judson dancers—Barbara Lloyd, Judith Dunn, Steve Paxton—were excellent technicians, their need to ignore their skills when performing at the Judson seemed wasteful and perverse to me. They argued that creative, difficult movements were seductive and cheap, that technique and virtuosity were beside the point, but to me these were the point. Virtuosity must appear in a context—even the most spectacular feats can become tedious—but audiences love virtuoso stunts for a good reason: they present the drama of the body being challenged to its physical limits. Although Judson dancers were sometimes almost nude (so, by the way, were Erick Hawkins's and many of Martha's men, much of the time), at heart they were very puritanical because they refused to enjoy the challenge, the juice of moving. "No to spectacle no to virtuosity no to transformations and magic and make-believe no to the glamour and transcendency of the star image no to the heroic no to the anti-heroic no to trash imagery no to involvement of performer or spectator no to style no to camp no to seduction of spectator by the wiles of the performer no to eccentricity no to moving or being moved"—Yvonne Rainer's mid-

Sixties manifesto did not attract me. All those nos would become my yeses.

Set in four sections and performed without music, *Re-Moves*, from 1966 (the name is a pun, meaning both "to do over" and "to take away"), began in the full rectangular area of the Judson performing space, the audience pushed to three sides. The second section, danced partially under a balcony, cut the space in half. The third section took place around a large plywood box, eight feet high, the audience seeing only one quarter of the action as we passed between them and the box, working our way around the perimeter. The fourth section was *inside* the box, the audience seeing nothing, only hearing shufflings and murmurings, the sounds of our next piece being rehearsed. After declaring the audience superfluous, we of course took no curtain calls, a practice we continued for five years because I was worried, first, that there would be no audience, and second, that even if there was one, they would hate what we did.

Most of the movement in this barren terrain was simply locomotive, establishing a unit of movement and repeating it ad nauseam until, like a repeated word, the gesture lost its sense. One basic unit was a small tap phrase—actually closer to a flamenco step. Another was putting one heel directly in front of the toe of the other foot and propelling an enormous hoop around the edge of a large space. I described the step around the box in the third section as follows: "You wiggle your heel and then you wiggle your toe and then you wiggle your heel, you wiggle your toe. You keep doing this on the same leg going around the plywood box. You cheat on the back side (where no audience can see) because your foot is very tired."

Re-Moves was steeped in death. We dressed for our ritual in black, stark nuns with one white glove and shoe on opposite hand and foot, the point of a white triangle glued to our foreheads. Many of the dance's images dealt with descent: a hard rubber ball was sent bouncing and allowed to die down, the dancers duplicating its paling rhythms; Sara lowered herself from the balcony via a rope ladder and then backed up slowly through the space, doubling up and eventually ending flat on the floor; I solemnly pulled three raw eggs from a black bag behind my back and allowed them to roll from hyperextended fingers to smash on the floor—a reference to my recent abortion. *Re-Moves*, made at the time of the Vietnam war, was an abstract on a bleak time. Its progress was to show less and less of itself, and it ended with its many elements splayed uselessly, smashed and spent; like the *1984* Newspeak we all knew the government was giving out, *Re-Moves'* gestures repeated mindlessly until they became a hypnotic babble, only filling air and time.

Now there were reviews, and I began to have to make peace with critics and criticism. What I hoped would be true seemed to be working: my abilities as a dancer compensated for my high jinks. Clive Barnes had moved to New York and now was the first-string dance critic at *The New York Times*. After *Re-Moves*, he wrote (one of my all-time favorites): "Miss Tharp herself is so cool she could use a refrigerator for central heating." But he slipped me the good with the bad, saying that while I was not yet a good choreographer, I was "bad in a rather interesting way."

There was more. We had sold out both nights (tickets were free, though the Judson took up a collection; I recall one of our takes was a respectable seventy dollars), and dance enthusiasts were appropriately baffled. I never heard of anyone loving *Re-Moves*, but at least they took notice. "There she was doing this two-step around a wall," Charlie Reinhart recalls. "I can see it now. And I

Re-Moves, below and right, 1966

thought, Oh my God, that's terrible—but interesting." Arlene Croce, later the dance critic at *The New Yorker*, who through thick and thin, good reviews and bad, has been a friend for twenty years, does not claim to have spotted genius at the Judson, but she did think, "This takes guts." She was most impressed by the tap dancing: "I knew this was authoritative—loony but authoritative. Something was going on, and I was just going to have to see the next thing this woman did."

We had not embarrassed ourselves; we had passed through the vale and come out whole. We knew we were relevant; we had situated ourselves in the vanguard of the investigation into how dance could relate to and deal with our lives. We worked in new forms, but by choice, letting our movements bridge the past and future. We were puritanical in our own way—rigid, self-righteous, stubborn, perverse, and antiphysical. *Re-Moves* was definitely not a good time; it was capital-A Art, directed to the heavy-hitters—as Sara said, "The painters came." But we were also dedicated to finding an honest starting point for ourselves—not in ballet, not in modern dance, but in something absolutely fundamental, something that could honorably be ours. I was getting down to the first building blocks for our dances—before the atom, before the neutron and the proton, down to the quarks, strange and charmed. *Re-Moves*, I always felt, earned us our right to begin.

5

When I work well with other dancers, I take up residency in their bodies. Any science fiction movie in which something invades someone is good by me, *Invasion of the Body Snatchers* best of all. But my bodies need to be intelligent, beautiful, and sophisticated, capable of the amazing, possessing the great and simple ease that makes you believe one thing: God lives here too.

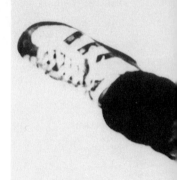

After the Judson season, the next step was clear: a European tour. "Twyla asked us if we wanted to go to Europe," Margie recalls, "and we all said yes. And she said, 'Well, call your parents.' Meaning, she couldn't pay for it. So we called our parents and they gave us tickets."

Through Bob's European dealers I was able to arrange evenings in several galleries and museums. Theatres in Paris and London were provided by two extraordinary patrons: Benedicte Pesle, who represented several American artists, including Cunningham, in Europe, and Robin Howard, who had brought Graham and Taylor to London. Robin's passionate commitment to dance made him risk his family fortune—wine cellars, restaurants, boats, and several Rodins—on a one-man crusade to introduce modern dance in England. Having trekked down to the Judson and seen a rehearsal, the two of them took a chance on their eyes and my talent, secured blessedly small and unostentatious theatres, and sent out the company's first press release.

"I suppose Miss Tharp could be called avant-garde," Robin wrote in the mailing, "though I never know what that means. I have only seen two of her works in rehearsal: one was too arid and dry for my taste and it was too long. . . . Newer work was not nearly finished but I found it more satisfying because my heart was allowed to be affected as well as my brain. . . . Anyway, Miss Tharp is one of my very few young 'dancer-choreographers' to watch out for." The release continued with quotes of my four reviews to date and concluded, "The performances will be without benefit of lighting and presented with every expense spared, but I still believe it well worth seeing."

Besides bookings, the other thing we needed for the tour was enough repertory to provide a second full-length evening. This I supplied by creating two new pieces, *Jam* (1967) and *One Two Three* (1967), before we left. The two pieces were complementary. *Jam* was Sturm und Drang Wagnerian, untempered and romantic, embarrassingly emotional in my minimalist, hard-edged world, so

One, Two, Three: Jenkins, Rudner, Tharp, 1967

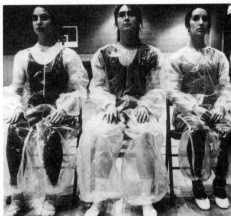

Jam: Rudner, Tharp, Dickinson, 1967

I staged it in the dark, only lighting the piece with battery-powered flashlights mainly directed into the audience's eyes. This novel form of theatrical illumination lent variety to the evening, a difficult task when all our scenery, costumes, and lighting effects had to be small enough to carry in our personal luggage.

In contrast, *One Two Three* was a strictly formal offering, consisting of a prelude composed only of fouettés—a smoothly hypnotic shifting from leg to leg intended as an homage to the great Act II chorus line of *La Bayadère*—and brief variations, the first solos in my company's history. Although we broke tradition by being the first modern dance performers in a long time to feature two dancing shoes per dancer, we were not corrupt enough to perform to music. Some avant-garde taboos were still too powerful to break.

In mid-February, Henny and Jenny—Sara's parents and the only people we knew with a car—drove us to Kennedy. We boarded an all-night flight to Stuttgart, sewed the unfinished, severe black and white costumes for *One Two Three*, and then tried to sleep, because I had no intention of not working the next morning. I was determined our discipline should not slip—we were *not* tourists.

And indeed it didn't. We arrived at 5:30 A.M. German time, took public transportation to our sponsors' house, woke them up, moved into our attic rooms, where sleeping bags had been laid out for us, and went directly to the performing space, the Kunstverein Museum. Finding it didn't open until 10 A.M., we got our sponsors to let us into the basement of their art gallery, an empty space with a concrete floor and a huge American jukebox of Fifties hits, did our barre to the music of the Everly Brothers and Elvis, saw some catacombs and cathedrals, ate an early dinner, and went back to the Kunstverein to start our tech. We were the entire crew, from wardrobe mistress to press agent. We set up chairs in the space, improvised the lighting cues, changed floor patterns to accommodate specific peculiarities of the space (there had never been two pillars in this dance before) and figured out how we could reach the johns to change into our next costumes before the public overran the facilities. We checked all the props, clocked our changes, and coordinated our various jobs, so that when the last ingredient—the audience—was added, we would be ready.

The performance went off smoothly, but then came the party. Never having been honored this way before, we were new to this part of the game. On our arrival we had been impressed by the elegant surroundings. But as our sponsors, the gallery owners, began introducing us to this person and that, I began to realize our performance had been a shill: the audience had been set up to buy paintings. I was shocked and mad: we were being used. My only commercial gig to date had been at the Alaskan Pavilion and at least that had been up-front. Furry hootchy-kootchies done for money was one thing, but our art quite another. Throughout my career this issue would prove a thorny one. The distinction is not pious but practical. One clear difference between art and commercial work is that commercial work is exploitive: the work may be high quality but the intention is to sell product or tickets. Art exists with or without ticket sales.

There were other shattered illusions. Touring bored me—no time for inventions, just get the show up. Of course there were always new problems and reactions—different difficulties with each space, different responses from each audience—but I found that making discoveries in the studio while I worked my way out of the white zone was much more rewarding than restaging work already done.

This first tour was brief, less than three weeks in all. But it immediately created a dilemma, pitting home life against being on the road. All dancers must travel, to build audiences and to gain a livelihood. Even now, with video, there is no product to send into the marketplace that captures the real vitality of dance. The best dance takes real bodies, and these cannot be in two places at one time. I missed Bob at the parties, missed connecting with him into the art scene, missed sleeping with him, eating with him, but I also loved our little band of three. Out on our own we were proving capable of handling everything, including trains that split, with Sara and the luggage going in one direction while Margie and I went with the coats and the hoop in another. A self-contained community that experienced other cultures and audiences through their responses to our performances, we had begun to build our own history. We pulled ever tighter in our conviction that we were waging a holy war with the infidel all around and we would triumph. "Three girls, one called Twyla Tharp, appeared at the Queen Alexandra's House, Kensington last night," wrote Susan Lester of *The Sun*, "and threaten to do so again on Thursday." All the same, when the tour was over Margie Jenkins stayed in Europe to teach a work of Merce's in Stockholm. I regarded this as a personal betrayal and I retaliated by not speaking to her for fifteen years.

I used Margie's departure as the opportunity to become a quartet, four providing so many more opportunities than three. Theresa Dickinson was a quick-witted Radcliffe graduate who had studied with Merce and had come to see *Re-Moves*. "There Twyla was, sitting on the floor," Theresa recalls, "and she chain-smoked in those days, so she was smoking, smoking, smoking. I was the first person back there to see her, and I said, 'It was really wonderful;

I think you're awfully good.' She said, 'Oh. Wanna try being in the company? Come to rehearsal on Monday.' " Margery Tupling was also from Merce's studio. Blond Margery made her income modeling part-time, and looked as though she had just stumbled into her dancing, a naturalness I found appealing.

Demanding a greater commitment than ever before from my dancers, practically making them sign in blood never to leave me, I decided to scrap the old repertory entirely and create new pieces, working every day but Sunday at the Judson. I missed Margie and I knew I could never really replace her, but the pain would be less if I moved on.

In my personal life, too, I wanted to make a stronger commitment. I had come off the road a more independent person, a better artist with a clearer sense of who I was and what my work communicated. I felt I was on the way to becoming Bob's peer, and I agreed to marry him. However, I added some stipulations. None of our friends could know, and I refused to change my name or wear a ring. Bob agreed. My parents flew in from California, and after a civil ceremony at City Hall, we all gathered at Bob's parents' home on Staten Island. Both sets of parents were pleased at this move in the direction of conventional respectability, my father and mother even participating in the champagne toast—the only time I saw them sip alcohol. But when it came to the hugs and kisses, my family held back. I was embarrassed to be marrying a second time, and to be marrying this time partially for the same reason I had before: to correct the past. Peter and I had slept together; we had to marry. Bob and I had lost a baby; marriage would prove our love and confirm us once again.

Now feeling anchored personally and professionally, I made eight dances in the next two years. I was determined to build my choreographic arsenal rigorously, one step at a time. The dances came from the work we did in the studio over thousands of hours. We parsed movement into its components, recombining the pieces in various ways. We looked at movement as energy; we looked at it as rhythm; we looked at it up close and far away. We asked, How slow can you go? How fast? We rehearsed and performed in silence because music communicates emotion and structure more easily to most people than movement, and it was movement we wanted to explore. Still, many of the questions in our investigation of movement came from lessons I had learned in music. Every morning my work began with improvising in the studio to music—any and everything from Bunraku to Renaissance music, Bach, the Romantics, early American jazz through Earl Hines and Coltrane, Webern. I did not tailor movement specifically, steps to measures (that would begin much later), but rather worked within the context of the music, sensing its larger flow and momentum, measuring its pulse. The energy of sound produces a spectrum; what were the equivalent reds, blues, and purples of movement? Gradually I began asking questions about counterpoint: where were the harmonies and tensions of movement? Unrelated single lines of movement began to seem chaotic and monotonous to me, crossing one another without purpose. We began exploring movement to learn ways of building harmonic possibilities. We inverted phrases, turning movements upside down, flexing instead of extending the feet, changing circular motions from en dedans to en dehors, rotating parallel positions out and vice versa. The permutations were endless, and Theresa argued that the only true inversions would be done under the ocean in China. We learned to retrograde movements, running them backward, like film images in reverse. Although I shunned unison movements—why subject these wonderfully unique minds and bodies to an abstract standard of uniformity?—I still tried to make my questions about physical potential universal, applicable to all bodies. Wanting to determine the common denominators of movement, I found it invaluable to work with bodies so very different from my own. Sara, Theresa, and Margery provided me with a priceless laboratory.

At the same time, the point of these investigations was never purely theoretical; these exercises built a foundation for us as performers. Turning a movement phrase inside out gave us more options in performance, a security and confidence as dancers, that resulted in performances rich in depth and authority. Our efforts, Sara says, were "frustrating, very difficult, but doing that work formed a whole style of dancing, which I always thought was a very intelligent style. It gave a lot of information and a lot of resources."

The first public display of our group's work was *Disperse* (1967), commissioned by the Bang Festival at the Richmond Professional Institute in Virginia and performed in the college's gym. I chose

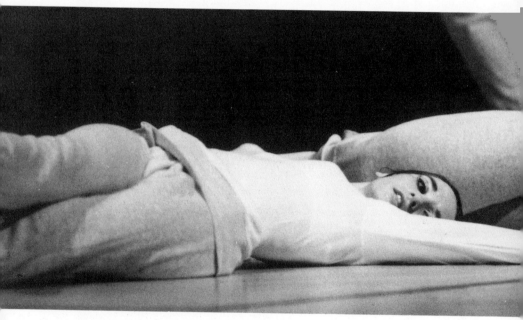

Disperse: Dickinson, Tupling, 1967

this space because I defined reality as the sweaty tangibility of the gym, not the make-believe of theatre.

Inspired by the mathematical proposition that since all matter can be subdivided to infinity there will always be a little bit left over, I used the sixty-by-forty-foot proportions of the Richmond gym, structuring *Disperse* to be danced in progressively smaller spaces: these areas were clearly marked by masking tape boundaries—forty feet by twenty-six feet, twenty-seven feet by eighteen feet, fifteen feet nine inches by eleven feet nine inches, and twelve feet by seven feet nine inches. I then divided the time segments according to the same ratio, beginning with six minutes for the first section—a twisted turn with one hip thrust forward, snapping around with dead stops on relevé between each turn. After each section the lights went off and the dancers moved into the next, smaller space. Each section introduced new material, and by the fourth section we were dancing practically on top of one another. The point of the work was stated when I brought in a child's

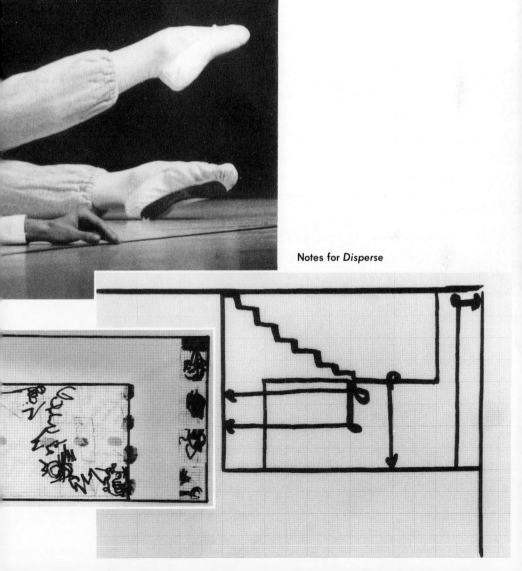

Notes for *Disperse*

wooden chair, abruptly spun, and smashed it on the floor, representing a little chaos in this pristine, artificially controlled world. Only the form of the chair was altered; its matter retained all its energy.

After the performance at Richmond, we drove back to New York in a rented station wagon (when asked why he made so many quartets and quintets, Merce replied that four or five is the number of people you can fit into a station wagon, with sets and costumes). We always had adventures in the car—especially since neither Sara nor I drove, although we tried to learn. Once, when Sara was behind the wheel, we sat a long while in a line of cars, missing light after light, until Theresa finally and lovingly pointed out we were in a parking lane. More rambunctious than Sara, I liked traffic circles, flooring the gas pedal while holding the steering wheel at a right angle. The Richmond performance provided one of my favorite escapades. When Theresa started the car, we found ourselves rolling down some wide steps. The surreal entered the picture in the form of a squadron of college men, out for a late-night walk, who simply picked up the car and carried us back to the parking lot. No one else remembers this event, so perhaps I was only dreaming, but I'm sure it was later the same night—Margery was driving—that the hoop used in *Re-Moves*, now with canvas stapled to it as scenery for *One Two Three*, began to billow, threatening to blow away. When a state trooper pulled us over for speeding, Margery dissolved in tears (almost convincingly) and explained, "Well, officer, I was just hurrying to get home before this thing on top blew away." Thank God, I thought, you can always count on a blonde.

Like *Re-Moves*, *Disperse* was a study in diminishing returns, but concluded infinity, not death, from the evidence. This optimism reflected my enthusiasm for the work and the group, which was becoming tighter all the time. Theresa had recently married Lewis

Party at 104 Franklin; company rehearsing at Great Jones Street, 1969

Lloyd, an administrator for Merce's company, and everyone hung out in their home, an old floor-through above the Pocket Theatre on Third Avenue and Thirteenth that offered a homey atmosphere none of the rest of us could provide. The camaraderie was so wonderful that even I—who thought my position as leader required me to remain socially aloof—couldn't help showing up more and more. "They had the best senses of humor and the best times of any group I've ever observed," Lewis has remarked. "They really had fun. And yet the public perception of the company when they performed was 'Jesus, this is tough stuff.' "

Working daily in the Judson gym—I had the key copied and always made sure to arrive before anyone else, effectively monopolizing what was supposed to be space shared democratically—we were beginning to reap the benefits of our intense collaboration. With no music cues, we had to work off one another. This meant our work did not have to be frozen, each performance an exact duplicate of the previous one; we could revel in being caught off guard. Dancing with each other was a real treat. We knew one another's abilities and sensibilities so well that each of us became an extension of the others, moving as a genuine team of spirit as

Judson Gym rehearsal: Dickinson, Rudner, Tharp, Tupling, 1967

well as body. The support within the group strengthened us as individuals, and together we felt we could move mountains. We were a true ensemble, the dancers free to come and go—no one had been hired and no one could be fired. We committed ourselves voluntarily. Watching us, you sensed no fear: we were not stuck in a career, but were our own people, independent, doing what we understood and endorsed. One rare Sunday when we were rehearsing at the Judson—we usually took the day off—a janitor came in and asked us how dare we dance on a Sunday. I replied how dare he disturb a bunch of broads doing God's work!

Our confidence extended to our performing. Although we still didn't take curtain calls, we were beginning to acknowledge the audience's presence. We were also learning the first lesson of capturing and maintaining their attention: do something—do *anything!* We employed all our resources as dancers—manipulating tempi, energy, and dynamics—to keep their eyes on us. We also tried to look great, Bob's costumes never failing to draw notice. Don McDonagh noted in the *Ballet Review:*

> Bob Huot is well on his way to making the company the best-dressed
> in American modern dance. Huot, a purist painter, is in the process

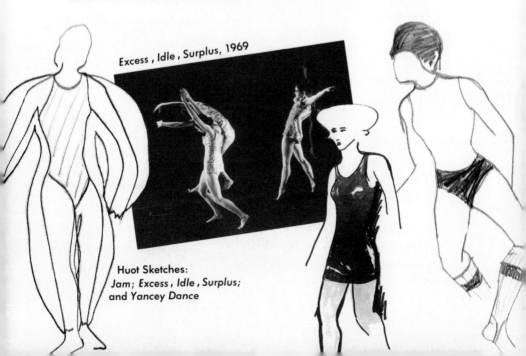

Excess, Idle, Surplus, 1969

Huot Sketches:
Jam; Excess, Idle, Surplus;
and Yancey Dance

of creating one of the most alive and consistently interesting sequences of costumes for any company in America.

Slowly our style—too balletic to be modern, too modern-dance to be ballet, too everything for the Judson—which had first won us enemies, was beginning to earn critical appreciation, often expressed in sentences as flamboyant as the movements they attempted to describe. Here is Jill Johnston's *Village Voice* review of a dance called *Generation* in 1968:

> . . . the fast stuff, a lot of intricate run-jump-slide-hop-leap patterns and explosions out of neutrality into wild flinging floppy gyrations with great complexities (thrusting, retracting, rotating) from hips through shoulders. I liked the floor business too, recalling only some splat falls, split falls, a fall into a reaching slide, a worming backward in a prone sprawl and a rump-first back-arched recovery with head impossibly twisted against the floor.

Our artistic development began to require more range, and this was made possible by the addition of three new dancers over the next two years.

The first was Rose Marie Wright. A breathtakingly precise dancer—we say a "clean" dancer—Rose had been in classes with George Balanchine, and I was sure he would take her for his company. However, Rose at six feet five inches on pointe was declared simply too big for the New York City Ballet—or probably for any ballet company. There were no men big enough to partner her, and I counted this unfairness as my blessing. But how would I get her into my company? I didn't have the nerve to ask her: unlike the rest of us modern dancers, this was a real ballerina.

So I posted an audition notice. "Twyla was rehearsing in a gym in East Harlem, at One Hundred Thirty-fifth Street and Lenox Avenue," Rose recalls. "I didn't know the subways very well so I took the train up to One Hundred Thirty-fifth Street on the West Side. It took me three hours to walk across town and find the gym.

Rose Marie Wright, Give and Take, 1976

I arrived late, nobody else was there for the audition, but Twyla told me to go and change. Then she and Theresa gave me some things to do, a number of little phrases, and I thought, God, this is really serious dancing. Please let me get this. Then they said, 'Well, you know, you're a ballet dancer and we'd really have to work with you, so we'll have to think about it. Why don't you get changed?' Two minutes later they showed up: 'We've thought about it. Why don't you start working tomorrow?' Years later, I found out they had staged the entire audition for me."

For the next fourteen years Rose worked with me, appearing in every piece I made. Throughout, she embodied the tenets of classicism, from her precisely folded clothes, neatly stacked in the dressing room, to the simplicity of her dancing and her mental clarity. In due time, Rose became the repository for the dances she was in because, unlike Sara or me, she *remembered*. We tended always to be moving on and sometimes liked to assume we should forget as much as possible to heighten the adventure. If ever we tried to lie, Rose called us on it. "This is what it was," she'd say. "Are we changing it?" And Sara and I would answer sheepishly, "Oh, no." We always acknowledged Rose's rightness.

"I was sort of dancing around in a corner somewhere, because I just like to move around, but Rose was the keeper of the flame," Sara says. "She was Twyla's notation." There was a strictness about Rose; things were always "exact" and in good taste. Although she had had less than a dozen modern dance classes in her entire life, she was so well centered—the result of her beautiful Balanchinian training—she didn't have to be taught a contraction: I said, "Bend there," and she bent there and that was it. Forever. Fixed. Done. In rehearsal, I would look at her even when she was standing still and feel centuries of classicism wash over me, images and essences from fifth-century Greek sculpture, Renaissance architecture, Mondrian. Then I would remember where we were going in our work that day.

The other two dancers were Graciela Figueroa and Sheila Raj.

They were polar opposites. Graciela was probably the most powerful woman I had ever seen dance. There's a film called *Our Dancing Daughters* in which Joan Crawford dances and Theresa—who had found Graciela at a class at Merce's—remembers, "Graciela was like that. Everything about her was broad and huge. She would make these sweeping gestures and chop off a piece of the room. Really dramatic. She learned a lot of the same parts we did, but she just did them her way. Graciela was the most different dancer we ever had. She was like a plow dancing or a truck dancing."

Sheila was Graciela's alter ego. Tiny—I sometimes thought of her as a fife to Theresa's flute—and unbelievably fast, not just physically but mentally. "She was one of the original natural dancers of all time," Theresa recalls, "and she also had a brain like a computer. She could learn anything Twyla showed her. She knew things Twyla hadn't figured out yet." Sheila came to this country on scholarship to the Graham company; the child of an English mother and an Indian father, she would go on to study hatha-yoga dance forms and the intricacies of tabla counting.

As a company we were a spectrum of unique bodies and personalities; as a community we had a powerful mission. "I really felt it was the beginning of something new," says Margery. "I always felt when I was looking at Twyla that she was on the edge of a new frontier and we were all working for that and had great faith in her vision, even though we didn't know what her vision was."

Theresa has a similar sense. "That company," she recalls, "was my first experience of what partnering could really be. It was possible because we trusted each other as much as we did and worked together as much as we did and tried to make things right as much as we did. We didn't wait for Twyla to make things right. She would describe what she wanted and it would be up to us to make it right. We must have been very dedicated, because now I find it extremely hard to get people to work with you that way." Dance critic Laura Shapiro has written, "Their commitment to the work

Tharp, Figueroa, Raj, Dickinson, Tupling, in best street clothes; center, Figueroa, Rudner, Raj, Dickinson, Wright in practice clothes; right, Rudner, Tupling, Dickinson, Wright, Tharp in *Generation* costumes, 1968

not only made it possible to survive the life, but informed the choreography itself, and made the dancing an expression of seven unique, but interdependent bodies."

Our spirit—communal, feminist—was part of the times. "We would rehearse together, perform together, take class and socialize together," Theresa remembers. "We lived with each other, we fed each other. One year Sheila and Graciela had no money and couldn't get unemployment, so Sheila got half of mine and Graciela got half of Sara's. We really were completely interdependent." When we got paid for a performance—not often—the money was divided equally. Sara continued to type, Theresa worked at the Composers' Bureau, Margery modeled, and Rose baby-sat— "They feed you when you baby-sit."

Yet within the world of the avant-garde we were considered hopelessly commercial. The Judson kicked us out, deciding we were monopolizing the gym, and worse, that we were successful, even *professional*. Theresa solved the space problem temporarily: she came upon a city listing of condemned properties which led us

to—among other places—an ancient Brooklyn school gym and a
Lower East Side police station. But the sites were far from ideal.
We abandoned the Brooklyn gym after blood dripped into a re-
hearsal from a stabbing on the running track overhead.

Bob, too, was critical of our growth. The more we talked the
pure language of dance—not simply breaking chairs or taping tape
to the ground—the more foreign we became to him. In particular,
he criticized my daily barre, condescendingly arguing that the classical exercises limited rather than increased my physical range.
Our brief performing stints were not popular at home—Bob didn't
like my absences. He also claimed that our "professionalism" was
destroying the integrity of our work. I vehemently disagreed. I was
moving away from the avant-garde tenets and ideologies. If people
wanted to see our work, great. If they wanted to pay, even better,
because the dancers were still living in Alphabet City, where
Rose's rent was $37.50 a month, and eating three courses of Jell-O
for dinner. When Rose came to work one day after being mugged,
I felt responsible. Unlike Bob, I didn't work alone; these were my
dancers. Yes, we were pursuing an ideal, but in the midst of a very
real world; if I wanted to continue, I had to help support my part-

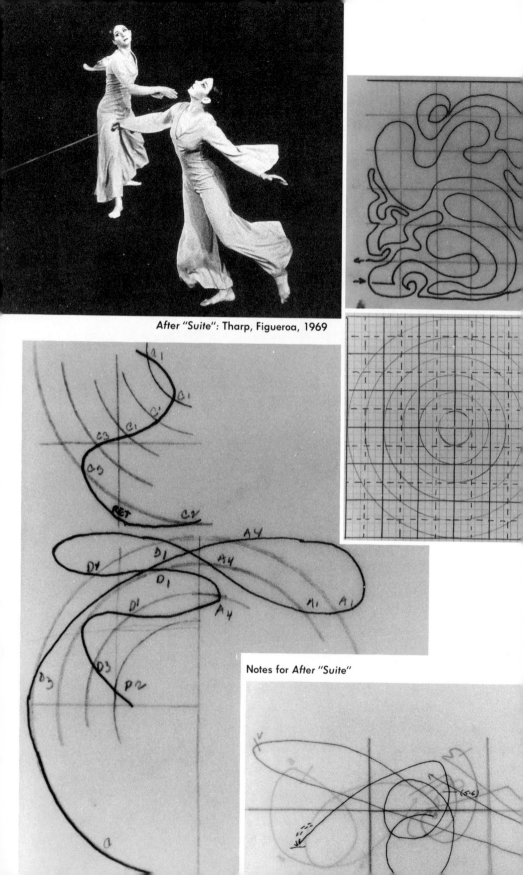

After "Suite": Tharp, Figueroa, 1969

Notes for After "Suite"

ners. Sure, I preferred working in the studio, but the performances paid the bills.

This group of seven cut its teeth on *After "Suite"* (1969), named in tribute to Merce, after his dance *Suite for Five* (1956). *After "Suite"* has seventeen different sections. From a notebook I kept then (without video, my notes were my only record) it's clear I was obsessed with continuity and differentiation, maintaining a pattern —what I call a matrix—while providing contrast to fend off monotony. Take the November 3 entry setting out the trio called "In a Flash." The specifications state a "short, continuous movement of very quick, effortless style. Canon with two dancers moving at very quick tempo, the third doing the movement slow-motion. The slow-motion dancer 'bumps' one of the fast dancers and they reverse roles; the process repeats again and again as they pass the movement back and forth like a sort of relay baton." The November 6 entry documents an "Exercise" called "Varied Constants #13," so titled because the phrase could be executed either with a "heavy pulsed movement: bouncing in knees, torso mvts over and back," giving rhythm to the phrase, or with a "non-pulsed mvt, rhythm provided by the action," simply through the shifts of weight. The "Exercise" itself begins, "Swing R arm front of body to side, L arm behind, L arm side high front cut to Rt side, to round by side of deep bent knees, R swings forward rounds, carries up as knees straighten, going as far back as possible. Legs go to parallel releve, high back arch, R hand flexes, carries forward to chest-hi as body rights self. Holding releve allow arm to relax, swing at side easily, fall, take wt on L long enough to get R down to outside of leg." The rest of the exercise is work on the floor and a recovery to a position with "continuous stretch."

The audience perceived little of this specific detail. But they did invariably note our seriousness and intensity. Anna Kisselgoff, in a February 1969 review in *The New York Times*, wrote:

> Pure movement is Miss Tharp's concern, with a special fascination for the uses of time and space. Having said that, it is almost

easier to describe, within current dance avant-garde references, what her choreography is not. No media were mixed last night, dancers acted as dancers and not as nondancers and no nondancer loped across the stage. Above all, this is a company of top-rate professionalism, where each member's technique is seen rather than scorned.

Deborah Jowitt in the February 13 *Village Voice* observed:

Twyla Tharp has changed a lot since I last saw her work in 1966. She has purged her dances of almost every element but movement. Tharp's mathematical space ratios, the chaste atomism with which she sprinkles her dancers all over the stage, their rarely colliding orbits, the purity of their attention on the movement give her dances an almost Spartan feel—a super-cool college of vestal virgins. And this despite the beauty and richness of her movement. She has been able to do what I thought might be impossible; she has transferred her own incredible style to her company. This style—speaking very superficially—involves acquiring a strong classical technique and then learning to fling it around without ever really losing control. The dancing is difficult, quirky, beautiful, stylish.

Jack Anderson in a *New York Times* article stated:

Twyla Tharp's methods are related to those of current systemic painters and sculptors and such serial composers as Schoenberg and Webern. . . . All this is curious to behold. Contrary to expectations, the effect isn't mechanical. Quite the contrary: the movements, so logically derived, so rigorously ordered, look mysteriously arbitrary. And the dances seem simultaneously rational and incredible.

But the very best was Arlene Croce, who wrote of *Group Activities* (1969), another premiere that year:

You grasp immediately [the dance's] difficulty and then its beauty of precision. It's so complicated that a timekeeper has to sit by, clocking the "score," now and then calling out the main count. The individual counts (in relation to the main one) and individual paths of movement of the ten dancers are uncanny in their symmetrical and asymmetrical play. The ten dancers are divided into two groups of five. Mirror-image opposites are offset by irregularities that keep the eye jumping. Oppositions occur in time as well as space. The animation is so intense, the stop-and-go action of the piece so unpredictable, that one hangs on in quasi-dramatic suspense. The unforeseen logic of these calculations has a peculiar relation to the imagery of abstract ballet. I mean, no matter what they are on paper or in the dancers' heads, they look—the near collisions, the sudden crowding or circling in a gang (in a jumping phrase), the as-sudden dispersals—brilliantly irrational to the eye. I know only two other choreographers who give the same effect, and they're Mr. B. and Merce.

Arlene's last sentence, written just four years after I'd begun to work, set me up for life. Ever since that sobering morning after *Tank Dive*, when no review whatsoever appeared, I have always been grateful for press. Even if a review is negative, reading it helps me better understand what exactly it is I think I'm doing in dance. Sometimes I may feel a reviewer is using my work to make his or her own points, but for the most part, critical attention has helped me put my work into a larger perspective.

The reviews were just the beginning. A picture of *Tank Dive* made the cover of *Dance* magazine in February, and in less than a year four separate head shots appeared in *The New York Times*. The most important of these was a publicity shot—the Ford Foundation was subsidizing a season of modern dance at the Billy Rose Theatre—featuring the pioneers and vanguard of modern dance.

Graham, rightfully, sits in the center; everyone in the photo but José Limón had either performed or studied with her. She looks intensely forbidding and deeply saddened, as though on the verge of tears. To her right stands a wry, distinctly cryptic Merce. Then Paul, a small relaxation at the corner of his mouth, attempting a smile but only managing to curl his cheeks upward as though he were already enduring his painful, future isolation; behind, Erick Hawkins, who looks too scholarly and decent to survive this brutal world. Next to Martha is Limón, his face already showing extreme suffering from the cancer that would kill him a few years later; then Don Redlich; Yvonne Rainer, dressed casually, with no makeup—a foolish merger of publicity, life, and art, I always thought; and finally me, scowling into the camera with what I hoped was a perfect deadpan public persona. We all look dug in, tenacious, fiercely determined. None of us looks the least bit pleased, honored, or relieved but rather deeply suspicious of the world, one another, and what would come from all this.

Certainly I was. Even as the photographer snapped the shutter, I knew that the moment was historic, representing an end to the generous "greenhouse period" I'd been blessed with, abruptly closing the time when I could escape the expectations, definitions,

Martha Graham, center; to her left José Limón; Counter clockwise: Don Redlich, Yvonne Rainer, Paul Taylor, Erick Hawkins, Merce Cunningham, Twyla Tharp, 1969

and cubbyholes of critics and audiences. My company's four years of relatively obscure investigations—when we'd been left alone to ask ourselves daily about dance and our own vision within its sphere—was over. Now we would have to factor in all manner of elements outside our private world. With *After "Suite"* we were a public presence.

The success drained me. After all the exposure, I felt dry in the studio. I had begun to worry: we would find we couldn't live up to our reputation; we would get too many proscenium opportunities and become caught in our repertory, chewing the gum long after the flavor was gone; we would lose our creativity, which maybe came only with being outside the system. To top it all off, I felt hypocritical standing on picket lines with the Art Workers' Coalition to protest admission fees at the Museum of Modern Art, while having to sell tickets to our own concerts.

Questions had inspired creativity in me before; now they throttled me. The eight dances from *Disperse* to *Group Activities* formed a cycle that gave me a primary education in movement analysis, design, and structure, painstakingly recorded in longhand notebooks with accompanying series of diagrams documenting space and time patterns. I thought of these pages as illustrated manuscripts representing thousands of working hours. These had resulted in new approaches to some of art's great themes: continuity, tradition, death, proprieties, courage, procreation. But now I sensed we were spinning our wheels. Rehearsals were becoming boring; we seemed caught in systems for generating movement and structure. To me, ennui is the only thing more fearsome than the unknown, and this restlessness gives me the strength to go on. Although we were only fledglings, I felt we had to escape our own traditions.

Medley, the dance that came from this period in 1969, mirrored these conflicts. Our years of working had kept us isolated for long hours in the studio, and in *Medley* I looked for ways to convey to

Medley rehearsal, New London, Connecticut; This page, counterclockwise from top left, student; Tharp; Dickinson, Figueroa; Wright and students; Opposite page, counterclockwise from top left, students; Rudner; Wright, Rudner, and Figueroa; notes; Figueroa; students, 1969

the audience, myself, and the dancers that art and life could co-exist, that they need not be mutually exclusive. The dance was developed and performed out of doors, free to the public. I attempted to loosen some of the constraints that had helped create the dances since *Disperse*—there were far fewer notes, diagrams, and schemata for this work—and I tried to allow as many elements of real life to penetrate the dance as possible. Based on everyday movement—running, walking, skipping—*Medley* became our "danci-est" dance yet. I tried to get this work out of the head and into the body.

Sponsored by Charlie Reinhart at the American Dance Festival, which was then held at Connecticut College in New London, the commission came with ten thousand dollars, an absolute fortune for us. Each dancer received thirty dollars a week for twenty weeks so they would be eligible for unemployment payments—fourteen dollars a week at the time. These were our first regular paychecks, and we made sure Charlie got his money's worth.

Rehearsing in New London, we worked in a deep meadow overlooked by a hill, which provided me a perfect vantage point. Watching—as Lee might have watched the Second Battle of Bull Run—I saw the sixty dancers acquire the personalities of their leaders: no-nonsense Rose; limpid, languid Sara; sharp, precise Sheila; huge and open Graciela; Theresa, beautifully accurate and measured; and good-natured, generous Margery. At the same time, I gave each of my dancers an individual moment. Sheila performed her "gnat," conceived to be the fastest movement possible for a human being, backed up by her "movement machine," a group of thirty dancers performing staccato chunks of her variation, arranged according to one of my few remaining fiendish systems. Graciela had a vast, arching solo, covering an enormous acreage of space, embodying her longing for the great, open Uruguayan pampas. Rose did a variation on pointe, set on an eight-by-eight-foot sheet of plywood. Theresa led off the "audience mirror," her solo backed by the student dancers reflecting the actions of the public as they entered the performing area, people suddenly seeing the

movement of their hands and heads in canon, as the dancers duplicated them a split second later. And she began the Adagio, the
piece's finale, a phrase that could be executed in less than a minute
but which was drawn out as long as possible, making it a nonmove-
ment: the record was Theresa's—winning is almost as important
for her as for me—her time being well over forty-five minutes.

Medley was backtimed to begin so that the Adagio commenced
at the official setting of the sun, the last section then progressing
well into darkness so that no one could see the end—or even know
it had ended. But the plan didn't work. At its first performance,
long before the Adagio ended, another concert, by Yvonne Rainer
and the Grand Union, began in the college gymnasium, after which
there was to be a party for the two groups in one of the dorms. So
most people left before our performance had stopped completely
in the darkening meadow. Charlie Reinhart remembers the party:
"I went looking for the john," he says. "I walk down the hall and
open a door and there's Sara in a closet, in arabesque. I said, 'Sara,
what the hell are you doing in here?' She said, 'Twyla came out
and felt sorry for us because the mosquitoes were biting us all up,
so she brought us in here, where we can continue.' "

With *Medley*, for the first time I was not in one of my own
dances. I had wanted the experience of seeing the dance from the
front, joining with the audience, but once I was there I found
myself very uncomfortable sitting in their midst. Hearing the com-
ments felt too much like eavesdropping, and many of the remarks,
positive as well as negative, made me blush. I used to fantasize
about having a large circle attached to my person overhead, with a
two-way curtain drawn all around me so I could watch performances without having my privacy abused. It has taken years to
find the strength to connect with an audience without jeopardizing
my own ego, detaching myself to find a director's objectivity. At
the party after *Medley*, I was particularly miserable. Never any
good with small talk and party behavior, skills I would need to set
about consciously acquiring, I realized how much I depended on
Bob to keep things going in social situations.

Bob was in the city mounting a show. The nearly four weeks of work in New London had been our longest separation yet, and with the intensity of the company's rehearsals before that, our marriage was definitely strained. Now, feeling that this dance *Medley* had become me, that my dancers had replaced me, that even Shakespeare probably was not as popular at Old Globe parties as whoever was playing Lear center stage that night, I went to my room feeling I did not exist. I desperately wanted to be held, to feel my body against another and to begin again. My misery would be duplicated often in my life, after premieres and alone in hotel rooms. But now was the first time, and I snuck back into the dorm's party room, found an unopened fifth of gin, went back to my room, drank myself into oblivion, and annihilated myself for real. Soon I was stinking drunk for the first time in my life, spending the early-morning hours retching out of the second-floor dorm window.

In September, we presented *Medley* in Central Park and then regrouped to begin a new work. But the group was no longer the same. Margery became pregnant and went off to San Francisco. In the midst of her marriage's breakup, Theresa also left. "Twyla really took care of me. I loved the work and really felt sad to be leaving it," she recalls, "but everything else was just pushing me out. That was the year when everybody was trying to examine their moral existence and see if they were leading the life they wanted to lead. I was feeling frightened by the intensity of Twyla's ambition, what she would do to be successful. I think she could see how I was being pulled toward other lifestyles—something more experimental, less involved with New York, less involved with the established art world."

So there we were, less two. Knowing we couldn't replace Theresa and Margery—the shared experiences were too great—I decided our next work, commissioned that year by the Wadsworth Atheneum in Hartford, *Dancing in the Streets of London and Paris*,

Dancing in the Streets of London and Paris, Continued in Stockholm and Sometimes Madrid, Wadsworth Atheneum, Hartford, Connecticut, 1969

Continued in Stockholm and Sometimes Madrid, would be both a retrospective (excerpting all the works from the beginning through *Medley)* to be performed by seven new "baby" dancers (as I thought of them) in the auditorium, and a new piece, which the veterans would dance in the rest of the museum. That way we could retain our past while disconnecting ourselves to move on.

Reeling over the two defections, I designed *Dancing in the Streets* to break down every conceivable wall put up to separate life from art. I was saying desperately to one and all, "Hey guys, don't pull out, we've got all the life we need right here."

We opened by warming up directly in front of the museum entrance so the audience had to walk over and around us to get in. They were provided with a large program, which was to serve as a road map to the action, then it was off to the races as the dances occurred in many different areas simultaneously—galleries, elevator shafts, broom closets, hallways next to guards. Thus a young lady might be calmly talking to a friend before a partial wall—one of those surfaces museums love to construct in the middle of a room—when a pointe shoe would pop out from the edge of the wall, the extended foot of Rose, performing a solo on the opposite side. During other sections we literally reconstructed moments from our lives. Graciela mimed talking in Spanish on the phone while she took a bath, Sara waited on an unemployment line, and all five of us danced one section while reading a book, changing clothes, and chewing gum. But for all my resistance, the realities of life were becoming overbearing. We were entering our fifth year of work and we still could not even begin to earn a living; the dancers were living well below the poverty level, and Sara's mother had begun to question the investment of her hard-earned money in Sara's Barnard College education. *Dancing in the Streets* was restaged in the Metropolitan Museum (with the Great Hall under construction and closed to the public, I talked curator of twen-

Dancing in the Streets, Metropolitan Museum, New York City: Dancers and audience, 1969

tieth-century art Henry Geldzahler into letting me use the space) and I got my picture in *The New York Times* again. But an overflow crowd turned aggressive when the promised television cameras— providing closed-circuit access to the many simultaneous performance areas—did not show and the throng, trying to find the action without the television to guide them, jeopardized the dancers performing on the marble staircase and on the treacherously slippery Spanish patio.

In March 1970 there was one more premiere, *Pymffyppmfynm Ypf*, named from a misprint in *The New York Times* and commissioned by Sullins College in Virginia. The dance was subtitled "predicted on theories of supply and demand," meaning the work had as much material and was as long as the commission money would allow. When the money was gone—thirty dollars a week per dancer—rehearsing was over and the dance done. We spent nothing on wardrobe, and to make this very clear (and also to protest the fact that Sullins, an all-girl school, had a male dean) Graciela performed a solo twice, first topless, then bottomless. The concert was a hit with the student body.

We had nothing left. We had worked nonstop for five years, with very little income and no vacations. The immigration bureau was after both Graciela and Sheila, their visas long since expired; much worse, Sheila was unable to work, her left metatarsal permanently damaged from dancing on the concrete mezzanine at City Center, a space we had found that no one else seemed to know existed. Feeling personally responsible for her injury, I decided I had to stop asking people to make sacrifices for me.

"What's going on?" Rose and Sara asked me after two friends they saw at a Lucas Hoving concert had expressed condolences upon hearing rumors of our demise.

"Oh, didn't I tell you?" they swear I answered. "I gave everything away to the Public Library and told them I was disbanding the company, in the hope somebody would take pity on us and give us money so we could go on."

The best I could do for my dancers, after five years, was not enough. I was still applying for grants, still accepting commissions, but in my mind I had stopped. Over the course of the last four years, since we had begun work in the Judson gym, I had built a group of dancing women who worked brilliantly together. An exclusive club, we went about our business with no male voices challenging our authority nor male bodies overpowering our accomplishments. Martha Graham too had begun her company as a devoted band of women whose husbands and boyfriends acknowledged themselves as "the men of Martha's women." Eventually all the women left to be closer to their families, leaving Martha alone—no family, no children to take her focus, nothing between her and her destiny as she saw it. I understood Martha's commitment, but I also believed she had shortcircuited both her life and her art. I had worked very hard to maintain a balance in my life, believing that work informed my life with Bob as well as the other way around and that each was about love.

Now, given the difficulties at hand, my frustrations and disappointment at learning of the near impossibility of my calling—not that it was any easier for Martha or anyone else in dance—I questioned the wisdom of the decision I had made to commit myself to dancing. That winter, Bob received a National Endowment for the Arts grant. He hadn't applied—a sponsor had put up his name—and at first he thought of sending the money back in protest against the Vietnam war. However, his friends convinced him it would only buy more napalm, and instead we took the money and bought, for nineteen thousand dollars, a badly-in-need-of-repair, ornate four-bedroom farmhouse with a barn and two hundred and fifteen acres, including pine forest and cherry and apple orchards, in upstate New York's Chenango County. We went up in the dead of winter, and by May I was pregnant. This time by choice.

6

My greatest fear in working
is always the end. Lately I have
taken to tricking myself into
finishing by leaving a hole
in the middle somewhere, then
stitching the two pieces together—
the Union Pacific approach.

The farmhouse and land

Pregnant and living on beautiful farmland that reminded me of the Indiana of my childhood, I spent my days contentedly stripping coats of green paint from the Victorian farmhouse on Spurr Street. I had definitely retired from the art world, never intending to make another dance, determined to clear even my dreams of dancing. The only traces of the outside came from the radio and from old T. M. Foster, a local farmer who hand-milked his cows and carted silvery containers of whole milk to all the neighbors in his ancient pickup truck. Bob bustled about, shoring up one side of the house or the other, learning about cows, scrounging used farm equipment in anticipation of the haying season, keeping a sixteen-millimeter filmed diary of our new house, and painting huge, elegant cartoons, antic drawings that were as far from his earlier hard-edged minimalism as we were from Franklin Street. We both felt newly respectable and independent. Chenango County is on the edge of Appalachia, and its dairy farmers work hard to keep up minimal living standards. To anyone with money, it would have been a dirt-poor economy, but to us, it was reasonably affordable. We were providing for ourselves and confident we would be able to manage the upcoming baby expenses. Our diversions were limited to grocery shopping once a week and Bill's Auction on Saturday nights. Here I could glut my mania for American memorabilia, buying an ancient pine blanket chest, buried under coats of paint, for only ten dollars, and huge pottery crocks that would do just fine for spring dandelion wine. In New Berlin there was no upper, middle, or lower class, just working people, and it felt good to be part of the community. The days Bob drove into New York to teach at

Hunter College, providing the money for our staples, I studied the *New Berlin Gazette*, Burpee's seed catalogue, or the *Chenango County Pennysaver*, believing myself up on the only current affairs that I needed to know about. My life had taken a simple shape but something was missing.

We had only been in the farmhouse six weeks when I found myself coveting the large, high-ceilinged attic. Spurr, with four daughters to marry off, had built the room for dancing: why not use it? The rhythms of daily chores—the stretch of my arms to reach faraway corners, the tension in my muscles as I carried laundry baskets, the pulse of sheets flapping on the clothesline in the wind —made me think again of dances. I started to work, but tentatively, and only when I really wanted to. Bob sanded and varnished the attic floorboards and framed them with a brilliant blue-painted band, a wonderful gift welcoming me back to my daily barre and brief stints of improvisation. I began working regularly.

The dancers came soon after—Rose on Memorial Day, Sara a couple of weeks later. They too were happy to be free of city grunge, of the crowding, the high costs, the impossibility of getting what was needed to work. On the farm we could provide for ourselves just waking in the morning and walking out to a field to work. Life was so simple. We all felt a dignity, a wholeness and wholesomeness that we lost hustling in the dance world. And anyway, who could be angry or disappointed in the spring? The farm was at its most glorious, the orchards and wild berries in bloom, the stream warm enough so that I could reach in for the watercress, the land constantly full of surprises.

We had a new member. Isabel García-Lorca, also a Barnard graduate, had seen us perform a brief protest piece at Columbia University while she was still in school; for an event to benefit the Chicago Seven, I had cordoned off an area six by six feet (the dimensions of a standard prison cell) and stuffed all seven of us in it to dance at once. Isabel is the niece of the late poet and playwright Federico García-Lorca, and her blood ties to classical theatre, peasant folk dances, and the Spanish elite excited the romantic strain in my imagination. I fantasized about her as I do every dancer I work with. Part of loving my dancers is seeing much more to them than meets the eye, and part of my challenge is to make these feelings tangible to the audience. Possessing an elegant bearing and great rhythmic sensitivity, Isabel had never studied either ballet or modern. She belonged to that rare category of performers who move with an unstudied grace that allows an audience the ultimate in wish fulfillment. Watching, they feel they could do it too and without so very much practice.

Both Rose and Sara lived in the farmhouse but Isabel had to stay in a rented house down the road. Her boyfriend considered himself a political radical although his family, to Bob's disgust, was one of the wealthiest in America. For this liberal aristocrat, Bob said, a revolution meant a Cadillac in every garage. Secretly, I didn't think this was such a bad idea. Everyone else had to earn their keep, so after morning class the girls who were not rehearsing with me joined in stripping paint, cleaning, laundering, sewing, ironing, baking, working in the garden, sanding floors, tending cattle we would slaughter and freeze, refinishing furniture, baling hay. To keep everyone from cracking, a bit of free time was built into our daily schedules for quiet reading or walks on the land. I made more dance that summer than I ever had before or since.

The reason for my prodigious creativity was simple. The phone did not ring for days; there were no distractions, no artificially imposed schedules or meetings, no inconvenient commuting. On the farm, everything was efficient and focused. The profoundly physical activities that seemed to link me to ancient chores—rowing, kneading, mowing—informed my work, and everything from sweeping out corners to thinking about the workings of a compost heap gave me new elements and purposes for the dances. All this daily enriched my ongoing concerns of conservation and continuity, and I always knew that if I got stuck I could just stop and walk in the cool forest, discoveries everywhere making me easy.

The Fugue was the first work completed in this new cycle. I dismissed everything up to this point—our first five years of work —as lessons. Now I used the contrapuntal techniques I had gained from our early work to put my craft at the service of creating and resolving tension.

The Fugue is twenty variations on a twenty-count theme, an idea I took from Bach's "Musical Offering." Each variation follows the same pattern. At the start, the three dancers—Rose the bass, me the alto, Sara the soprano—are in complementary repose; then the voices separate, repelled into various, isolated torments, finally re-uniting at the last possible moment. For the sake of both suspense and satisfaction, I tried to make each episode a cliff-hanger, with the age-old motif of bitter wandering repeatedly followed by reassurance and resolution.*

* The fugue phrase has four counts revolving clockwise, four counterclockwise, two counts traveling backward stage right front, two moving backward on the upstage front and arcing around the corner (temporal change being introduced by a double-time beat on the twelfth count). Beats thirteen, fourteen, and fifteen move forward on the upstage front, lowering to a kneeling position (thus including the vertical possibilities in the theme). Sixteen is a quarter turn to stage left, seventeen a scootch backward in the stage left front, eighteen a scootch forward, thus inscribing a cross with its four right angles in the theme's floor pattern. Nineteen steps back, and twenty, the only circular movement in the theme, sweeps open and drops heavily to punctuate the end of the phrase. If good construction can bring beauty, this phrase covers all the bases, moving through space vertically and horizontally, forward and backward on lines and circles, with the possibility of different tempi and meters built into the theme.

The Fugue, 1971

I set a variation each day for twenty days, indoors if it rained, outdoors if not. Each of these came from exploring the initial phrase—reversing it, inverting it, resequencing, exploring the various attacks and coordinations. We "ironed out" the phrase by taking all the angles out of the pattern and created stylistic variations that governed the execution of the theme. One goes as quickly and tautly as possible, usually with the eyes scrunched tightly closed, the arms folded rigidly across the chest and the head "ticking," moving erratically in tiny brittle movements from side to side, diagonal to diagonal; another, by contrast, is as large and heavy as possible. The "mush" was so called because it is seven different phrases of amorphous, fluid movement which can be

scooped into and out of at random; the "stuffing" was little ornamentations that fit between the counts. With all of us taking a shift cooking and baking, the language of *The Fugue* came out of the kitchen.

Although describing *The Fugue* makes it sound intellectual and dry, creating it was deeply sensual. The theme was made on a hillside; counts eleven and twelve twist around waxy, white-flowered blackberry bushes, while thirteen, fourteen, and fifteen drop to a kneeling position to accommodate the land's downward slope. The controlled, sustained lowering of the weight through the feet comes directly from creating *The Fugue* on grassy fields and softly padded beds of lichen, textures that promote different speeds and transitions.

When these moves were transferred to the attic, I was very aware of the thumping sounds our feet suddenly made on the hard surfaces: without the lichen moss, we heaved onto the floorboards like cossacks. Earlier in the year I had gone to the tacky ballroom of the Dixie Hotel with Arlene Croce to see the reunion of some of The Hoofers—Chuck Green, Sandman Simms, Rhythm Red, and Jimmy Slyde. I admired their camaraderie and engaging ease, all the more remarkable since several of them had just reemerged as dancers after twenty years as garage attendants and night watchmen. Their taps forced my attention to the integration of sound and movement. Making *The Fugue*, I sometimes closed my eyes to hear the dance; sometimes I actually *heard* the piece first—some

The One Hundreds, 1974

sounds swift and delicate, others almost brutal—and designed the movement accordingly. When the piece is performed, it is danced in silence on an electronically amplified stage so that the sound of the movement becomes an audible representation of the work's structure.

From the beginning I worked to make *The Fugue* into a rigorous, accurate, authentic, elegant, original dance. I had the notion this could be accomplished because of the ballets of George Balanchine. I had never met Balanchine and I didn't know his repertory well. But each time I'd been to see the New York City Ballet, I'd seen that no detail went untended—everything was in good order. In the attic, outside the pressures and biases of the

New York art scene, I used Balanchine's eye. I found that if I imagined what he would say about what I was doing, I could see how things had to be. I parked him in the corner of my studio and I kept him there for the next twenty years, steadfastly refusing opportunities to meet the real man because my invisible mentor was so very useful. The insistence on thoroughness that I felt from him formed my standard, and if ever I tried to move on too quickly, leaving a loose end or taking an easy solution, I saw his head shake and I went back to work. *The Fugue* is not a ballet, but it is an attempt at a classic dance, one Balanchine might recognize and maybe even claim as a bastard offspring.

While working on *The Fugue* I also made *The One Hundreds*, a dance I simply and modestly designed to represent the entire universe. The idea came on a sunny spring afternoon. I was lying on a hill; bees buzzed about pockets of wildflowers; a single bird's call pierced every now and then through the general cacophony; the grass and nettles bristled up; the clouds moved swiftly. I saw this marvelous mix of smell, texture, movement, sound, and touch— feeling my heart beating, and imagining I could feel my baby's

Jennifer Way and France Mayotte teaching *The One Hundreds*, 1978

heart beating too—all this dense completeness of God's creation reflected in one theatrical moment. One hundred people would fill a reasonably sized space with one hundred different and carefully crafted eleven-second phrases. In and out, on and off, in eleven seconds, simultaneously grand and humble. As I worked, choreographing these two pieces in a great rush, my life was more balanced than ever before—my happiness was complete. I had a marriage that worked, a child on the way, and work I cared about deeply which I developed with a community of loyal and talented friends. Nothing was missing. For me, life, love, and work cycled back and forth in a healthy flow. For a few brief months, in the spring and summer of 1970, I truly had it all.

Making *The One Hundreds*, I began to see this was a great deal of labor for an awfully short period of performance time, so I extended the eleven seconds according to a formula I described in *Ballet Review:* "It's a hundred eleven-second segments separated by four seconds between segments, performed by two dancers in unison. Then five people each do twenty different segments simultaneously so that the one hundred segments are represented in one-fifth the time, and then one hundred people each do one segment in eleven seconds. The two dancers take twenty-five minutes to do their segments, the five dancers take five minutes, and then a huge crowd materializes and the whole dance flashes by in an instant."

Both *The Fugue* and *The One Hundreds* have vocabularies built from everyday movements. *The Fugue*'s phrases, worked and refined, became quite sophisticated. The movement for *The One Hundreds* remained instantly available to all bodies with almost no rehearsal time. But for the two dancers who would present the movement initially, the enterprise was Herculean. Rose and I struggled for hundreds of rehearsal hours, side by side about fifteen feet apart, giving us only peripheral glimpses of each other and making every error painfully blatant. And then, after all the hours of rehearsal we still attempted to give the illusion of perfect naturalism that graced the uninitiated in their first run-through.

How to keep the audience's interest during such a dry and academic exercise? When the company performed the work several years later, we would move into a town and shill the performance by teaching the phrases to one hundred locals in an afternoon session, each company member responsible for up to twenty people, the rehearsals providing opportunities for amusing press and TV coverage. When the performance was finally given, our audience was expanded by local friends and relatives of the one hundred; having been told about the work, they were sympathetic to the first two performers' dilemma and tolerated the second five as they waited, hoping to spot their loved ones—who, if they were clever, sported an absurd getup to stick out in the eleven-second, one-hundred-person rush. The ploy worked; audiences loved *The One Hundreds*.

Both *The Fugue* and *The One Hundreds* premiered during a summer residency at the University of Massachusetts at Boston in August 1970. I had also made a solo variation for Rose, a forty-five-minute meander through the campus, which she performed daily as classes broke. "The local police were getting calls every day from people saying, 'This woman is freaking out, she must be on LSD,'" says Rose. "Classes were changing, people were

Sowing of Seeds: Dunn, Rudner, Tharp, University of Massachusetts, 1970

walking by, but mostly they tried to ignore me. Except the construction workers at the library, who would hoot and holler every day. Then on the last day I did the piece, they applauded."

Our University of Massachusetts residency was cosponsored by Boston's Summerthing, and I had built several community service projects into our program. Along with a planting ritual, the Sowing of Seeds, for the Parks Department, there were special materials designed for children we taught in Roxbury, south of Boston, as well as a proposal for the Boston Patriots football team.

Following our works in Boston, we danced *The Fugue* and *The One Hundreds* at New York's outdoor Delacorte Theatre. This audience was much broader-based than our usual college and avant-garde crowds, and their responses fascinated me. During *The One Hundreds* several fights broke out between hecklers and supporters —first shouting, then fisticuffs—but after *The Fugue* there was a long, loud ovation.

Although we took no curtain call, true to our old artistic puritanism, I longed to acknowledge the audience's response. With a child on the way and about to have a life separate from me, I took a new interest in our audiences and I no longer wanted to pretend that I did not care. I wanted to see dancing recognized as a daily part of everyone's life. There were different ways of doing this. One was to project our work into an audience's living space, as when Rose performed her *Cross-Country* solo among the strollers; another was to suggest that you, the audience, could do it too, as with *The One Hundreds*. But another way of accomplishing the same goal—old-fashioned as it might be—was to capture the audience's attention. Our company's Delacorte success suggested we had a shot at accomplishing this, and this conviction, coupled with a growing sense of isolation once we returned to the farm, made me restless. Doing business from the kitchen phone, I tried to arrange future engagements for the company, but it became clear the farm was no longer capable of containing all our activities nor all our members.

The dancers were reluctant to stay away from their friends and lives in New York City for much longer. Evenings at the farm could be very quiet and long; for entertainment, Sara and Rose often took the company's old Rambler into town and practiced parallel parking. So I cooked up a scheme: I would work with half the group in New Berlin for two weeks, then they would leave and the other half would come up from the city and work. However, this arrangement entailed doubling the size of the company, so I took on three apprentices.

Fine in theory, the plan fell apart in practice. When the time came for the first group to leave, I found I wanted everybody on the farm—all the time. So suddenly there were strange girls traipsing through the house, invading Bob's space and privacy. The wife he wanted to live with was away working in the attic; the company he wanted to leave was camped permanently in his living room.

Bob tried to impose a schedule so that he would be out while we practiced, but the ever-widening cracks in the second-floor ceiling —caused by our rehearsals in the attic—were sinister signs of the dancers' wear and tear on the house and its major shareholder.

To make matters worse, I panicked. Up until now I had been able to call upon my body as I wished. Performing *The Fugue* in my first trimester, I was concerned about miscarrying but I danced

Big Rose in the attic, 1970

full force anyhow. Now I fatigued easily. Working more slowly daily, I decided to compensate by working longer.

To this end I found a tool that finally allowed my ideal of dancing from sunup to sundown. A Panasonic video system, it was promoted as portable, although the deck alone weighed seventy pounds. Already secondhand when I bought it, the machine worked infrequently, seemingly ruled by the weather, but its temperamental fits didn't stop me from doubling my productivity. With the video system I could work with one group of dancers while the others watched a tape, learning movements I'd done earlier. "We'd all go out there and do stuff," says Rose. "Then we'd watch the video and Twyla would say, 'Well, that's working, that isn't. Let's do some more of this, and let's try and feel that.' " Both Rose and Sara remember weeping over the frustrating complexities, but videotape became an extension of my body, essential for dance notation, teaching, and coaching.

Every day still began for me as it had for the last five years: I improvised in the studio. But now I could tape these sessions for future viewing. Each morning I put on the same music, a Commodore recording of Willie "The Lion" Smith's solo piano, and as my body changed, I documented what I could do with my new sense of weight, ways of moving that I had known nothing about before.

I continued doing a full barre, only toward the end cutting out the battements to the back because I was afraid of straining my stomach muscles. I felt it was safe to work this much because, dancing daily, I was constantly monitoring my body and very aware of its changes. Bob, however, worried that all this was dangerous. He had been unhappy about my absence that summer and let me know in the fall, as I began to prepare for a winter residency at Oberlin College, that he would hate that even more. One night at dinner, he said the inevitable: "You love your work more than me." The words have echoed since, but at the time I didn't know what he meant. On the farm I had lost track of the life-work division. I continued to dance as hard as possible in order to guarantee the success of our Oberlin engagement. I refused to let my body take its natural course, tapering off into a peaceful and quiet late term, cementing my relationship with Bob and luxuriating in all the preparations for the baby. I was driven by my work ethic, but I was also determined not to sacrifice my life to my child as my mother had done, keeping her baby eternally indebted and herself institutionalized at its center for a very long while. I wanted this child born with freedom on the horizon.

The material we developed late in 1970 went into *The History of Up and Down*, a full-evening work I created with computer programmers at Oberlin. This involvement, plus the classes the company taught, made the residency the hoped-for success. Although nearly eight months pregnant, I still had enough energy to get through full days of teaching, rehearsing, and performing, although trudging up into the attic of the dorm where we were staying nights took the last of my strength. Returning to the farm this time, I put the company on sabbatical while I waited out the six weeks until delivery, the sabbatical my only obeisance to the coming event. I had heard Melissa Hayden did a barre the day after delivery and I was determined to be at least as Spartan as she. I refused to practice Lamaze—I didn't want anybody telling me how to have a baby any more than I wanted anybody telling me how to dance—and refused to change my schedule an iota, even as delivery day neared. The night of March 8, against advice but within the realm of my own common sense, I ate a huge portion of Bully Boy, a steer we had killed and dressed ourselves. The next morning I worked in the attic, doing some foolishly dangerous slides and falls that eventually ended up in *Eight Jelly Rolls*. Late that afternoon, the pains began. Bob and I carefully made our way over icy roads to the county hospital in Norwich. There, I stubbornly continued my regimen, insisting I would give birth as God intended. Fifteen hours into labor, I was still refusing the aspirins the nurses offered in little paper cups. I wanted my baby to begin life on the up and up.

History of Up and Down, Oberlin College fieldhouse, 1971

When, after twenty-eight hours of labor, Jesse Alexander Huot finally emerged—head first, healthy, and squalling—I had never been so glad to be done with anything in my entire life. As Jesse touched me, and our skins pressed together for the first time, my tears and love could not overcome my rage at the agony and possible damage to my own body he had caused. I banned him from my sight for an evening and refused to nurse, wanting nothing to do with him. Acting as though my behavior were normal, nurses kept bringing him back for little visits. And we finally took to one another. When we brought him home, I made Bob run ahead into the house to put on Mozart, because I wanted the baby's life to be good and I hoped against hope music would deter his crying. Mainly I figured it was going to be downhill all the way now, and we should try to make the best of it. I worried about my capacities to mother, Bob's to father, and our society's to educate and nurture.

The county nurse called regularly those first few weeks, checking on the baby's feeding and weight and on my maternal skills. But I felt confident handling Jesse, and I enjoyed nursing him. My one steadfast rule was not to force anything on my son, his toilet

Bob Huot with Jesse, 1971

training or his weaning. I wanted to let him do things in his own time and find his own ways early in his life, a privilege I felt I was still struggling to gain from my parents.

About ten days after Jesse's birth, my mother and father arrived. Mother, with so much baby practice, would help with Jesse in the traditional ways. Daddy came to work on the farmhouse. He helped remodel the kitchen and planned to build a fireplace, assistance that Bob—who had labored hard on his own to make the house dry and fully heated—didn't necessarily want. He had gotten rid of my dancers, and he understandably resented that my family—Twanette was also with us—seemed to be overrunning his house so soon after his son's birth.

One morning Daddy came down early as usual and settled into the gloomy north parlor where he'd set up a workbench and sawhorses. He'd already finished some kitchen cabinets and plumbed a new sink, and now, before starting in on a fireplace for the dark northern rooms, he was making a light day of it with a small task: stripping an old oak door with a chisel. I was cleaning in the kitchen a couple of hours later when Bob came down to breakfast, complaining about sawdust from my father's new shelves falling into his soup. Then he went into the room where my father was working.

Both Bob and my father had violent tempers. Both had frightened me: my father when he threw the hatchet at my mother, and Bob throughout our life together. His seemingly uncontrollable outbursts were particularly scary to me because he was so big. I had warned Bob I would leave if he was ever violent with me or the baby and had lectured him for many months to quit yelling.

Twanette and I were in the laundry room next to the parlor when both men exploded. The argument was over the chisel my father was using. The tool had belonged to Bob's grandfather, Alexander Comrie, who had also been a builder and an engineer. Jesse was named after both my father's father and this grandfather of Bob's.

"I'd take that tool away and slap one of my students for using it to strip paint," Bob said.

My father, who knew perfectly well how to use every tool, retorted, "I'm not one of your kids."

The argument never came to blows but afterward my father was strangely winded; he seemed to limp from the room on his way upstairs to rest, something he never did during the day. As he passed me in the hall he put his arm around my shoulder—something else I cannot remember him doing, since physical touch was not how my family expressed its love. Like Egyptians to their gods, we built huge edifices instead, as my father had so many years before and was attempting to do again now with his renovation of the house. He whispered that but for me, he would have left long ago.

Rest didn't heal the chest pains Daddy felt all day, and that night my mother insisted we charter a plane and fly him to Johns Hopkins in Baltimore. Bob said she was being hysterical and that the Norwich Hospital was as good as any. We put my father on a mattress in the back of the station wagon and while Twanette stayed with Jesse and me, my mother drove with Bob on the back roads to get Daddy help as quickly as possible.

The next two weeks were the most painful of my life. I shuttled each day between Jesse and my father, whispering prayers not to let my daddy die, while sensing my chants were only preparing me for the unimaginable.

But my father clung to life. Even partially paralyzed in the hospital bed, he liked to demonstrate with a certain glee how he could still draw with a pencil clenched between his toes. Once I brought Jesse with me. I set the baby next to him, and my father and I both began to cry. When we embraced, finally, after so many years, I wondered how much time he had left.

Doubtless my mother was right about Johns Hopkins. My father's nurses were not the most attentive, and although he had apparently suffered several minor strokes in the past two or three years, his condition would probably have been helped by advanced technology. Instead we brought him back to Spurr Street after several weeks in intensive care, and a few days later, Twanette took him to her house in Vermont. There he seemed to improve;

still, my mother did not want to risk taking him home to California, and she had to attend to their businesses. He was still asleep on the morning she left, and she decided not to trouble him with a good-bye. She never saw him again. Two weeks later, while picnicking with Twanette, he died of an aneurysm.

Bob and I were in the city and I heard of my father's death over the phone. Although she didn't say it, we all knew my mother held Bob responsible for Daddy's death. He did not attend the funeral. I took Jesse to Indiana with me, partly to console Grandma Cora, who had outlived her only son. The pulleys lowered the casket and the box hit the ground. But there were no caretakers to shovel earth over the coffin. Everyone was already filing away. I felt I couldn't leave him like that, uncovered. I picked up a shovel and threw the first bit of earth on the lid.

With Jesse, I flew to California to help my mother start her life alone. Trying to pack my father's effects and face the businesses single-handedly, she weakened visibly. Suddenly it was painfully clear that my father had been much more the mainstay in every way than any of us had recognized. While my mother was still capable of monitoring the estate, putting the house up for sale, and leasing both the drive-in and the car agencies, the expansionist days were over. Her life was on hold. She remembered everything through its connection to Daddy, and it was obvious she would never marry again, insisting at fifty-seven, "Any man would only want to be with me for my money." Unschooled in talk or the expression of sympathy, my efforts to extend love to her were awkward, and my gestures felt hollow. I wanted her not to be so lonely and I wanted her not to blame me. But there was so much distance between us that when Jesse and I left six days later to fly back to New Berlin, I knew she would be out of my life now almost as much as my father was.

Back in the Spurr Street farmhouse, I felt torn in my loyalties between my mother and father and Bob, caught in a Greek drama where all solutions are painful ones. I knew things would never again be quite right.

7

Art is the only way
to run away without
leaving home.

Jesse was in the attic studio a lot that spring, and except when he was sleeping, I felt an enormous conflict: to hold him meant I was not dancing, to dance meant I was not attending to my child. Holding him and dancing did not really work—although of course it was tried—because I was always afraid I would drop him. For some strange reason, I worried about jiggling him around too much —my son, who no doubt was born addicted to movement. I remember being so torn that often I would just sit in the middle of the attic and do neither. Somehow that seemed fair.

Sara and Rose were back on the farm and we had another commission from Charles Reinhart, its only requirement being to perform in New York City. I decided we would stretch even this rudimentary mandate by asking for a barge to circle Manhattan. We would dance phrases so large they would be visible from apartments miles away on both shores. We could reach thousands. Unannounced, we would enter the spectator's mind in unexpected ways. As the three of us started literally hurling our bodies into developing our barge dance, Bob and I came to loggerheads over Jesse's care. The camel's straw was probably the afternoon I reminded Bob of our prebaby agreement—fifty-fifty with the child care. But when I said, "Now it's your turn, I'm going to work this afternoon," his surprising reply was: "Fifty percent of the time means you take care of Jesse until he's ten years old, and then I take the next ten years."

I needed help trying to gain conditioning as a dancer at the same time that I struggled to become a mother, nurse a child, be awake at night when Jesse needed me. Earlier that spring, I had received my first establishment grants in response to applications filed the year before. To the pages of baffling forms I had simply attached a handwritten note saying, "I make dances, not applications. Send the money. Love, Twyla." And they had. Ten thousand came from the National Endowment for the Arts and a couple grand more from the New York State Council. I also received my first Guggenheim, another ten thousand dollars, a personal award that I could spend in any way I wanted. Why not use the Guggenheim to pay someone to take care of Jesse part of the time I worked? No, said Bob. On this he was adamant. He didn't want anyone else in the house, all these girls were already making him nuts, and I was the mother.

It wasn't only because of Jesse and Bob that I had trouble concentrating in the attic. My body seemed to be in rebellion. I grew easily nauseated as I threw myself about, occupying as much space as I possibly could, swinging my legs in massive arcs. Working the body at its maximum of energy might not have physically been the wisest approach to postpartum recovery, but my depression— the infamous blues compounded by my father's death—was such that I felt I needed this kind of jolt to get going. Work in the studio was also interrupted more frequently as I found myself going up and down between the attic and the kitchen phone more and more. I spoke almost daily with Charlie about the status of our barge, which was proving difficult to arrange, and he advised me to get plan B going. I also spoke more and more often with a lawyer who was helping me become a not-for-profit foundation. Before the Oberlin residency I had gone to the Volunteer Lawyers for the Arts to get help in applying for Chapter S Not-for-Profit status. This would allow me to become a tax-deductible charity, eligible for contributions from individuals and foundations, which was a necessary first step if I was to begin the fund-raising I would have to do to pay the dancers. One of the volunteer lawyers, William Kosmas, had expressed interest in assuming the company's business management. I was very grateful for Bill's interest and complimented by his regard for the company, and I allowed myself to read into all this a personal interest in me as well. For the first time since Bob and I had met eight years before, I began to be attracted to a man other than him.

On May 27, Bob drove us down to the city and took over with Jesse while plan B went into effect beginning at about 3:30 the morning of the 28th. Without the barge I would circle Manhattan in a different way, locating the work in three spaces: a baroque *Sunrise* jump-starting the day in Fort Tryon Park at the north end

Sunrise: Wright, Rudner, Tharp, 1971   Tharp

of Manhattan, a *Midday March* parading all the way downtown in Battery Park, and an *Evening Raga* to herald the night at City Hall.

We began our preparations with a barre in the Franklin Street loft. Rose supplied us with ten cups of coffee from Dave's, an all-night restaurant on Canal Street. We forgot makeup and didn't bother with costumes. The day began with a bang as we performed our huge (non-barge) phrases to a tape recording of Torelli's Concerto in D Minor a few moments before sunrise. Our audience was even smaller than the one attending *Tank Dive*. However, when seventy-five more people arrived near the end, I insisted we repeat the dance from the start, performing the only 6:30 A.M. matinee I've ever done.

Noonday was the marches, played by a Brooklyn high school band (a badly tuned echo of the recordings by Her Majesty's Royal Brigadiers that we had been using in the attic). Finally, we concluded at dusk in City Hall. We had planned to have three musicians playing Indian ragas in a rotunda and a player piano knocking out rags in a judge's paneled quarters, the dancers and audience shuttling back and forth. But at the last moment everything went wrong: city officials would not let the player piano enter the building, and everyone crowded into a single room that was different from either room I had selected. Somehow we got some of the dancing done, but by then I'd altogether forgotten what connection I'd imagined existed—other than linguistic—between rags and ragas.

At the end of the day I was a mess. Everyone was understandably exhausted, but in addition I was embarrassed to have Bob and Bill in the same room at the same time. Bill was very elegant and sophisticated, a dapper dresser whom Bob would predictably find a dandy and obnoxious. Of course Bob also resented Bill's eagerness to help promote my career, but I was determined to set the company on a path toward fiscal responsibility, and Bill and I were planning a second European tour. The dancers could no longer be away from family and friends, and life on the farm was unduly complicated now, what with Jesse and the girls and Bob and the attic and the phone, and I thought that I could perhaps sort some of this out by leaving the dancers in the city and commuting between the loft and the farm. Jesse and I would drive down with Bob on the days he came into the city to teach, and sometimes I might remain in the city with Jesse until Bob's next trip, or Jesse could go back up to the farm with Bob. Those were the possible combinations, and we would all try to be flexible even though four hours each way was a long commute. In addition, after several trips it was clear that the queasiness I had been experiencing for the last month or so was not just motion sickness. I was pregnant again, and once again Bob wanted the child. I knew that having two babies within a two-year span and caring for them would be the end of my career. Although my second abortion was legal, the Chenango Hospital nurses' crusty behavior made it clear they had no sympathy for a perfectly healthy woman stopping a pregnancy. Even though the Dalkon Shield had not been adequately tested, I had one inserted immediately after the second abortion. It might mean sterility or even cancer, but I didn't want the responsibility for another abortion. Bob, feeling that I was already splitting my attention too much between Jesse and my work, was furious. His sense of family was always more, as he put it, "traditional" than mine—meaning the wife should stay home and take care of the household. He gave lip service to my working but he wanted our family life to be my main focus.

As we drove between the farm and the city, Bob and I had begun to argue more and more, and these arguments seemed to center on money. Bob was defiantly anticommercial. He wholeheartedly disapproved of the transformation of the company into the Twyla Tharp Dance Foundation, and while I didn't particularly like the idea of becoming a charitable foundation, dependent on gifts to make ends meet, I knew that was the reality if I was to support the dancers. "Twyla was from the entrepreneurial class," Bob says. "I was from the artisan class, so my class consciousness was very different from hers. She was more of a careerist, she wanted to make a corporation."

Bob insisted that the public schools were good enough for him and they would be for Jesse, but I felt that having the opportunity to attend really good schools could give you a better start in life. It was a whimsical undertaking in the dance world, but it now seemed that in addition to finding money for the dancers I was going to have to support Jesse's education.

Bob's countercultural revolt was serving him well. He felt independent, free from all the art world intrigue and politics. To give him his due, by removing himself from the art world altogether he had moved away from a fundamental hypocrisy in the avant-garde: namely, talk a tough line on the purity of art, but continue to sell it from your booth at Max's Kansas City. The dollars from this setup, according to Bob, were poured into the military-industrial complex, and that in turn was sucking the world's blood. Bob would continue teaching two days a week at Hunter in order to provide the basic necessities, but he would do no more.

I had deferred to Bob's work and its greater importance since we had first been together in 1963, trying to make my thinking consistent with his. He was older and established. His male circle of friends were on the cutting edge, and they could be both intimidating and maddening. Carl Andre liked to go around saying he was the world's greatest expert on Dostoyevsky because he'd never read any, or that "A thing is a hole in a thing it is not." Or Bob Morris: "The problems of solipsism and autism hang in the air. Here the labyrinth form is perhaps a metonym of the search for the self, for it demands a continuous wandering," and so forth. Art as philosophy had been a feature of twentieth-century Western culture since Duchamp.

But dance is real; you don't talk that much about it. You either go round eight times or you don't. Because it is preverbal, the intelligentsia of the art world in the Sixties chose to see it in the same light civilized people have for many centuries: a divertissement, a light entertainment, a pastime not really challenging or worthy of serious attention.

Dance is the stepchild of the arts. Modern dance in particular—without even the splash of money or dab of power that exists in the ballet world—is an art form in which women have been allowed to rise to the top simply because there is no profit to be made by holding them down. Painting, sculpture, and even the avant-garde film world, which, after all, you might outgrow by moving on to Hollywood, are certainly of far greater importance—just look at the economics—than anything happening in the cloistered and subsidized world of modern dance. So, of course I had felt Bob's career was more important than my own, even after we came to the farm and he removed himself and his work from the art scene.

Commuting between the attic and the city, I trudged into the studio daily, but I was not productive. Finally I just gave up on new work for the moment and returned, for the first and only time in my life, to rework an old dance. *The History of Up and Down* would become *Eight Jelly Rolls*. In so doing, I broke one of our most sacrosanct taboos, and this was only possible because of Jesse.

After five years of performing in silence, I finally let the music play. In the attic, with Jesse still inside me, I had improvised to the 1927 jazz of Jelly Roll Morton and his Red Hot Peppers, and I had suddenly thought, "Yes, letting music play with the dance is old hat, but, hey, having babies isn't too original either, is it? But it's still one of the wonders of life so let's keep the music." Performing at Oberlin in my eighth month, I had realized a part of me would soon be sitting out there among all those faces, and I wanted to connect with them. Reworking this material, I tried to remember all the places we had really hooked the audience, zeroing in on the humor in both the dancing and the music. I ruthlessly cut out all my academic concerns and unless the technical dancing problems were so fiendishly difficult that even the audience could delight in their perversity, those went too. I was determined to reach our audience more viscerally than ever before.

Bob called the new work commercial, geared to success, but I argued all I was doing was taking the liberal argument to its extreme by allowing the people the final word. I had no intention of being like Carl Andre. When the town of Hartford wanted its money back after he moved thirty-two granite boulders from outside the town limits onto the green, he replied: "People who think I'm putting them on believe I have them in mind when I work. I don't." That was precisely the point; more and more, I did have them in mind. I wanted someone in the forest to hear the tree fall.

What really happened that spring on the farm was that with the birth of my son I became more and more unwilling to feel second-class, to subjugate my readings of things—how one lives daily life, what the proper concerns of art are, what a dance is—to those of my husband any longer. I had no more time for manifestos, shoulds, and don'ts; all a mother knows is that her child's body must be kept clean, warm, and fed. That is the priority. As the work on the new piece moved into high gear, I could no longer take the commute, or lugging things in and out of cars, up and down steps. Over the summer I decided to stay at 104 Franklin, keeping Jesse with me.

Life with Jesse was not easy in the loft. There was just enough hot water for one shower every four hours; the kitchen consisted of a single electric hotplate, the only sink was a tiny one in the bathroom. I had seventy-seven steps to climb with the laundry and

Right middle, *Eight Jelly Rolls* rehearsal, Franklin Street loft; Upper right, Wright and Rudner; top left (fourth from left), newcomer García-Lorca with Tharp, Wright, Rudner, and two apprentices; middle left, Rudner and Jesse; 1971

groceries and Jesse—in addition, living in the loft was still illegal, and I had to dispose of all his diapers inconspicuously. Each evening I put his crib in the center of the studio, as far from my bed as possible, in the hope that he would finally bless me with an uninterrupted night's sleep. In the morning, the sight of our family of two saddened me profoundly, adding to the endless guilt I felt at depriving Jesse of his father. I was bitterly lonely, but Jesse was a wonderful baby and made a difficult life easier.

During the day Jesse crept, crawled, and actually cried very little. He seemed a very tolerant child—"The one rule in the studio," Sara remembers, "was no one steps on the kid." In a way, Jesse conducted rehearsals as we all took turns changing diapers and feeding the baby. We called him Mr. Baby, a moniker derived from Jelly Roll Morton's joyful interjection, "Oh, Mr. Jelly," in the recording of "Strokin' Away" I was using for a solo I was making.

I had cast myself as The Drunk, a down-and-out independent who lurches about the stage, escaping from the company drilling away upstage in close formation. My inebriated state ranged from tipsily arrogant to straight-out splats—the material coming from my last improvisational session before Jesse's birth and the memory of my queasiness and the weight in front of my tummy. This source kept my drunk from being too literal, and this first extended solo of mine has actually always been at least a duet to me. Keaton and Chaplin also flowed through my veins as I staggered and reeled. Women do not usually have either the stomach or the

strength for the brutality of knock-'em-down clowning, Lucille Ball being one of our century's only female comics comfortable with physical slapstick.

Premiering at the Delacorte on a program featuring the Lar Lubovitch company in black masks dancing to music by Luciano Berio, *Eight Jelly Rolls* was going to seem not very serious and might even, who knows, cross over and become popular. And so it did. Rose kicked the piece off with a solo stagger onstage, looking a bit lost but having the presence of mind to acknowledge the audience, then Sara and I crossed over, and from the second we exited I knew we had them. I have always considered that moment, when I sensed we really could reach an audience, the biggest thrill of my career, and I probably would have wept with gratitude except that tears would have smeared my makeup. Instead I jumped insanely up and down.

Arlene Croce's *Ballet Review* article called "The Drunk" "one of the great individual set pieces of modern dance," and added that if we'd been willing to take bows—at the very next performance, we began trying—the company would have received a standing ovation. Later Deborah Jowitt wrote: "Remember that up to now, Tharp dancers did not 'perform.' This was the trend of the time

Eight Jelly Rolls, London Weekend Television, left to right: Wright, Weiner, García-Lorca, Rinker, Rawe, Rudner, Tharp, 1974

among more adventurous choreographers—no emotional indulgence, no role-playing, no trying to please an audience which you nevertheless hoped might be pleased." Arlene concluded *Eight Jelly Rolls* was "not only magnificent choreography but magnificent entertainment." In *The New York Times,* John Rockwell called it "an astounding masterpiece." And word came back that Jack Cole, one of the most talented men ever to choreograph for Broadway and Hollywood, had remarked on the skill with which I deployed my backup choruses—always a difficult chore, keeping masses onstage engaged but not pulling focus away from the downstage action.

Eight Jelly Rolls: Tharp

Immediately after the *Eight Jelly Rolls* debut in September 1971 we were back in the studio working on a new piece to premiere in Paris in November. This one too would break a taboo. With *Dancing in the Streets*, I sensed that I had a solid feel for what women alone could accomplish, and the next logical step was to bring men into the action. *The Fugue* was a reach for women and, in my mind, was always intended to be danced by men when we had them. Now, perhaps because of Jesse, I felt our work had to reflect the male presence. I had been coveting Kenneth Rinker for the company since first seeing him at Merce's studio in 1969. Wonderfully musical, his dancing was unusually fluid for a man, capable of extremely small, precise articulations and possessing an acute rhythmic sophistication. I figured his virtuosity could be quickly absorbed into our company, and after a careful courtship, he said yes.

With Ken's entry we began an investigation into partnering—the infinite ways in which dancers physically support and extend one another's movement—that has continued to this day. Before, I had worried that including men in our group would automatically bring up the issue of clichéd partnering, its sexual implications and limitations. But when Ken came in, we all tested the waters together; I did not automatically assume that the guy would be doing all the lifts, or even that there would be lifts. After all, Rose was probably as strong as, if not stronger than, Ken. Instead, we developed a kind of group partnering based more on friendship and trust than on sex, and here too Jesse's presence was evident. Not only did I lift his little body many times a day, but the way he went about discovering the world with his fingers reawakened my sense of touch.

In the end, there was one lift in the work we rehearsed with Ken. When Deborah Jowitt came to an open rehearsal she wrote: "The dancers lifted and supported each other in slippery fumbling ways; before this, Tharp dancers had moved as if they wanted neither help nor to be responsible for anyone else's state of balance." She also observed, "Tharp, dripping wet, plunks her seven-month-old son down on the floor and fields questions while adroitly changing a diaper. Rudner and Wright bring in damp rags and warm bottles. These are some possibilities that George Balanchine and Merce Cunningham haven't dreamed of."

Dancing continuously in the studio, I had never stopped to mourn my father, but plunged daily back into working, where I could address his death without feeling I would break apart. Perhaps I felt I could keep him with me in the dancing. I began to work on a piece to the music of trumpeter Bix Beiderbecke. Coming from the same period as Jelly Roll Morton, the Beiderbecke music was as light and airy as the other was rough-edged and earthy, as sophisticated in its arrangements as the Morton was raw and close to the belt, as white as the other was black. Most importantly, Bix Beiderbecke was playing music my father would have heard as a young man. Part one of *The Bix Pieces* was five songs— first me alone (twirling clear batons), then Sara and me swooping and swooning to Beiderbecke's arrangement of "Tain't So, Honey, Tain't So" sung by Bing Crosby, then Sara and me backing up Rose, then the three of us behind Isabel, and finally Ken joining the women to Crosby's "Because My Baby Don't Mean Maybe Now." I began to sense that the dark subtext behind the movement would never come through in the sprightly dancing, and I wrote in a narrator to account for the reservoir of emotion that prompted *The Bix Pieces*. "I hated to tap dance, when I was a kid," says she, and I proceeded to do just that. "But this dance is about remembering. My tap dancing lessons, my baton twirling lessons, my acrobatics, the hula-hula. My father." As the Adagio from the third quartet of Haydn's Opus 76 begins, she explains that much of the dancing was made to this adagio, because I did not want to be too literal in following the Bix music. You can begin to see, as Ken dances in the vernacular and Rose in ballet style, "chassée is really slap ball change: Exactly and not at all the same." All things are related, and as the Haydn winds down, she observes its theme was a folk melody existing long before Haydn. There is continuity and

The Bix Pieces, Paris: above, Tharp, opening solo; below, with Rudner; 1971

development in all things, "for while my father died this spring my son was born." And then comes Part Three, a very short revision of the dancing in "Because My Baby Don't Mean Maybe Now," this time reset to the John Coltrane "Abide with Me." "Nothing new has been added, much has been forgotten, and it is all different again."

As I worked on *The Bix Pieces*, Bill Kosmas tried to help me make sense of my life. He seemed willing to do whatever was necessary to help us establish ourselves, even suggesting I find a dancing student who could apprentice as an understudy and also help me by looking after Jesse in the studio. Bill had introduced me to Kermit Love—a wonderful designer who had worked with both Balanchine and Jerome Robbins and, along with Jim Henson, had given birth to *Sesame Street*'s Kermit the Frog. Bill had also taken on all the company's bookings and overpowered the grant writing with his legalese. He also took a hand in our style, his upper-crust, expensive taste beginning to dictate the packaging of the company, giving it a glamour that made it attractive to some and corrupt to others. Gone, for instance, were the down-home street clothes in which we had originally performed *The Fugue* and *Eight Jelly Rolls* at the Delacorte. Now, *Eight Jelly Rolls* was put into classic black tuxedos with the backs scooped out, and *The Fugue* was danced by svelte cossacks, our suede boots complemented by uniform mandarin collars and fitted gabardine jackets, but with my pants cut as shorts, Sara's as knickers, and Rose's as flowing gaucho pants. Both these dramatic costume-sets were designed by Kermit Love.

Our chic wardrobe, combined with our virtuosic dancing skills and our complex choreography, belied our old conceit: we no longer even implied that you, the guy on the street, could be up here with us. The real point of no return was the haircuts. Bill took us to Vidal Sassoon, where, after the hairdressers practically tied each of us down, we were transformed from our gruff, natural, bohemian selves into the epitome of fashion-plate chic. Sara's

The Bix Pieces: Tharp, Rudner

frothy mass of pitch-black curls was artfully arranged to frame her face. Rose's indiscriminate ponytail was shaped into a shoulder-length bob. My superfine, waist-long nothingness became a traditional Sassoon cut. Quite liking the emphasis on my high cheekbones and the feeling of it swirling ever so slightly behind me whenever I turned, I answered the critics in my mind: what's wrong with setting your hair in a flattering, eye-catching mode? I knew my classicism was rooted deeply enough to allow a little modish dalliance, and I was convinced my art could survive packaging.

Kermit finished our Bix costumes—gorgeous gowns, lounging pajamas, and short backless tuxedos in pearl gray satin and chiffon —and we went off to the Paris premier in the fall.

I had looked forward to the tour for some R and R. Without Jesse for the first time since his birth (Gram Cora was staying with him and Bob on the farm), I would fulfill, I hoped, two long-treasured desires: a full night's sleep and a tryst with Bill. Neither was to occur. After registering at a tiny hotel, we showered and went to

Sara Rudner, 1971

check out the performing space, a historic building where the IX International Festival of Dance was being held. Eagerly we stepped out onto the beautiful parquet floor on which we were scheduled to perform, and disaster struck, our feet practically sliding out from under us on the thick wax as we walked. Dancing was impossible.

Immediately Bill turned the problem into an international incident, insisting that the floor be stripped for us, then sanded, varnished, and rewaxed once we left. This suggestion was anathema to the custodians, who were worried—quite rightly—about damaging their historic treasure. Why couldn't we simply move to another space? they asked. There was no good answer except that Bill had negotiated the contract and would lose face. On and on the battle raged until finally a truce was called and Bill and I went out to dinner. Bill promptly celebrated our first night in Paris by splurging on a fine Burgundy. Intent on seducing him, my concern —passion, sex, love, or any combination of the three—was far from his. He had steadfastly shied away from an affair, saying he was afraid of a divorce action. Becoming my boyfriend would undercut what he really wanted, which was to be our producer. He wanted to dictate everything from haircuts to wardrobe and publicity, everything that had to do with the company's appearance other than the choreography itself, which didn't seem to interest him very much. Eventually, he would even demand and receive the billing "William Peter Kosmas Presents" in letters as large as mine and the dancers'.

His power play made life impossible; Paris became a series of late-night dinners, with Bill complaining about the company—particularly Jennifer Tipton's lighting, a matter on which he felt his taste and sensitivity were impeccable. Since Jennifer Tipton, whom I had known since my Paul Taylor days, was already well on her way to becoming the best lighting designer of our generation, I felt stranded between him and my better judgment. But hell-bent on reunifying my life, putting all my interests under one roof again, as they had been when Bob and I were first together, I persisted with Bill until one night, my mounting frustration generating an

order for escargots *after* the ice cream, we finally slept together—
almost. (Don't ask.)

The Bix Pieces was well received in Paris, and in performing I
found consolation for my various conflicts. Then I returned to the
farm, where I hoped to reestablish our little family over the
Thanksgiving and Christmas holidays. Bob and I confessed mutual
strayings—his were evidently more successful than mine—and we
tried several sessions with marriage counselors. But for all the
honesty we were still stuck without any clear answers to our dilemma.

Working in the attic, I tried to steady myself with dance, but I
seemed to be lost even in movement. The choices I made felt
arbitrary, without any clear right or wrong. I had hoped the focus
of my dance would clarify the decisions I had to make; instead, the
confusion of my life was paralyzing me in the studio. Christmas
came and I gave Jesse noisemakers—drums, gongs, chimes,
gourds, bells, and wood blocks: I wanted my son to learn early
about talking back. Finally, on New Year's Eve, I couldn't bear my
confusion any longer. I decided to stay in the loft at Franklin Street
all the time. That was it. After eight years, Bob and I would never
be together again.

That gloomy winter, the company toured a lot. I was the only
one glad for the distraction, because anything was better than lan-
guishing alone in the studio. There I was lost. After *The Bix Pieces*
I could not find a place or reason to begin new work. My body was
still trying to adjust to its various traumas, and without either my
husband or my father I felt estranged from almost everything. Only
the touring seemed accurately to reflect my condition. We were a
gypsy band, uprooted, carting our wares, together in a warm car.
Jesse was almost always with me now because I had taken on most
of the responsibility for his support; Bob had no intention of compromising either his politics or his art by attempting to go the
gallery-dealer route once more, so it was left for me to sell out. (I

Left, passport photo from 1971; right, from 1973

took no alimony and Bob agreed to contribute two hundred and fifty dollars a month in child support, but this was my only regular income—three thousand dollars a year for food, housing, clothes, toys, and tuition to come.) Bill Kosmas didn't accompany us on our meat-and-potato-runs—grueling drive-out, teach and perform, drive-back affairs—and inside the Rambler I found momentary respite from all the bickering.

Our performance fees barely made a dent in the expenses of the company, but all the same we began working with a group of seventeen young dancers. Calling them The Farm Club, we taught them some repertory, sent them on a State University of New York tour and watched their progress. I was already toying with the idea of keeping one group on the road—performing and generating income—while another worked with me in the studio on new dances. This arrangement would address a problem particular to dance. The fees we received were for performances or classes, but the money covered little more than the direct costs of touring. Except in the case of a rare grant, the actual work of making the dances or creating the teaching materials was apparently perceived by the world as being done by elves during the night.

In addition to making the drive-outs, we traveled on a residency-touring program sponsored by the National Endowment for the Arts. Splitting the fee with the NEA, each presenter received a package of one performance, one lecture-demonstration, and one master class, which allowed us to stay in a single place longer. The official imprimatur of the program helped us expand our audiences and develop critical response, and lured by the growing visibility and glamour of these tours, Bill often accompanied us on the NEA-sponsored residencies. His presence was a blessing and a curse. I wanted him in my life, but, Svengali-like, he criticized my interviews, oversaw my personal appearance, monitored my public behavior, and only displayed affection to me in public and on occasions when it served him. One of the only pictures of us features Bill with his arm around my shoulders. It was taken in April 1972, when I received my first award, a citation from Brandeis University. I asked to have the one-thousand-dollar prize paid in two checks. During my acceptance speech, I turned them over to an astonished Sara and Rose.

The sourness and frustration in my life with Bill began to seep into my work, or what work I was able to do, because I was still blocked in the studio. My real-life problems would no longer be

Brandeis Award recipients, among them, back row, left, Louis I. Kahn; fifth from left, Alfred Lunt; sixth from left, Merce Cunningham; front row, third from left, Lynn Fontanne; fourth from left, Katherine Anne Porter; far right, Twyla Tharp; 1972

squashed into dances. I allowed all my feelings—all the sadness, loneliness, guilt, and frustration—to be mushed into misery, and this weakened me as I tried to handle my dilemmas rationally. How was I going to earn a livelihood for myself and Jesse and also build new work in the studio? Could I ever find a man to take both my sides, becoming a father to Jesse as Bill certainly could not and allowing for my work as Bob could not? Was I trying to make my work more accessible because of money, as Bob insisted, or was it more profound concerns that drove me? My confusion was so great that I began seeing a psychoanalyst on a pay-as-you-can basis. Dr. Murray Stern is a man of direct observation and plain talk. His first task was to help me understand and then accept human emotions.

In my family no one spoke to anyone about much of anything concrete, let alone about feelings. Talking to an outsider about such problems—for feelings were automatically a problem— seemed unimaginable. Therapy was for sickness. Trouble was kept to yourself or taken into the wilds on hunting trips. My Quaker grandparents had actually been more emotionally advanced than my parents, participating in Wednesday-night church gatherings which were a form of group counseling. Without any preacher, the membership sat silently assembled, waiting for any troubled Friend to speak up. If no one did, it was a silent meeting. As Stern and I began, all I could say was that Bill was making me miserable and that somehow it was all my fault. Feeling for so long that my mother's many lessons added up to the message that I was not good enough, I easily believed that all I had to do was work harder on my own shortcomings to change my fate and to stop the pain. Stern and I got to "work." That was his word, and it would take me twenty years, on and off, to understand how appropriate the word is. Eventually through Stern I would see that pain is a reality in our lives—something that finally cannot be put off.

Jesse and I lived now uptown on 116th Street in an apartment I had been able to sublet very cheaply through Isabel's father. It was near a nursery school, and I had found a Paraguayan woman,

Azusena, who would look after Jesse in exchange for room and board, which meant the couch in our living room. Working downtown in the Franklin Street studio, I was completely alone except for a video camera. I had begun to work practically nude on a series of complex, syncopated phrases, and as I looked at tiny shudders and muscle vibrations blown up on the monitor, it was as though I had to start relocating myself in very small tentative movements. I worked to music Bill had given me, the Joshua Rifkin recordings of Scott Joplin rags, which were becoming very trendy. I took the most famous of all these, "The Entertainer," to make a bittersweet solo for myself as a stripper, sad and sexy. This role, like The Drunk, fit into a theatrical genre I could identify with emotionally: the victim. The pathetic and dangerous part of my stripper's routine was that, since nothing else was working, I hoped to entice Bill with it. Art developed in this way is bound to prove embarrassing, and this was no exception. "She dances for a long time, looking with every passing minute smaller, lonelier, tireder. A stripper seen through the wrong end of a telescope," wrote Deborah Jowitt. After the first few performances, I gave the solo over to Isabel. On her it was a dance, on me it was an indulgence.

Other parts of this work, *The Raggedy Dances*, were more successful. The gentleness and simplicity of the Joplin rags recalled some of Mozart's piano works, and I mated the two composers, adding a coda for Rose and Sara to the variations K.265 (aka "Baa Baa Black Sheep" and "Twinkle Twinkle Little Star"). Even though this dance was well received by both press and audience when it premiered in 1972, *The Raggedy Dances* failed to nab the man and so the superstitious primitive in me judged the whole thing a failure.

Fortunately, however, my career was suddenly to change. A few weeks before *The Raggedy Dances* premiered at the ANTA Theatre in October, we presented a sampler from the rags at the Delacorte, also giving the New York premiere of *The Bix Pieces*. Robert Joffrey—the founder and director of the Joffrey Ballet, New York's hippest, most popular company at the time—was in attendance.

An astute showman, Bob recognized my awareness of the audience. He was also a historian, always looking at dancing within a context. His revivals of Massine, Jooss, and Ashton were meticulous, and this grounding gave him the authority to believe he could recognize quality in new work or find tradition in the avant-garde. The narrator in *The Bix Pieces*' performance at the Delacorte helped him, pointing out the parallels in Rose and Ken's dance— "tendre," to stretch, "battre," to throw. Bob trusted his intuition and by the end of the week I received an elegantly drafted invitation asking me to dinner—a dinner that would push me into the mainstream of dance.

The Raggedy Dances: Rudner, Wright jumping; left, Rudner, Wright, Weiner, García-Lorca, Rinker, Tharp, 1972

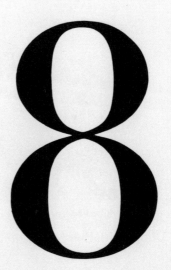

8

I think of
music as fuel, its
spectrum of
energy governed
by tempi, volume,
and heart.

KEVIN O'DAY AND TWYLA THARP, 1991

Robert Joffrey, 1981

Dining with Bob Joffrey at the Carnegie Tavern across from City Center, I was my usual brash, no-bullshit, direct and rude person, and when Bob said, "I'd like to offer you a commission to make a ballet for my company," I said I'd really never seen his company but maybe I could do a new full-length *Swan Lake*, which I'd also seen very few of. Bob tactfully—and one thing Bob always was, was genuinely diplomatic—suggested that perhaps a slightly less ambitious undertaking would be good for my first dance ever in the ballet world, for my first dance ever choreographed for more than six people, for my first dance ever with a production budget. I said I'd think about it; he should give me a bunch of tickets to see his company and then I'd let him know.

Going into its ninth New York season, the Joffrey's repertory mixed revivals, critically respected for their precision and authority, with contemporary works Bob commissioned. While his company lacked both the virtuosity of American Ballet Theatre's stars and the thoroughbred purity of New York City Ballet dancers, Bob himself was a meticulous and loving teacher with a regard for the niceties of several classical techniques. Through his efforts, his dancers were well disciplined with a coherent stylistic sense. Bob's historical perspective allowed him to cull from the classics of twentieth-century ballet masterworks that no other company was presenting—Kurt Jooss's *The Green Table* and Massine's *Parade*. However, the new works his company performed tended to be a kind of punchy hybrid, a glossy Broadway/jazz sort of ballet, and while I had no intention of subordinating myself to this Joffrey image I also had no idea what sort of ballet I would make instead.

As I attended the Joffrey performances, I watched the stage less and the audience more, trying to gauge what got through to them —rather like Mother stocking the drive-in candy counter. The ballet to come represented my first commercial work since the Alaskan Pavilion's furry hootchy-kootch. I never lost sight of the fact that Bob Joffrey was hiring me to make successful art.

Originally I thought of making the Joffrey ballet to a Beatles score. I had been listening to the White Album all winter, and now that their music spanned well over a decade, there was a wide range to their work. It was also very danceable and very popular and it seemed this might fill the Joffrey bill. But I stopped myself when I realized if I was going to make a ballet in the vernacular I should use slang I had grown up with. So I selected the Beach Boys instead. A distinctly American band who were slick about not being slick, they too had range—some ballads, some highly driven music, even some ecological songs. Their music was all about being in movement, all about cars and motorcycles and kids surfing in southern California. Perfect; that was me, or at least the me I would become. I would make a ballet in celebration of my generation's teenage years, going back and redeeming that era for myself. I would pump some vicarious fun into my memory of the halls of Pacific High. Along with the proprieties of the ballet I would blend a vernacular style composed of running, skipping, sliding, and tumbling, plus all those magical steps I never did—the bugaloo, the mashed potato, the slop, the go-go—the whole of this funneled through a little bit of Broadway show biz via the authentic energy and personalities of my dancers. I had remained loyal to my company, and Bob agreed that my dancers could be onstage with his. In 1959, Balanchine and Graham had shared a program, Balanchine using Paul Taylor in his *Episodes* and Graham using the Balanchine dancer Sallie Wilson in her *Mary Queen of Scots*. But my collaboration with the Joffrey marked the first time ever that a modern company performed in a ballet.

Getting a jump on the Beach Boys' music, I began to work on the new ballet with my dancers—Sara, Rose, Ken, Isabel, and one of our farm-club dancers, Nina Weiner—downtown at Franklin Street. After a couple of weeks we moved uptown to Bob's studios at Sixth Avenue and Tenth Street in the chic West Village. Here there was a lot of space—much more than my loft's seventeen feet of depth, even though Bob's largest studio did have two foam-wrapped pillars in the middle of the floor. I was very excited. This was definitely the big time. We would be getting our first weekly paychecks since *Medley*, and the Joffrey dancers would get the chance to dance in a new way. I naively thought this mix would be a piece of cake.

Instead, the resistance was intense. The first few days and weeks at the Joffrey, all the ballet dancers kept their distance, letting us know by their demeanor that there was only one way to dance: the old way, the proper way, their way. The worst of these dancers were slackers—snobs who took long breaks, marked most rehearsals, and never worked full-out. But even the best held back.

Franklin Street loft, 1972

Insecure, frightened of looking bad and/or getting injured, the Joffrey dancers were threatened by my dancers and how comfortable we looked executing some of my more demanding movements. I sensed the male dancers were particularly unhappy. They were not used to taking orders from a woman, for in 1970 you could count on the fingers of one hand the number of female choreographers who'd been allowed to create ballets in the twentieth century. Many of the Joffrey dancers maintained that my movements—which, granted, were a lot of work—were impossible and they made me and Sara, Rose and Ken show them otherwise. But slowly they relented. Drawn in by the movement, they began to see the dancing might be fun to do and might even feel good. As they began to understand the work they were challenged by the fact that it was actually an extension of their classroom studies and came to see they too possessed the tools for this dancing. It was just that they had never used them this way before. Bob had seen this right off in the Delacorte performance of *The Bix Pieces*, and we both felt a small degree of righteous pride, in ourselves and in his dancers, as they came round.

Still, all the dancers working on the project were nervous that they were going to be asked to be something they weren't: Ballet dancers were going to be modern dancers, which was beneath them, and modern dancers were going to be ballet dancers, which was what they'd been rebelling against from the get-go. I tried to explain that actually neither would be the case: all the dancers would be particularly and singularly themselves.

As themselves, they broke down into several camps. All by herself was Erika Goodman, a Balanchine-trained member of the troupe who would be the center of the ballet, performing the entire canon of ballet steps from *Ailes de Pigeon*—"pigeon's wings"—through *Voyager*—"to travel," a sauté in arabesque I gave her to get off the stage. Erika was well cast for her role as the concentrated fanatic: a serious little Twyla doing her lessons in the principal's office, avoiding contact with any other living soul while presumably perfecting her future. All around her everyone else

Deuce Coupe: Erika Goodman, left and far right; García-Lorca, center, 1973

was having a ball, frugging, swimming, jerking, and monkeying. In real life I never saw Erika do anything but darn pointe shoes and eat lettuce and carrots to keep her weight down.

Another faction was the Joffrey converts: Rebecca Wright, one of Bob's principal dancers; Henry Berg, with whom I'd taken classes from Michel Panaieff in Los Angeles; Starr Danias, because she could see I liked her quick delicacy; William Whitener, willing as only rookies can be; Glenn White, a principal dancer who compensated for a quiet personality with a very clean technique. Then there was my gang, and finally, the bigger guns of the Joffrey who would wait for a smash tryout in Chicago before really committing themselves to my work.

As the dancers came along, so did the rest of the ballet. One day I heard a vaguely romantic melody in "Cuddle Up," a tune with a bit of languish to it, as though Schumann or Chopin hovered nearby. I had already placed this song in my mind as the finale. Now I saw this melody could be developed as a through-line to pull the whole thing together and keep the score from being just a suite of songs. I found a composer, David Horowitz, to write four small variations on the tune—one for the opening, the others to be dispersed throughout—and during three consecutive nights in a recording studio we constructed a montage of Beach Boys songs from 1962 to 1973, speeding up a section here, cutting a single note there, then adding the "Cuddle Up" variations—with minimal orchestration because we could only afford a piano—for continuity.

Set design came a little later, although I actually had been looking at it for a long time. In 1972 graffiti was a subterranean art form: newly painted trains came in on the tracks with wonderful explosions of color and design that made you want to applaud. You knew the designs were done by underprivileged kids—who else was idealistic and desperate enough to find this mobile home for their work? One night, traveling on the IRT, I thought: Aha! An ongoing upstage mural by adolescent boys—what could be better decor? The inspiration was not without its problems. The aerosol spray cans the kids used made the air unbreathable; acquisitive types, the six street kids we located—Rick II, Coco 144, SJK 171,

Deuce Coupe, 1973

181

Stay-Hi 149, Rican 619, Charmin 65—had to be banished to the warm-up studio before shows or they stole everything in sight. They also rejected my suggestion that for the final number we white out the fifteen-foot rolls of paper they had painted during the dance. This I felt would legitimize their work as process rather than vandalism. However, these kids were definitely not into conceptual art; they intended to sell the rolls later.

Finally, the wardrobe was designed by Scott Barrie, a hot young Seventh Avenue fashion designer whose costumes made the dancers look like people—like you and me at our best, or perhaps our most bizarre: short flashes of shocking orange for the women, cerise trousers for the men, with Hawaiian print shirts. Jenny Tipton lit the stage with just the right touch of shadows and gobos, colors, blackouts, and silhouettes.

I choose to remember my pre-premiere state of mind as cool and casual, but Sara and Rose remind me that I tried to check myself into a Chicago hospital, convinced I had stomach ulcers. Prompted by their memories, I now recall that I suffered a panic and fear

greater than I had ever known, proportionate to the higher stakes
and greater visibility of this premiere. Bob held my hand, as he had
throughout the rehearsal period, quietly reminding me that the
clock was ticking and wisely not telling me everything was going to
be all right.

Then we were on—*Deuce Coupe.* The ballet's name came from
a Beach Boys hit titled after a two-door vehicle. This seemed an
auspicious metaphor for our two companies working in tandem.
We began by letting the audience know this would be a ballet for
real as two of the Joffrey dancers, Becky Wright and Billy Whitener, performed a schmaltzy ballet variation set to the "Cuddle
Up" theme, played by a solo piano, while Erika began the "A's"
center stage. Then—*powie*—"Little Deuce Coupe," our title song,
max volume, a snake line with the wonderful, sexy, gorgeous Beatriz Rodriguez first out and Sara batting cleanup. After this came a
long ballet passage which was followed by character bits: a loose-
swinging "Alley Oop"; Rose dominating the stage in "Long Tall

Deuce Coupe: Beatriz Rodriguez, Rudner, Goodman, García-Lorca; right, Rodriguez,
Rudner, 1973

Texan"; "Papa, Ooh Mau Mau" in which the dancers, their hair
slicked back in ducktails, mimed smoking pot and revving motorcycles; a cool, nightclublike trio patterned after Fosse's "Steam
Heat" for myself and two men; a female octet danced to rock and
roll's first ecological protest song, "Don't Go Near the Water"; and
then a solo, "Got to Know That Woman," by Sara that reduced
every person in the audience to the breathless heat I used to feel
after watching the steamy love scenes on Mother's drive-in screen.
There were duets, trios, canons, "Wouldn't It Be Nice," a choral
section—now fully painted, the graffiti rolls looked like beautiful
stained-glass windows—and the Grand Pas, led by Erika, a final,
swollen, full "Cuddle Up," for which the first ballet variation was
repeated, developed, expanded.

We were done. The curtain came down. There was a shouting
whistling stomping standing ovation. Ushers carried huge floral
bouquets onstage. This was the first time in my career I had ever
been presented with flowers, and as I took mine from the usher, I
looked at it for a beat and threw it back to him. I didn't know how
else to handle it. But we came back and back and back and finally
Bob came out with me because his love for dancing, his sympathy
and intelligence, had made it all happen.

Deuce Coupe was an enormous hit. "The Joffrey Ballet's decision to ask Twyla Tharp for a new ballet for its own repertory was
daring and sensible," wrote Nancy Goldner in *The Nation*. "Twyla
Tharp's *Deuce Coupe* is the best thing to have happened to the
Joffrey Ballet in a long time," said Dale Harris. "It is also one of
the best things to have happened to dance in America."

Deuce Coupe became more than a ballet, spurring *New York*
magazine to do a cover feature on the graffiti kids; it also brought
a new audience to the ballet. *Dance and Dancers*, a British publi-
cation, wrote, "*Deuce Coupe* is one of those works that totally
comes together in all its aspects, choreography, music, and decor.
Whenever *Deuce Coupe* was given, it sold out the house and

brought in lively new audiences that included not only pop music fans but also an assorted crowd of theatre directors, artists, and others who are rarely seen at dance performances."

At the same time, the critics understood the love for dance that inspired the work. About Erika Goodman, Deborah Jowitt wrote:

"She becomes a kind of testament to the dancer's discipline and endurance. Through it all there is the shining thread that holds it together and is the ballet's signature. That is Erika Goodman who goes through a fair lexicon of classical dance while the world breaks up around her. She is the symbolic glory and salvation, the one who, after all else has failed, proffers hope in the palm of her outstretched hand. In the end, *Deuce Coupe* doesn't contrast ballet with rock dancing; it points out their kinship. . . . Boy, is it nice to see *people* up there dancing."

Then we went on the road with the Joffrey and the bubble burst. Success came with a price tag, and *Deuce Coupe*'s was a big chunk of my innocence. Gradually I came to disapprove of the audience I had worked so hard to please. I had thought *Deuce Coupe* was a success because it was a well-crafted dance, challenging and developing techniques and traditions. Instead I came to realize there

Backstage at the Joffrey, 1972

was a large portion of the Joffrey audience that liked almost anything as long as it had bright lights, scenery, or loud music; sexy people in all combinations were a given.

I also began wondering about what it took for dancers to survive life on the road, constantly dislocated, constantly having to deliver: just get the show up. Drugs were commonplace in the world of professional dance. I had banned recreational drugs in my own company since 1967, when one of our members had started sweating over half an ounce of tinfoil-wrapped pot stashed in her luggage as we crossed the Canadian border. However, as we toured with the Joffrey it became impossible to disregard not only recreational drugs but therapeutic ones too—shots of this or that injected directly into damaged muscles or tortured tendons.

The promiscuity of life on the road was equally unsettling. I too experienced the insecurity and loneliness of the road—you come off an intense high onstage to an empty hotel room, from ovation to nothing, hello Spokane. I wasn't at all sure about life at the top being worth the struggle, but I wasn't sure I wanted to climb down. I also wondered if I could even find the ground anymore.

In the summer, my company left the Joffrey and went back out on its own. Our group was expanded with two men, one of whom, Tom Rawe—a cab driver with an engineering degree—had been understudying with us for a year and would be with us up to the end, fifteen years later. The other was a curly-haired Adonis who made a living doing carpentry work and would not survive the summer. Following a residency at Jacob's Pillow, we moved into Washington, D.C. to teach and perform at The American University. Bill had made the room assignments. Even though he would be driving back and forth to New York, not planning to be with us much of the time, he had nonetheless given himself the best room. Sara blew up. Emotionally quick, Sara doesn't brood; this makes her a great performer but it also made quite a scene. I was still tormented by Bill, part of me attached to him but part of me also resenting him terribly, as did everyone else in the group, because of his blatant self-interest. This time I sided totally with Sara, but it was too late. Sara had recently spoken of wanting to do her own work, and now she told me she wanted a leave of absence as soon as it could be arranged.

Furious at Bill and hurt by Sara, I looked for sympathy among our newcomers, who provided a breath of fresh, untangled air. Tom Rawe had been around long enough to know that things could be complicated, but our other newcomer knew none of the history and we spent one night together. However, if only instinctively, I have always been aware of a very sensible navy regulation: don't fraternize on duty with subordinates, not because of the subordinate but because of the ship. I was using him and when I told Bill, even though we had not been close in a long while, his response was instant: he bashed me, leaving my eye black for a week. Dependent on Bill for the company's support and perversely tied to my hopes of a relationship with him, my reaction was no less sick. "This proves he really loves me," I told myself when he held me in his arms afterward. I meekly followed Bill's command that the dancer be sacked and his name be stricken from the company posters. We still billed the company with all the members' names; we were now Tharp, Rudner, Wright, García-Lorca, Rinker, Weiner; however, about this time it was decided the tradition could no longer be afforded, each change of personnel meaning a change in stationery, and we became the Twyla Tharp Dance Foundation, a performing troupe named for its office. I didn't know the theories about victimization and codependency then, and Dr. Stern was not particularly interested in having me learn the terminology. But he did continue to tell me that my relationship with Bill was not good for me. However, instead of confronting Bill, my solution was to withdraw from everyone. Embarrassed and confused in my own group, I went back to the Joffrey.

After *Deuce Coupe*, Bob had asked me to write another ballet, this time for his company alone, and as I thought about a second

Jacob's Pillow, 1972

Joffrey ballet, I felt I was betraying my own company. I have always demanded absolute loyalty—no one would have dared ask for a leave to work with another company or do commercial work—yet here I was planning a major dance without them. I had no justification for this double standard, but the opportunity to write another ballet for the Joffrey was too attractive to refuse. Not financially: I was paid only seventy-five hundred dollars for each ballet with a per-performance royalty of seventy-five dollars. But professionally and artistically the offer was irresistible, providing me with an opportunity to work away from Bill, and most of all, to write a real ballet—not a *Deuce Coupe*-like semblance of the real thing, set in a specific time and place, and inventing a new vocabulary but a work within the constraints of dance history. Clive Barnes had sniped that *Deuce Coupe* was a "disposable masterpiece." With the new dance I would proclaim my true breeding, my ancestry reaching through Collenette back to Louis XIV, fashioning something built to last, a dance everyone would have to acknowledge as a true classical ballet.

Long before my family had left Indiana, I would put on music, close my eyes, and see dancing—ladies whirling on their toes when the music was light and high, men jumping when the music got lower or slower. To me the vision—which I thought everyone had, once they shut their eyes—of these spinning, dipping bodies extending the structure of the music into space was ballet. The vision is Apollonian—cerebral, balanced, effortless. While I no longer believe everyone sees these gossamer figures when they close their eyes, I do still believe that when dancing is *right*, the movement possesses a logic common to us all, an inevitability that takes it beyond the personal and egocentric and makes of it classical art.

This sense of dance was what I plugged into in 1973 when I began to work. I called the new ballet *As Time Goes By* because ultimately time is the only test of classicism, not whether the work is highbrow or lowbrow. My music was Haydn's 45th Symphony—

the "Farewell" Symphony, noted for the slow exit of the different orchestral voices at the end—and my title taken from a pop standard: both are classics.

As in *The Fugue*, Balanchine was at the core of my new ballet; however, his influence here was different. *The Fugue* is in my own idiom; *As Time Goes By* is anchored squarely in the traditional ballet vocabulary. I wanted this ballet, like Balanchine's *Agon*, to throw off some new possibilities.

As Time Goes By opens in silence, its ballerina presenting a brief synopsis of the entire ballet in about forty-five seconds. This opening solo, set on Bea Rodriguez, my favorite from *Deuce Coupe*, emphasizes Bea's strength and pride and is delivered in an absolutely straightforward, direct fashion. She leads in five dancers who begin a sextet to the minuet of the 45th Symphony. This section features tightly designed ensemble work, set in a world of genteel manners, and requires split-second timing from everyone. The sextet then brings in the full company of seventeen dancers to begin the finale which accompanies the symphony's presto. This music is some of the most blisteringly powerful in the classical repertory.

As Time Goes By: Rodriguez; right, Jan Hanniford, Larry Grenier; 1973

Originally I had told Bob I only wanted to use the very hottest part of the symphony—twelve bars twenty in from the beginning, looping them over and over. He, however, talked me into using the last two movements intact, with repeats as Haydn wrote them. As the last strains of the symphony wind down, the musicians literally leave the pit section by section until only the first two violins are left. By legend, Haydn was dropping a hint to his patron, Prince Esterházy, that summer was over here in the bucolic Esterhauz Palace, the mosquitoes were biting, and it was time to return to winter life in Vienna. The ballet ended with Larry Grenier, a very laid-back, almost passive, self-absorbed dancer, left onstage while the others departed one by one.

I have always felt one of the things dance should do—its business being so clearly physical—is challenge the culture's gender stereotypes. Because almost all ballet choreographers have been male, most of the major roles have been written for women. As Balanchine said, his women are the queens, the men their princely consorts. Clearly the choreographer is king. In excluding women from its power center, the ballet world has forfeited the roles for

Anna Marie D'Angelo, Grenier, Christine Uchida

Company

men as kings that women might create. In *As Time Goes By*, Larry was the soft one, Bea the firm one, yet Larry's vulnerability had everyone longing to support him, while Beatriz's drive was a relief.

My company had had a brief break while I was in the heat of the *As Time Goes By* rehearsals, and then I started to work on a new project for them while I finished the ballet. Working with two groups at the same time, I began piggybacking projects. This would become a dangerous, unhealthy, sloppy way of life for the next fifteen years. While I was committed to working with my group most of the time, there would be work opportunities that challenged me, such as this pure ballet, that were inappropriate for my dancers. As it turned out, the success of the new Joffrey ballet, rather than undermining my company's popularity and bookings, as we had feared, pushed us further into the vanguard of the dance world. We were hot, and wanting to capitalize on this momentum, I plunged into rehearsals.

In the next months we produced a critically and commercially successful six-week London engagement, as well as two television specials—taping *Eight Jelly Rolls* and *The Fugue* for London Weekend Television—and beginning a multi-media project for Public Television's WGBH that addressed the question "How do we know what we know?" with graphics, language, and advanced technology as well as dance. I welcomed all this activity—the television was especially important, providing us with a way of expanding dance audiences—but by the end I was exhausted. Jenny Tipton left the London engagement because of Bill's interference in her department; Sara was gone, ostensibly to choreograph her own dances although I couldn't help but believe my confusion and ambivalence about Bill had damaged her faith in me; and Bill himself finally left the company for other ventures. I had made two of the season's most popular and critically successful ballets, had one of modern dance's best ensembles. Still, I felt a complete failure. With Sara gone, I couldn't bear seeing *Eight Jelly Rolls* or *The Bix Pieces* and the only way I could see out of this morass was to let go of the past. I decided to drop the old repertory and cut back to the bone. Entering the studio every morning, I accosted the first one I saw of the three surviving dancers—Rose, Ken, and Tom—with an orgy of self-pity. "We'd come in every day," remembers Rose, "and before we did anything we'd have these heavy conversations about life and relationships. It would be very emotional, but not very specific. Twyla was always asking, Why, why, why? She didn't understand why relationships weren't simple. She'd cry and then we'd go into the studio and work all day."

In the midst of this misery, I discovered a line of discontinued Fats Waller recordings pressed on translucent green plastic in Chambers Street Records' one-for-a-dollar bins. All the greens were slightly different, "Honeysuckle Rose" paler than "Ain't Misbehavin'," but no matter what the color, the music was all great and provided us with something that felt real and right. We started

Sue's Leg rehearsal, Minneapolis, 1975

working to it. In half an hour, I wrote an opening variation for Rose; in two days, I did "In the Gloamin'," extending the group partnering begun in *The Bix Pieces* into many moments of slippery suspensions and counterbalances, the four of us never letting go of one another's hands for the first two minutes of the song. When the piece was later taped as the first *Dance in America* television program, directed by Merrill Brockway, an introduction suggested that this section was related to the dance marathons of the Depression, the era in which the music had been composed. This implied I had researched and lifted movement from that time, which wasn't true, yet the past did sift in, summoned by the Waller music. "In the Gloamin' " does show four desperate people clinging to one another for dear life—but the dance's desperation came out of our lives, not our parents'.

The Waller pieces eventually became *Sue's Leg*, the Sue of the leg being Sue Weil, our sponsor at the St. Paul–Minneapolis residency where the dance had its premiere in the winter of 1975. Sue and I had met in 1972. I had wanted to find a location to house our rehearsals and performances that would be inside the community, and that could help us make the dancing familiar and inviting, rather than intimidating and foreign, as so much dance is in so many theatres. We came up with an old abandoned firehouse. Sue delved through the bureaucracy to find out which city department owned it, located money to get the firehouse brought up to code, and secured clearance to use the building for open rehearsals, as well as a performance space, all within ten days. With her moxie, our first residency had proved a real success, and when we were finished we left the firehouse as a work space for the community.

Three years later, our second collaboration presented Sue with a new problem. Since we had scrapped the old repertory, there was nothing to which a sponsor might sell tickets. Nevertheless, Sue was undaunted, bringing us out for a four-week residency and trusting we could come up with an evening's presentation during our stay. *Sue's Leg* became the first dance in a renewed journey.

Sue's Leg rehearsal, Minneapolis: Wright, Tharp, 1975

Money was tight for us all. Gathering at Kennedy for the flight to Minneapolis, Rhoda Grauer, a fledgling arts administrator who would replace Bill as our executive director, took one look at four-year-old Jesse, wearing pants so small they dropped below his belly button and came up above his ankles, a shirt with only two buttons, and a down jacket that fit him like a vest, and decided she had to make some changes. The next morning, while I did barre, she slogged through shoulder-high snowdrifts to buy Jesse proper clothes and enroll him in a Montessori school for the duration of our stay. That afternoon in a meeting with all of us, she pledged that from now on the dancers would receive two hundred and fifty dollars a week (AGMA scale at the time was two hundred and forty for principal dancers), fifty-two weeks a year. I would get the same as all the others, with an extra weekly thirty-five-dollar allowance because of Jesse. I would have to supplement this income with commercial projects—part of the infamous piggyback plan—in order to pay his tuition, but this commitment to the equality of all our company members was critical to me. It meant the dancers would never go on unemployment lines. They would be paid during rehearsal periods, injuries, and vacations, not just performing periods, which meant they would be treated as though dancing was a real job, not just a pastime. In 1975 my company became the first in America to pay its dancers fifty-two weeks a year.

We would respect this policy without interruption for the next thirteen years. In order to do so, we took on a range of projects unorthodox for a modern dance company—ballets, films, television projects, commercials, Broadway shows, and self-produced seasons. Since we also worked to develop all the usual teaching, touring, and residency opportunities, we would often be seen by the funding sources in the not-for-profit world as muddying the waters —going commercial as we crossed boundaries working to support our membership and our goals. However, it was through this extremely aggressive and creative management that we managed to sustain a payroll. Issuing checks fifty-two weeks a year is a standard yet to be matched by any American company—including ABT and the New York City Ballet. Rhoda Grauer was with us for four years before becoming director of the dance program at the National Endowment, and during this time she worked imaginatively and unstintingly to honor her pledge and make our lives more reasonable.

At the heart of our second Minneapolis residency was my determination to confront head-on one of the basic problems in dance. People often introduce themselves to me with: "I know nothing

Sue's Leg, 1975

about dance but," as though the general public does not have the right to know what it likes or the background to understand what a dance is. This sense that dance is an esoteric venture, its product beyond the comprehension of the man on the street, makes dance understandably hard to support. There is an element in the dance world that wants to keep dance closed off to a broad public, keep it caged in big gilded theatres at sixty dollars a pop. But the truth is that dance is simply the refinement of human movement—walking, running, and jumping. We are all experts. There should be no art form more accessible than dance, yet no art is more mystifying in the public imagination.

To demystify the process, we finished *Sue's Leg* in public, rehearsing in the old lunch halls of the St. Paul auditorium, and we created another piece, *The Double Cross*, during daily periods that were open to any and all. While this is not necessarily a comfortable way to work—I always worried that *this* would be the day I'd be dry, not an idea in my head, and the dancers, professionals and perfectionists all, didn't love being watched as they struggled with new material—I felt it was important for our *Sue's Leg* audience to understand we didn't always have the answers either. We didn't always know what a dance was any more than they did.

The result was deeply gratifying. As Sue said, "By the time the work premiered, it was like an old friend. New work always intimidates people because they are afraid they won't know what to say when it's over. It makes people feel funny because they don't know how to respond. You can't hum it. But because the whole process had been open to everyone, *Sue's Leg* in its premiere was both new and familiar at the same time. And when it was done the second time, in just the work light, it was really very touching because that was how we had first known it." Sue's reference is to our solution for not having quite enough new work to fill an evening: we performed *Sue's Leg* twice, sandwiching *The Double Cross*. The first time, we wore the exquisitely designed beige satin costumes Santo Loquasto, an extraordinarily talented young designer Jenny Tipton

Sue's Leg: left to right, Wright, Rawe, Tharp in Santo Loquasto costumes; right, in rehearsal clothes

introduced me to, had copied from the unraveling sweaters, torn sweatpants, ripped T-shirts, assorted tights, leotards, and leg warmers in which we had rehearsed the piece originally and which we wore the second time around. That way the audience got to see the grit and underlying work behind the virtuosic turns that had entertained them in the earlier, more finished version.

The daring program worked, largely due to the nature of the dance. Smaller and more intimate than *Deuce Coupe, Sue's Leg*

Tharp, Jennifer Tipton, Santo Loquasto, 1975

PBS *Sue's Leg* "Dance in America" taping: Rawe, Wright, Rinker, Tharp, Emile Ardolino, Merrill Brockway, 1976

was both my most tightly focused and artistically flamboyant work to date. Nothing was held back. In "Fat and Greasy," a trio for Tom, Ken, and Rose, I gave each dancer free rein with individual virtuosity and sophisticated phrasings. In my solo, "Ain't Misbehavin,'" I pulled out all the stops—big jumps, sudden freezes, a series of pirouettes and turning jumps in a circle that got progressively smaller until I spun so fast I felt as though I might go up in smoke. In "Please Take Me Out of Jail," I am caught in a conveyor belt of movement between Tom and Ken; I move around one, practically bash into the other, and veer offstage while Ken joggles tentatively into a split, finally hitting the deck long after the music is over. Compared to all this, my *Eight Jelly Rolls* Drunk was an exercise in restraint.

However, our Marx Brothers antics were at the service of the dance, the metaphor for community that emerged as we worked through that rotten winter in the Franklin Street loft. In "Tea for Two" Rose played with each of the men, bringing out aspects of their character. But there would be no choice between the two. At the end, all three recovered from a particularly chaotic and grueling moment and finished with arms linked in the best Hollywood tradition. In "I Can't Give You Anything but Love" we worked in unison, a kind of dancing most performers loathe because the demand to be in sync deprives you of the strength of your personal expression; but we had danced together so much that we appeared to be four independent bodies, each doing the movement in our individual ways, just happening to be aligned together, none of us forfeiting our independence in the collaborative exercise.

My sense of community in *Sue's Leg* came not just from the dancers but from Jesse too. At four, he was a real trouper. He enjoyed touring with the company, he loved roving the halls of the various hotels, going from one dancer's room to another. He remembers that everyone was nice to him and he passed the feeling on to me. When I began the commute between *Deuce Coupe II*—a Joffrey adaptation without my company that was premiering in St. Louis—and our St. Paul rehearsals, Jesse would say, "Don't let those dancers make you cry, Mommy." When I came home defeated, he would set up a stepladder next to the bed, put a piece of his huge white drawing paper in the middle of the mattress, and dive, always making me laugh. I began to think of dance, like Jesse's jump, as therapy—not ritualistically but literally, just as laughing literally helps the digestion. Jesse's resilience set a kind of example for me—what he remembers from the Minneapolis trip is not his cold feet but the red rubber boots Rhoda bought him. Ultimately it was my love for him that made me want our dance not only to be challenging but also to entertain.

Jesse Huot, 1978

For the longest time
I could not understand
duets between men
and women. "Why aren't
they just in bed together?"
I asked myself.

MIKHAIL BARYSHNIKOV AND TWYLA THARP, 1976

Shortly after *Sue's Leg*, I met with Lucia Chase and Oliver Smith, co-directors of American Ballet Theatre, and their associate, Antony Tudor, in a very large, fairly intimidating, sumptuously appointed, and appropriately high-up corner office in a Chase Manhattan Bank building. Wasting no time, Miss Chase asked me to make a ballet for Mikhail Baryshnikov, Gelsey Kirkland, Martine van Hamel, the entire chorus and ensemble of the company . . . and, oh, could I maybe find something for Fernando Bujones? Equally quick, I said I would consider the offer, but if I agreed, my fee would be ten thousand dollars for a three-year exclusive license.

Lucia gasped. "Young lady," she said, recovering her self-possession, "that is a great deal of money." No one in the ballet world set out to make money. Balanchine often gave his works away. Just who did I think I was?

The two men tried covering their surprise at my audacity, Tudor in particular looking as though he had just swallowed a whole chicken with all its feathers. I explained that I supported myself and my son and that while I was honored by their invitation, I could not afford to work for less. Further, I would not commit until I had seen Baryshnikov in a rehearsal. I wanted to be sure he would be able to do new work. I had seen him perform *Giselle* already and had been properly impressed. Physically, he was adorable—a short, muscular, manly body, an innocent, worldly face; his dance technique was perfect, genuine, and dominating; his stage manner was admirable—he had generously and warmly stepped into the shadows when the spotlight was on his partner. But performing beautifully in the nineteenth-century ballets was one thing. I needed to judge for myself whether he could do anything else, physically and emotionally, and how willing he would be to put himself on the line. My cool response masked my real reaction. As Tudor probably guessed, I didn't really doubt Misha's artistic commitment or ABT's financial one. I already knew Misha himself had proposed the idea after seeing *As Time Goes By*, and the company was going to give him everything he wanted.

It was myself I doubted. Could I pull it off? Making a ballet for Mikhail Baryshnikov was a tall order. Yes, he guaranteed great exposure for the choreographer working with him. But notoriety can harm as well as help: if the work failed, the choreographer, not Misha, would be blamed because he was already an untouchable. Since his defection in the summer of 1974, he had received enormous publicity, including the covers of both *Time* and *Newsweek* in the same week. The publicity, combined with his reputation as one of the century's premier—if not the greatest—dancers since Nijinsky, in addition to his profound sex appeal, made him a forbidding collaborator. Before the official announcement of my commission, I ran into Alvin Ailey. Alvin was larger than me in size, reputation as a choreographer, and experience. He just looked down at me and said with sardonic amazement, "Are you really going to do a ballet for Baryshnikov? You've got to be nuts. You'll be eaten alive."

Still, with the courage of the naive and the willfulness of the ambitious, I attended a rehearsal to see up close what all the hoopla was about. I came in a bit late, so there was no formal introduction. I crept around the edge of the space to my empty and waiting chair. Misha was rehearsing lifts with Gelsey Kirkland. Gelsey was evidently unhappy with the lifts but Misha kept doing them the same way: I was apparently witnessing a standoff. Then suddenly, just after Gelsey had stopped the pianist with a soft wave of her hand to go back for maybe the fourteenth pass, Misha paused and, instead of following her to the upstage corner, turned a cartwheel and a somersault and landed at my feet—literally—arms outstretched somewhere around my knees. And such a grin. The one thing I had not expected from the great Russian ballet stylist of our time was acrobatics and clowning. But then, I didn't know Misha yet. "Take me," he was saying. "I promise I'll never become boring or predictable." Well, what was a girl to say?

The next time I saw him was in June, in Spoleto. My company was there to perform repertory and premiere *Ocean's Motion*, a work based on material from Minneapolis's *The Double Cross*, set to Chuck Berry songs. Misha was dancing in a *Medea* choreographed by John Butler for him and Carla Fracci. The Arts Festival had been founded by the Italian opera composer Gian Carlo Menotti who, tired, as he put it, of being "the after-dinner mint of the wealthy," had transformed a beautifully quaint but deteriorating Umbrian hill town, with an ancient Roman amphitheatre and two nineteenth-century theatres, into an internationally renowned creative center. Misha arrived the afternoon of his first evening performance, and after watching him rehearse, I dallied on the way back to the hotel where we were both staying in the hope that I might run into him on his way home. Art and ambition surely guided my decision to work with Misha, but what finally got me past the fear was the same impulse that had drawn me to Paul Taylor: lust.

We both performed the matinee in Spoleto's opera house, the Teatro Nuovo, a picture-postcard fantasy done up in red plush, gilt, and marble—probably tacky as all get out for the old days but infinitely quaint now. Exquisitely small, with only eight hundred seats, the theatre has boxes so close to the stage that I could spot Misha the moment I made my entrance. I was doing *The Fifties* (half *The One Hundreds* with no mob) as a solo because the rest of the company had to be ready for *Ocean's Motion*; then we would close with *Sue's Leg*. I felt no response from the box during *The Fifties* other than an occasional gasp at the more outrageous references (a moment borrowed from *Les Sylphides*, Act 1, a sylph listening for James) or some of the athletic dancing, moves that are unusual for women and out of the question for ballerinas. But during *Sue's Leg*, Misha laughed often, and always with delight, never derision, his response coming from pleasure and surprise—a true compliment, since there is nothing a dancer likes more than the appreciation of another you think may be as good as yourself. I gave notes to the *Ocean's Motion* cast—missing Misha's performance—and went on to that night's party, at Gian Carlo's palazzo overlooking the town's main square, the Piazza del Duomo, and its

With Mikhail Baryshnikov in Richard Avedon's studio, 1976

eleventh-century cathedral. The traditional applause for performers who have just entertained greeted our entrance but clearly the evening's real guest had not yet arrived, a fact that the dancer in me wasn't too happy about: I had just given a remarkable performance too, but I hadn't defected from Russia.

A stirring began and the applause for Misha broke out. I pushed through the crowd but he had disappeared again—to take a shower, someone said; Gian Carlo, unlike the theatre, had hot water. Then there he was, suddenly by my side with a glass of champagne. I quickly put aside the one I already had to take his. He spoke practically no English, I no Russian, and we had hardly even been introduced. But we were already committed to each other and we knew it: as dancers, we were in love.

The party was much too crowded. We became restless. Outside, the evening was clear, the air warm; the moon lit the winding streets that pitched steeply down from the palazzo to our hotel. Soon we were running barefoot down the town's ancient sidewalks, laughing at the pleasure of moving together. When we arrived at the hotel we paused. We were both winded, speaking different languages; it seemed ridiculous even to ask. In my room, I found that the famous muscles I had only seen tensed in performance possessed an extraordinary softness. As we explored each other's bodies, the confidence we had as dancers let us invent transitions that flowed as smoothly as well-drafted duets. Afterward he fell asleep and I watched his body shake, throwing off the remaining tension from his incredible dance efforts. It was dawn before I closed my eyes and when I woke he was gone.

Back in New York we began work on the new ballet. We rehearsed in the old ABT studios on West Sixty-first Street, an ingeniously designed space that included an overhead walkway, letting you view the action in four large studios below. I asked for the last studio, the fifth, because it was not accessible to the walkway: concentrating on new and foreign ways of moving, Misha didn't need the extra trouble of thirty little faces analyzing each move.

Those who were hopelessly and desperately in love with the body and the image would have to wait for him at the downstairs door.

Almost instantly, two things became very clear about Misha. One, he was unbelievably eager for new movement, trying anything I did with complete sincerity and heart. And two, his concentration span was practically nil. After two or three minutes he would phase out, his eyes glazing over; he would pace the room as though the walls were confining him, then turn and go up close to the mirror, looking into his own eyes as though he were suffering amnesia and searching for a way to recognize himself. Frowning, he seemed to be saying, "Where am I? Who am I?" My heart went out to his bravery and pain. As he wandered toward the mirror he would run his fingers through his thoroughly drenched hair—in mid-July, the room was a hotbox with the fans turned off for fear his muscles would cramp—drawing it back off his face, but also to touch himself, "pinch" himself: "Am I really here?" Without language to distract him—earlier plans of learning Russian in two weeks had been abandoned after my first look into a beginner's primer—I clowned, waited, futzed, until I caught his eye with an interesting move and he returned.

Partly his inattention was the result of an intense, lonely culture shock. But his wandering was also due to fatigue. In Russia, he performed rarely; one performance a month was not uncommon in the large Kirov company. This problem was compounded by the structure of ballet classes, the morning exercises made into brief combinations that don't develop aerobic or muscular endurance beyond what is required for the short variations in the ballet repertoire.

Misha began to understand the logic of my movements. While I wanted a literal, athletic heroism from him, capitalizing on his unsurpassed virtuosity in the male domain of ballet—jumps, multiple pirouettes, batterie—I wanted it in a new form. At first, Misha couldn't locate his balance off center, and his face would cloud when I asked for turns and large jetés that twisted or lay far back from his supporting leg. Then I would demonstrate the movement

HERBERT MIGDOLL

I wanted, and, as though he had ingested my body, he would mime my action perfectly (trained in acting and music as well as dance at the Kirov, Misha was an excellent mime and he always loved becoming characters—including me). Actually it was easy for him to pick up my movements because our proportions are uncannily similar. Slowly, he also learned how to come out of the strange movement, watching me catch my weight just a little lower than normal, or in turning, reverse my momentum a hair before usual, coming to understand that the trick was in the timing—actually, I'd never left my center. I'd simply shifted it—a relief because it meant this new movement was not going to end up with him hurling himself untended into space. I also began incorporating parts of Misha into the dance, embedding his idiosyncrasies into the work, using as a signature for the opening variation one of his particular gestures: he dips his head, runs his fingers through his dripping hair, then tosses his head back. This delighted him, for this gesture

Once More Frank: Baryshnikov, Tharp, 1976

and this dance were his and his alone, and it was a desire for such freedom and personal expression that had drawn him to the United States in the first place.

When we began working, I intended setting the ballet to Bach's "Partita Number 2 in D Minor." Sublimely musical, Misha knew intuitively how to take his pulse from the Bach—pulling back from it, digging under it, soaring with it. But the music was getting a little heavy. I wasn't sure the American public—or I myself, for that matter—was up for such deep soulfulness from the Russian guest in our midst. The rehearsals had begun to drag. Misha's

thirst for artistic adventure, to be the first one there, was something I associated in my mind with his love for ice fishing. To witness his artistic process was like watching a man sitting patiently on a fjord in the middle of nowhere, just him and the frozen water, waiting for a fish to take the bait, for days, maybe weeks—any length of time so long as the mission was complete. In this regard we were alike—we both liked being on the edge of nowhere—but sometimes his tenacity would turn into petulance, intransigence for its own sake; there would be flashes of rivalry, and I could sense a stalemate brewing. Then we would both instinctively know it was time to recess to the water cooler, and there, at a safe distance from the studio, on neutral ground—and unable to speak the other's language, thank God—we'd waste no time talking it out. We'd simply look at each other, see ego coming out of our ears like steam, and laugh it off. A little hug and back we'd go, into the fray, pushing and racing each other toward another unique combination of our individual personalities, striving for that new boundary where the body has never yet been.

Push Comes to Shove: **Rehearsal with Baryshnikov, 1986**

That summer I worked hard not to fall in love. Misha, in his mid-twenties, was probably as close to physical perfection as anyone need ever see, but he was clearly alone and a loner. No one was going to change that. Perhaps if I could have acknowledged myself as his counterpart, also a person with maybe ten friends in the Western world, alone and a loner, then things could have been easier between us. But I was not yet ready to accept a personal life on the run. I also felt that to maintain the distance and clarity that sees without prejudice, I should fight to remain unattached. So, given the choice between a personal relationship with Misha and a great ballet, I was opting for the ballet.

Misha was scheduled to leave soon for a three-week barnstorming stint and, to get the ballet as thoroughly prepared as possible, we worked on duets in addition to his solos. His partner was Gelsey Kirkland, a wonderful dancer whose work habits drove me crazy. First of all, she always arrived at least half an hour late. The habit was worse than a mere irritation—her tardiness threw the whole ballet off schedule. But this was just the beginning. Once in the studio, she had to make the right selection of practice skirts, of which she kept a seemingly never-ending supply in her bag—long chiffons, short taffetas, plus thousands of barrettes and three or four pairs of leg warmers, all of which she had to pin, fold, and otherwise beguile into shape. And then the ankle still hurt, after all this.

It was this ankle that finally parted us. Always claiming she was frail—though somehow I found this suspect, because she was a workhorse when she wanted to be, pushing herself nonstop with a fierce commitment that even I found extraordinary—Gelsey asked to be released from the ballet because of her injury. But I wondered how much she really wanted out because of her temperament, her fear that this was going to be Misha's ballet, not hers. This wasn't my plan. I was determined that everyone in the ballet be shown to the very best of his or her abilities, and I very much wanted to explore Gelsey's natural love of movement and her exquisite New York City Ballet technique. However, her bottom-line fear of anything beyond her control made working with her an agony.

So now we had to find another partner. Natalia Makarova was the likely next choice, but there were problems with her. Rumors circulated, claiming friction between her and Misha. Misha said he'd go along if I wanted her, but I didn't: from the upper ramp that looked down into all the studios, I could easily see that she was temperament in spades. Her passion was also the wonder of her dancing. A wild, free spirit, she was capable of altering movement to her own divine purpose. But while this habit was great for her onstage, I decided her way of working might be something of a tension provoker in my rehearsals so I decided to forgo the opportunity of working with her just yet. Instead I opted for a much less famous, lovely dancer of exactly the right size and proportions for Misha to partner and one who would be grateful for the opportunity. Marianna Tcherkassky, a beautiful, small, dark-haired woman, fit the Gelsey mold but was much sturdier. I had a feeling she would need to be.

I drafted a drama for the ballet. Misha was a womanizer, and being perverse, I decided to give him his wish: every woman in the company. There would be two principals, the little one, Marianna, and a big one who towered over him, capable of squashing him, a terrifying, dominating Marta-esque figure in juxtaposition to Marianna's lovely petite coquette. Martine van Hamel fit this image perfectly; she was a gloriously expansive and still very feminine beauty, extraordinarily strong on pointe and capable of enveloping space in a way that ordinarily requires a masculine drive.

In addition I would give him the chorus—a double chorus, eight girls in each—for whom I developed some of the most difficult movement in the piece. I like to side with the underdog and I figured that the valiant among them would view this as a challenge, a promise of a future beyond the chorus and into larger things. Meantime, the chorus would be a little less boring place to be.

Then I changed the music. Inspired by Misha's birthday—the same as Mozart's—I decided to exchange the baroque for the rococo. I chose Haydn's Symphony No. 82 in C—"The Bear," an appropriate choice, I thought, for a Russian. The four movements would be the dramatic "acts" of the dance. The first would introduce Misha and his two dates—big and little—and end in an impasse: each would have to show more of her stuff. The little one, with the entire chorus as reinforcement, got the second movement (my double-chorus concept fit nicely with the music, which was essentially a series of variations). The third movement belonged to the big one, with the rest of the ensemble and her own cavalier (Clark Tippet in the original cast, one of the rare members of ABT with some modern dance in his background). Then Misha crashes this party—the fourth movement—and wins everyone in the ballet, another instance of art imitating life since he had already captured the heart of the dance world.

But what of Misha's original reasons for wanting to dance in America? How did they fit into the ballet? I sat at a restaurant alone on Thanksgiving (Bob had Jesse over the holiday) and contemplated this Russian so in love with American pop culture. Astaire was his idol—not a strange choice for a dancer. To Misha, Astaire was a mortal elevated to godhood, not the other way around, not the Apollo descended, that generic heavenly being that so many of Misha's ballet roles called for. Could I get more of this quality into the ballet for Misha? What of the Broadway part of Misha who wanted to dance Jerome Robbins' musical comedy and jazz? Did we have any of that in the ballet for him? We Americans wanted to see him dig his teeth into our culture. But I saw no opportunity for this in Haydn. To broaden Misha's range in the piece, I decided to start with him introducing the whole circus to come. Taking a page from *The Raggedy Dances*, where I had combined Mozart with Joplin, I mixed the Haydn with Joseph Lamb, a successor of Scott Joplin's. These were frontiersmen of jazz, America's pop culture, and this beginning was where Misha would start.

As I studied the Haydn fourth movement for the nine thousandth time—I wanted to be completely prepared for Misha's return because we would have very little rehearsal time before the premiere —the title occurred to me: *Push Comes to Shove*. A little trashy for such a grand institution as ABT, but then maybe a posh audience would be grateful for a little funk. Besides, there was a yin and yang to the words—as well as the obvious sexual hook—that suggested the juxtapositions in the ballet: the old classical forms of ballet versus jazz and its own classicism, the East of Misha and the West of me (though which of us was push and which shove was up for grabs). Then too, there was a personal reference I knew would please Misha: the name of the great Kirov instructor, responsible for Misha's development from the time he first entered the academy as a child, was Alexandr Pushkin.

So that's where we were when Misha returned: same material, completely different music, two paramours and two choruses instead of one, the responsibility of hosting the whole event resting on Misha's shoulders, and a joke for the title of his premiere piece. If he was shocked he didn't let on. Part of our deal always was— up for anything.

We started working on the Lamb rag, transforming this Apollo into Astaire by moving his weight down, centering him further back into his legs. Working into his new character, Misha looked horrible, hideously out of whack, his poor feet, locked into their tightly confining black slippers, trying to learn parallel movement, synco-

With Baryshnikov in Avedon studio, 1976

pated timing, and a new, lower-to-the-ground balance, all in one fell swoop. But instead of being daunted, Misha took delight in his clumsiness. Soon he had stopped looking in the mirror—because what he saw there was too awful. Instead he began to visualize the movement for himself through its feel, reveling in the dangerous risks.

At the same time, we worked on the two solos I had given him before he had left. Misha had put the time on the road to extraordinary use. He had parsed the movement by himself, working out the transitions in his own way. His solutions were breathtaking. He was learning to maneuver around an ever tighter base and the precision and audacity of his leaps and pirouettes astonished me. Everyone watched his rehearsals for the moments of greatness, all of us feeling we had participated in making him ours, changing him from our guest into a cousin. If you were a dancer you could not but love him. He was just that good.

The last touch was a hat. Misha would enter fondling a bowler, establishing his character with a single dramatic prop: he was the lovable rake. And in the course of the ballet he would live up to his reputation—every woman would be his, and we would approve. (Some feminist I turned out to be.)

Then it was time. Misha and I exchanged opening-night presents —he gave me a nineteenth-century crystal pendant shaped like a very fat heart with a diamond center. I gave him two photographs of himself taken in rehearsal—the orchestra struck the first (as requested) slightly off-key note, the curtain rose, Misha sauntered into the spot.

He was nervous, but the actor in him quieted the dancer, telling him to focus on his role, and the hat. He introduced the two women, and the audience started to fidget: "Is she going to cheat us? This guy hasn't gotten off the ground once."

Then the Haydn began, and there's nothing but darkness onstage, as I delay the inevitable for as long as possible. At the very last moment the spot hits him and he's off. He circles, runs his

Push Comes to Shove: Baryshnikov with, left to right, Tcherkassky and van Hamel, 1976

fingers through his hair, paces, gathers himself, and he's in the air. It was a moment every dance aficionado hopes for—a moment in dance history. From there on he's in perpetual motion, soaring, spinning, feet flying, back working overtime, releasing as much energy during his two variations as any audience has ever seen from any dancer, while never compromising his technical purity. Martine and Marianna follow, each with small solo passages in the first movement as well, during which Misha, unbeknownst to either

woman, observes them from upstage. We begin to see the dramatic question is not which woman he will choose but whether he will pick any at all. When, at the end of the second movement, Marianna pulls Misha in from the wings and confronts him with the whole chorus, he's only momentarily overpowered by this ocean of femininity; within moments he's vanquished them.

Martine dominates the third movement, and the company gets an opportunity to look as strong as possible, setting a high mark for Misha to top, which he does at the start of the fourth, entering on the deep diagonal with double sauts de basque, flying higher than anyone has ever seen and still keeping his bowler on his head with a free hand and a big grin on his face. Enter chorus, ensemble, and soloists together, and from now, wherever Misha goes, he seems to

Push Comes to Shove premiere: curtain call

be in the way, about to be trampled, his life in imminent danger. Ringleader as clown and underdog—a favorite role for those of us who are short—he tries to maintain order, getting bashed and ignored as he tosses out hats for everyone. Finally the whole chorus bears down on him and the music stops: he pauses with both arms formed into a cross over his head, warding off this swarm of vampires. Then the music resumes and so does the little one, interjecting herself between the girls and him, saving his life. Everyone else pours in to celebrate the final chords, Haydn thoughtfully ending the symphony about twelve times. On the last of the finishing flourishes, Misha tosses his own hat high in the air, and dozens of other hats, snuck onstage in the last moments of skittering chaos, fly up to meet it, celebrating his battering, bruising, incontestable triumph: "Hats off, gentlemen, a winner!"

10

One of the inspirations in my work is the trust my dancers show in consigning their bodies to me.

HAIR, 1978

Push Comes to Shove was an incredible high. I had choreographed a huge hit for arguably the greatest male ballet dancer in the world and building on the success of *Deuce Coupe* and *As Time Goes By*, my career in the dance world was assured for the moment. I could have coasted on this success with my company for some while.

However, Milos Forman had been to see *Push*, loved Misha's capers, and invited me to choreograph his next film, *Hair*. This was a unique opportunity to enter the broader world of entertainment, but it would take me many months to say yes.

While *Push* and *Deuce Coupe* both flirted with show business, they asked serious questions, and answering those questions meant more to me than making money. *Deuce Coupe* examined the division of dancing into the arbitrary worlds of modern and classical, and *Push* investigated the boundaries of the classical technique itself.

Now, deciding whether to work for Hollywood and meet its simple demand for entertainment, I had to wonder if I could remember who I was inside the massively commercial world of big-time show business. The director has final say, and I would for the first time lose control of my own work. As I anguished over my choice, I tried to balance my fear of being gobbled up against the challenges offered by a larger world. Each medium—film, television, theatre —has its own lessons, and the only way to really learn them is to go in and start to work. I might be tempted, in the course of this work, by whatever was involved in selling out, but I felt I wouldn't be destroyed. About that I was right, but about the degree to which I imagined I could manipulate the forces that put together mass entertainment—the vast budgets, egos, and fortunes that ride on the fate of shows and movies—I was wrong. I underestimated the cost, personal and artistic, of working in the commercial freelance world. Threatening to the ego, it is confusing and it is demoralizing, and its success will always be mixed. But I also found that each time I returned to my own work the lessons I learned in commercial projects made me a better artist—stronger, surer, a survivor. Besides, I went into *Hair* with an agenda of my own. I had already directed and, with NET funds and a grant from the Mellon Foundation, produced a television special, *Making Television Dance*. I wanted to learn more about film directing and Milos could serve as my Paul Taylor for the silver screen. Also, Milos wanted me to dance in the picture; if I came out a star so much the better.

We began to meet at Milos's Central Park South apartment, looking north over all Manhattan. On my first visit he brought out a special bottle wrapped in a linen towel and dispensed shots all round. We bottomed up. Then Milos unwrapped the bottle. Inside there was a massive snake coiled in the Marc de Bourgogne—"worm juice," as he liked to call it. I did not blink an eye, asked for another shot, and tossed that back. Figuring I had made the grade and with my new name, "Twilotka" which is, loosely, "Little Brown Twyla Cow," I was ready for this man's world. Milos loves dubbing his favorites with these Czech-style diminutives, for he is both a primitive Czech peasant and an incredibly shrewd politician.

Milos had come to America in 1968. Unable to get work, he had moved into a cheap room at New York's legendary Chelsea Hotel, celebrating his first American Christmas and last twenty dollars with a bottle of champagne, watching the Yule log burn on his TV, then sleeping for thirty-two hours. In his worst depressions, those moments when, as he likes to say, he can't even dream about a hot dog, let alone a woman, Milos simply goes to sleep. For days.

Then things turned around. After his success with *One Flew Over the Cuckoo's Nest*, the first film to win all five top Oscars since *It Happened One Night*, Milos was still pinching himself, not sure he believed his sudden good fortune. His doubt was reflected in his apartment. Even with its luxurious space and views, the place was a shambles. The few pieces of furniture were all heavy, ugly stuff that might have been carved from the densest Black Forest timber; stacks of books, manuscripts, head shots, and résumés were strewn everywhere, and the only paintings were the works of a

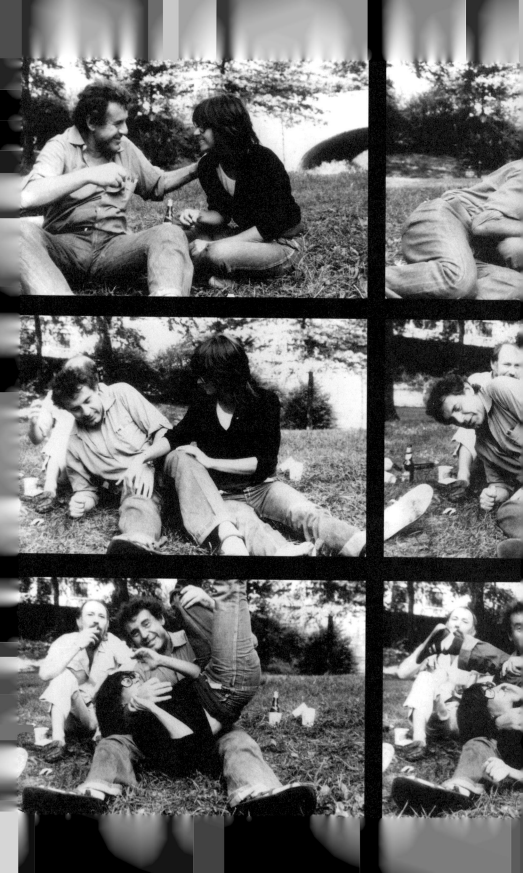

With Milos Forman in Central Park, New York City, 1977

Czech primitive that suggested a strange mix of influences—Felon, de Chirico, and Rousseau. An endless stream of Czech immigrants —often great tennis players and chess masters—passed through this mess, including occasional blondes who would appear suddenly, only to vanish within months or sometimes weeks. Milos was a classic chauvinist, open about his womanizing, and somehow managed to suggest he'd arrived at this condition because of the nature of women, not men. On the day shooting began he handed out the same present to every department head, all of whom were men except Ann Roth in wardrobe and myself: gold quarters from Tiffany's with the tail side featuring a naked woman's butt. Still, I knew there was a certain bravado here. Milos was missing a quite gorgeous French actress who had suddenly developed passport problems, and he still deeply mourned his wife Vera, who chose to remain behind in Czechoslovakia with their twin sons after the Russian invasion of Prague in 1968. Milos was working in Paris at the time but Vera did not join him because her homeland was all she knew; her career, family, and language were there. Milos characteristically hid his feelings behind a sardonic mask; having suffered at the hands of history—both his parents were killed by Nazis—his irony was a means of survival. Milos's humor lies in perceiving that we all get fucked sooner or later, it's just a question of when.

We began the project by screening Hollywood's ten top-grossing musicals. In buying the rights to the musical *Hair*, United Artists had acquired only the title plus the Ragni / Rado / MacDermot score. When I entered the project, Milos and the screenwriter, Michael Weller, had the outline of a plot—two very different young men serving their country in Vietnam while being attracted to the same young woman—but still needed to weave the music and the original dance numbers I would create into this narrative. After the screenings we all agreed on one thing: the musical numbers had to grow out of the dramatic action.

As our meetings progressed I came to understand a truth that would color my whole experience with *Hair:* of all the elements that made up the musical—book, music, dance—dance came last. Real dance passages never seemed to find a place in the story, and dancing ability was never considered in casting.

An actor or singer would be sent over to my studio—a huge ballroom in an old West Side hotel—for a dance audition.

"Milos," I would say, "this one can't dance."

"Well," he'd answer, "but this one is so good for the script, and this one is so good for sing. . . . I hire."

It was the same every time: John Savage, Beverly D'Angelo, Annie Golden. All were cast for singing and acting. I was supposed to put dance in after the fact, and that included teaching Treat Williams, the lead, who, although he was an excellent mover and an incredibly hard worker, had no real dance technique.

Afraid that dance would be overlooked in the film, I began searching for every possible situation in the script that might get people moving: young debutantes on pointe; recruiting sergeants dancing under their table; Hare Krishnas tripping around; military guards extending their drill routines; mounted policemen's horses dancing; T'ai Chi and Aikido experts working out in the park; kids in the park moving in trances, even if only in the background. I wrote my company in as members of an extended hippie tribe,

Dancers in *Hair:* "Aquarius"

augmenting my group with ten able-bodied and mostly overweight good sports to give the feeling that all the world moved as easily and freely as it sang, and included myself as the park jogger who accidentally gets fed acid and trips out, pulling the film into a prolonged fantasy sequence in which I am a high priestess wearing one Shiva-esque ankle bell and one heavy running sneaker (shades of *Re-Moves!*). But through-the-back-door ways of introducing dance were still far from the all-out dance sequences I had antici-pated at the start of the project.

"Dance, damn it," I'd say to Milos. "We need good dancing, excellent dancing."

"Why?" he'd answer.

Finally shooting began, and I saw how painstakingly Milos worked. A consummate craftsman, Milos provided himself with endless coverage—shooting scenes from different angles and lenses—doing elaborate setups before each shot, executing every take twice in case the lab messed up, and shooting until Milos was happy, Mirek Ondricek, the Czech director of photography, was happy, Michael Hausman, the first assistant director, was happy, and, if my work was in a shot, I had to be happy too. Milos never

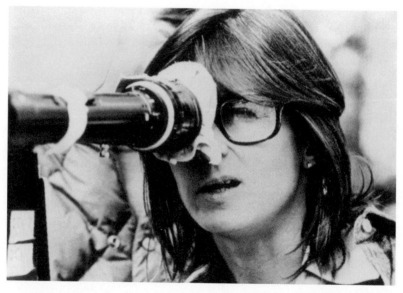

asked the actors. His perfectionism meant rolling a lot of film, and I often wondered admiringly at his nerves of steel; he sat there scowling, letting the dollars run up until he got his shot just right. Eighty thousand dollars was not an impossible sum for a "big shot" in an afternoon calling for principals and background effects, and yet Milos would continue shooting until he got just what he wanted.

Even though I believed he was right to persist, in time I personally began to resent his perfectionism. Milos would demand anything to get what he wanted, and this included my time—not some or most of it, but all. My own life was irrelevant. The only salvation was in dancing: rather than drinking one more cup of coffee and finding someone to attack—the sound or prop man, the gaffer, even a grip, to explain why cameras were not rolling—I would take an unused corner of the set and start a dance. Discovering something new, no matter how small, I could feel there was someone at home after all. And always, at that precise moment, a production assistant would come, saying, "They need you for a rehearsal, Twyla. The table sequence is coming up next."

The table sequence was one of the main production pieces in the film. Treat sang "I Got Life" while dancing on the banquet table to the amazement, shock, and disgust of the assembled guests of his beloved deb, the beautiful D'Angelo, the only spectator favorably impressed by his chutzpah and vitality. The number was Treat's one solo and he worked hard on it. No matter how many takes were needed, he had to look spontaneous every time, as though he had just gotten the idea to mount a table and sing and dance through and over a full-course dinner-party setting of Rosenthal crystal and china. He also had to be unfailingly accurate from take to take—if his performance was inconsistent, the takes would not cut together. Each time he crashed down on a predetermined dinner plate, his high-top black sneaker had to take the same size bite of the plate it had before. And to top everything, the linen, crystal, and china were all the real thing. Milos refused to fake it: these characters were wealthy people. This was what they would use.

Treat Williams in *Hair*: "I Got Life"

"Why must the china be real?" Lester Persky, one of the producers, would ask, after another grand of shards was tossed into the garbage.

"You want to use paper plates?" Milos would reply.

Each night our teamsters would drive us back to Manhattan and I would use the time to pump Milos with questions: how he planned his shots, why he selected which lenses, how the coverage was unfolding in his mind. He was always available and spoke generously, unless Mirek was in the car. Then the two would revert to Czech and God knows what mysteries.

Often, after a day of shooting, Milos would say, "Let's go to Victor's," referring to the great Cuban restaurant on the West Side. "There we have pig." He loved going out of his way to appear as barbaric and direct as possible. I liked this side of him, but thought that in his position, you had to be pretty sophisticated to pull it off.

We would push our way through any waiting lines, and the maître d' would find us a table, Milos or Robert Greenhut—the executive producer—slipping the guy whatever it is that ensures the right treatment, a ten, a twenty, or a fifty, one part of the male code I have never mastered.

Sitting at the table, fingers still numb from the cold, looking at Milos ordering pig, listening to the general table talk about "shots," drinking with the big boys, I would be reminded of the hunt and would bask in the ritual of ordering drink, warming fingers, awaiting the wild boar, bonding. Milos drank beer or wine but the others ordered hard liquor, and I joined in. Almost always, now, I'd have too much to drink by the time I got home, and in the mornings I felt lethargic and a little depressed. Only after I sweated some of it out in morning exercises did I begin to find the resilience to cope. I began to worry that I was drinking so much it would become a habit, but I loved the sense of community it fostered, whether with Milos in restaurants, the crew with their paper cups out in back of the trucks, or with Joey Tubens, the hairdresser, who passed out anisette-flavored espresso to his favorites.

As I watched the politics of *Hair* unfold—Milos getting his way one way or another—one of the classic moments occurred during the shooting of the Central Park Be-In. In the script the scene occurs in spring, but Greenhut, a long-time New Yorker, gambled on a mild December and scheduled the sequence for shortly before Christmas. If leaves had to be tied on trees, so be it.

Finally, after weeks of rehearsing on-site, constantly watching the skies for impending blizzards, we were all ready to go. The camper caravan was in place; hundreds of extras sat with steaming coffee in their Greyhound buses; the costume department was getting all the small featured players ready for the huge scene—including me, making my on-camera debut in a sequence for which I had been rehearsing a particularly harrowing, nasty, back-jarring pinwheel performed with four of my company men holding my arms and legs.

There was only one thing wrong.

It was snowing.

Milos arrived. He scowled and glared for a moment. He unwrapped a cigar, clipped the end, wheeled around and yelled at Greenhut, "You see, is snowing."

Greenhut explained to him that the bags of ice that had been placed everywhere were for the actors. They would suck on the ice, spit it out just as Milos rolled the cameras, and for eight seconds you would see no breath. Milos smiled sarcastically. "And then?"

Milos is a master at the movie production art of outwaiting your adversary. Now he dug in. He took to his camper and the clock began to run.

For three hours everyone sat it out—twenty dancers, a flatbed band with four vocalists, the tribe principals and all the extras (this was a very expensive shot). Then at ten, the ground started to thaw. It might even be dry by noon. But now Mirek balked: he refused to shoot in the flat, direct, overhead light.

O.K. We would wait until "the golden hour"—the wonderful last light of the day, named for its deep luster—and for everyone's pay to go into time-and-a-half.

At this point it was Milos who refused to go ahead.

"Look," he said, "read script. Annie's baby on the way. It is clear that things thaw down now, not freeze up. This is warm moment in script, loving moment. You cannot expect these people to want to hug the ground; ground push them away now."

He looked at Greenhut accusingly. "Nobody care about baby, just care about money."

This was Milos at his finest. He was playing Solomon, caring about the baby; everyone else was a monster of self-interest. A portion of this act was sincere. With his love of reality, Milos undoubtedly wanted the Be-In to smell like spring and for the extras to feel the soft air. But I suspected he had also masterminded this event. He had known he would shoot in the spring, but he had gone along with the scheduling hoping that when the time came, the resultant dispute would weaken Greenhut's standing. It was the executive producer's job to hold the budget line, and conflict between the two of them was ongoing.

Persky joined Milos in the camper.

"Lester," Milos began, a beguiling combination of sarcasm and pathos, "are we so poor that we cannot afford to shoot scene at warmer moment?"

Lester, knowing little of the difficulties of rescheduling and sensing an opportunity to be one of the good guys, said soothingly, "No, of course not."

Milos won. In doing so, he showed me something about the art of power plays, a far more valuable lesson in movie-making than conversations with camera directors about lenses or shots.

Early in January we went on location to Barstow, a small Western town on the edge of the desert in California. I spent days at an abandoned army base in Fort Irwin, staging Treat and John Savage in their boot-camp training sequences and using fifteen hundred National Guardsmen as extras. Milos knew I would be the perfect drill sergeant, gleefully driving everyone through hundreds of push-ups, chin-ups, pull-ups, and that rat's maze of training hell-holes, the obstacle course. I relished pushing myself through the regimen—me, a mere girl, pulling myself hand over fist, jumping barricades, climbing ropes that swung over deep mud holes.

Evenings I spent with Lynzee Klingman, *Hair*'s principal editor, who had set up a rudimentary cutting room in the dingy ground-floor suite of a local motel. Milos encouraged me to participate as much as possible. He wanted to see what I would make of the material, if there was anything I could suggest before he started cutting in earnest.

Life became unreal. I've subsequently found this is the normal condition of being on location, whether in London or Lisbon, but my first taste of the peculiarities of location life was intense and unsettling. We were a self-contained family, although our only real bond to each other was our attachment to the film itself. I admired Dickie Quinlan, Mirek's head electrician, for managing to find some normative security: he religiously did his laundry every

Thursday, the ritual assuring him that one day the film would be over and he would be going home to his wife and family.

Loosed from the responsibilities of daily lives, adrift, most of us wandered off, masking the terror of impermanence with indulgence —drugs, alcohol, sex, or a mix of all three. For me, double Scotches with a twist became a tradition at the end of the working day and helped me become a believer in the lies to come. I found myself in the midst of a passionate affair with a married man, and there in the Barstow desert, this attachment seemed more real than the other elements of my life. Jesse was now seven. Because of his schooling, he had not traveled with me for several years, and we had become ever more distant. "Please Mom write more," he would implore in his letters. We were both lonely and Jesse kept asking for a brother. That I did not provide, but I had replaced Azusena with Zoe Rygh, an ex-dancer who would become his surrogate mother over the next few years. From her I heard, with dread, reports of his progress: he was overweight and having trouble in school. My guilt at abandoning him overwhelmed me; when I called I almost hoped he wouldn't be there so that I wouldn't have to face my own sense of irresponsibility.

My work seemed equally distant. No matter how hung over, I forced myself to go daily to the studio, beginning with floor work and a barre, moving onto a center and improvised sessions, sweating out the alcohol. I concentrated on the yet-to-be-drafted sequences for the film and those that were done but still needed to be shot: New York and the Central Park Be-In, then a protest demonstration scene in Washington, D.C. that included a major production number for my company, and the fantasy sequence to be shot at Astoria, in Queens—the largest production number in the picture, revolving, as I saw it, around my own performance as high priestess. And there was still the Wall Street sequence with another five hundred extras. I tried to design the material for these scenes but nothing seemed to work; how could it? In Barstow, for nearly two months, I was surrounded by fantasy. Nothing was real;

none of the personal relationships around me were lasting. We had all been absorbed by the picture's world.

Returning to New York and rehearsing the company brought me back to reality. One of my ulterior motives for doing *Hair* was to secure employment for my dancers. Now we were together again —including Sara, who had returned after running her own group for several years. With her, and using Ken Rinker as my assistant, I could not have been happier. I was back with my Franklin Street family. We worked in earnest to finish the unshot sequences, trying to create new work that didn't repeat old material. This was a risk —it's difficult to be truly creative in such an intensely visible situation—but all of us felt the effort was worthwhile.

Jennifer Way and Shelley Washington, who had been with me since 1975, were, along with Rose and Tom, the nucleus of the group. Christine Uchida had joined in 1976, Raymond Kurshals and Richard Colton in 1977. Both Chris and Richard came from the Joffrey and had been in the original casts of *Deuce Coupe* and *As Time Goes By*. These dancers formed a loyal and talented center for all the large production numbers and had already proven themselves through the most testing situations. Whether slipping and sliding on mud, shivering through thirty-below nights, or camped around space heaters as shots were endlessly deferred, they had never failed to give one hundred percent. Whatever happened, they would make it work. They were veterans.

We finally moved into the fantasy sequence, *Hair*'s major number from the production point of view. A very big deal indeed, the scene presented me with production values on a scale I had never handled before. Several weeks of shooting were required in the Astoria studios using the largest sound stage on the East Coast. Thousands and thousands of candles, a treadmill that carried all my dancers in front of huge fires, John Savage on horseback, dancers writhing in dry-ice mists, Rose walking in air and flying through fire, water sequences with drenched dancers barely able to stand, and a corps of baby ballerinas on impossibly pitched inclined slopes representing a flock of harpies that kept John, the bedazzled hero, from his beloved Bev as Treat swooped in now and then from nowhere—all this had to be executed with a convincing naturalness that conveyed the effortless way impossible occurrences happen in dreams.

Loving physical challenges, I tested all these contraptions myself before letting the dancers use them: I flew, braved the fire temperatures, sampled the slipperiness of the water platforms and the pitches of the inclines, fell from heights of fifteen feet plus into catch boxes. We knew there could be an accident at any moment —a wire might snap, a gas jet could suddenly flare. Rose later admitted she had been terrified to fly through the fire with her blue "Virgin Mary" robes trailing behind her. Only the image of her paycheck with its double hazard bonuses—for fire and flying—got her through her terror.

Hardworking, excited, conscientious, none of us missed a mark or caused a retake; it was a matter of pride. In their makeup and costumes, the girls were gorgeous beyond belief, the darlings of

Hair fantasy sequence: left, dancers receiving oxygen after take with dry ice; right, Uchida, Shelley Washington, upstage

Bottom left, D'Angelo flying; above, Tharp; right, Wright flying

the set. The moment Milos yelled "Cut!" the crew ran in to rescue them, pampering them like prize racehorses.

One by one the sequences were shot. "3-5-0-0," a huge number set in Washington on a platform between the Lincoln and Washington ("Big Stick" as Milos called it) memorials. My company was exquisitely costumed by Ann Roth as ghosts dancing to lyrics from *Hamlet:* "What a piece of work is man! How noble in reason!" They were backed by a drill team of fourteen men while Melba Moore sang the lyrics for a mob of over twenty thousand extras— homegrown hippies fifteen years after the fact, faces painted in patterns inspired by old copies of *Life*. The Central Park Be-In was finally executed on a hideously windy day that left dust in everyone's hair, eyes, and teeth, but it looked great onscreen. My jogging sequence was set among hundreds of extras instructed to behave "naturally," and I got knocked over on the first take, tearing a ligament in my ankle so that I wore a cast for the next two months.

Finally we completed the Wall Street sequence as well, and filming was over. Dreamtime was up. We moved to the United Artists Burbank lot to edit the picture. What had pretty much been working all along would still be working; what hadn't wouldn't.

Milos tried everything possible in the cutting room. Even when a cut worked, he tried improving it, from shaving frames to starting with the end at the beginning and working backward. He had to be absolutely certain; he had to see, literally *see*, the different orders on the Steenbeck: the mind's ideas were no longer enough.

Hoping to get a frame or two more onscreen and wanting to be certain all the choices made about the dancing footage were the best ones possible, I sat through editing right up to the last sound mixes. My reward for this time was ultimately not on the screen, but in the lessons I learned from Milos. In the cutting room, his mastery is secure. Over and over—the exact timbre and accent of his voice is still fresh in my mind—I heard him say, when asked if he thought a cut could work, "Try. I don't know." There was no

Hair on location at the Lincoln Memorial

arrogance in Milos now; he took nothing for granted. Everything simply had to prove itself. I watched his list of "if onlys" grow and I sympathized with his anguish as he labored with the realization that the back third of the picture was in deep trouble. I had warned him that this final third, with its minimal production numbers, would be a long stretch—but that didn't matter now. If the picture didn't work, it was my problem too.

Hair opened in Los Angeles, complete with a wildly flamboyant fete that made me wonder if Lester hadn't produced this film simply to throw the finishing party. The fancy trappings and exposure just made the obvious more painful: *Hair* did not quite click. Rushing to the first screenings of *Grease* and *The Wiz*, I had been relieved when each, in its own way, had been unsuccessful because these musicals were opening in direct competition with us. *Saturday Night Fever* was another matter. A commercial smash, the film had the elements lacking in *Hair:* a terrific performance by a star who portrayed a hero with whom the audience could clearly identify. In contrast, our "protagonist" was multiple; no single performer was ever free enough to take over. And the timing of the release was miserable. Before long *Rambo*, not our confused, ultimately noble pacifists, was about to dominate the box office.

But those of us close to *Hair* kept up the charade. The New York opening was even bigger than the one in L.A. Shortly after, I met Greenhut and Milos for the film's European kickoff in Cannes, where we continued the games and kept up appearances. But we all knew. *Hair* might have taken our hearts and souls and every ounce of focus and commitment we had for two years but, hey, the handwriting had been there all along. At any place along the line we could have simply acknowledged that nothing was working well enough.

Then it was over. All of it. That spring of 1978, I was so worn I had to work hard to reclaim myself. Where was the energy current

I could connect to? Now that I was no longer swept up in someone else's project, where was my anchor?

I found myself back on the farm in New Berlin. Not in reality, of course, but as I watched the video of improvisations I'd done eight years before in the old attic—twenty-six hours of movement to the same Willie "the Lion" Smith recording—and saw myself on tape growing bigger and bigger with Jesse, I felt as though I could connect to a strong beginning. I recognized what I needed in the pure work force Sara, Rose, and I had shared before the Hollywood fling.

Invigorated by the tapes, I began to create *Baker's Dozen*, a piece made for twelve dancers and one more presence, the baby in the oven. *Baker's Dozen* represents an ideal society. Artists, I've always believed, have the opportunity to make the world a more righteous place through their work, and *Baker's Dozen* was made to extol economy after the flamboyant wastefulness of Hollywood. All the same, it gives just that little bit extra, the baker's generous measure of thirteen.

Capitalizing on the virtuosic qualities of the company—my *Hair* veterans plus newcomers France Mayotte, William Whitener, and John Carrafa—I let the dance play with the tension between indi-

Baker's Dozen cast; Osgood Hill: Back row, left to right, John Carrafa, Richard Colton, Raymond Kurshals, Rudner, Tharp, Washington, Uchida, William Whitener, Wright. Kneeling left to right, Anthony Ferro, Mayotte, Rawe, Jennifer Way, 1978

Baker's Dozen: Wright, Ferro; downstage Rawe, Way, 1979

viduals and the group. I introduced the dancers first as six couples, then—like the ancient game of jacks—gathered them as four trios, three quartets, then two sextets, the sections flowing easily one into the next with no demarcations. Finally the whole ensemble of twelve worked as one, dividing into a community of eleven which first delivers then reabsorbs its twelfth member, presenting each dancer briefly as a soloist backed by a chorus.

In *Baker's Dozen*, there is a place for everyone, time after time, a place into which each dancer comfortably and naturally fits. Maybe this is the reason I've always associated Edward Hicks's "The Peaceable Kingdom"—the famous painting of a wolf lying next to a lamb—with the dance. At any rate, the success of the piece—from the outset it became one of the company's signature works—lies in the ease of its society, the sense that everything has a context and that chaos is only momentary. Everything fits; there will be no cutting-room floor. From the simple elegance of its design (Santo Loquasto and Jenny Tipton's good work) to the grace and economy of the dancers, *Baker's Dozen* has always assured its audience that Biblical order is possible in this world.

During the making of *Baker's Dozen*, which premiered in 1979, the affair with my married man was on and off again many times. When finally he returned to his wife and family, I was glad that loyalty was being expressed in some direction. I think from almost the beginning of our affair two years before, I had suspected it would not last. And because I had been quite nervous about it the whole time, I began to wonder if I didn't thrive on anxiety. As I talked with Dr. Stern, I began to ask whether some of my dances required loss in my personal life. Making *Baker's Dozen* gave me a pleasure and focus lacking in my affair, and I started to see this new work as another of my "rebound" dances—like *Sue's Leg*, made to distract me from Bill's leaving, or *The Bix Pieces*, to cauterize the wound of my father's death. Maybe I needed loss to create art. Perhaps I made the "rebound" dances to give me a happiness in art I didn't want to find in life. How else to account for my selecting unavailable men for relationships.

"Nonsense," said Stern. He helped me see all this reasoning as highly self-serving and suspect. He cut through all the theorizing to insist on the obvious: the dances and the disasters were not really connected. After a bad night I could go into the studio and the dances I made would *become* optimistic simply because dancing makes me feel better. Gradually I would realize that when I start to move, I shuck off the world and its worries, enter a new environment, gain a new outlook. This is one of the things I mean when I say that to make a dance you must put yourself in motion. A sort of chemical optimism builds inside me that buoys and strengthens all my efforts. But all the same, my psychoanalytical ramblings sometimes became self-fulfilling prophecies. It would take me a while to feel my chemical optimism on a good day as well as a bad one.

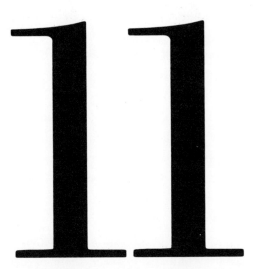

11

From a graffiti nude I
once saw scratched on the
side of a truck—her
breasts so exaggerated
she needed its power
moving under her to keep
from pitching forward—
I create a duet resolving in
a gyroscope. My woman
needs her man no
more than he needs her.

TWYLA THARP AND DAVID BYRNE, 1981

Suspiciously, nervously, after *Baker's Dozen* I began a dance realizing I felt a need for language. All along, dance to me has been as Joyce Carol Oates described boxing: it is not a metaphor. Of all sports, it alone is not "played" as are other games. Dance to me is the same: simply the thing itself. So why suddenly distort the medium as I know it with words? Dance even without language is perfectly capable of communicating all fundamental story elements. But then, silent ballets are usually based on stories everyone knows, and I didn't want to repeat fairy tales.

I had a personal theme I felt could be developed theatrically: a single mother on the eve of her fortieth birthday, none too happy and wondering why she wasn't born a man anyway. I realized I couldn't just throw myself and my problems onstage. I needed to dramatize my conflicts, to place them in a narrative outside my immediate experience. I began looking for a playwright.

Through our agent in common, Robbie Lantz, I met Thom Babe, a protégé of Joe Papp's whose play *Kid Champion* had been a notable success at the Public Theatre. A definite up-and-comer, Thom was willing to work within my company's limitations—little money and a cast accustomed to being seen and not heard.

Rehearsal of *When We Were Very Young* with Thom Babe, 1980

I was certain there was more than enough drama in my life to go around, and when we began I had visions of a great tragic struggle onstage. But Thom simply proposed we incorporate the A. A. Milne poem "Disobedience"—a favorite of his eight-year-old daughter Kirisa's—into the dance. Thom sat on a scaffolding overhead at the Winter Garden Theatre, where we opened, and read out loud:

James James
Morrison Morrison
Weatherby George Dupree
Took great
Care of his mother,
Though he was only three.
James James
Said to his mother,
"Mother," he said, said he:
"You must never go down to the end of the town,
if you don't go down with me."

The poem was a good choice on Thom's part. The verse stylishly suggests the necessity and difficulty for James's (read *Jesse's*) mother to grow up, a resentment I dramatized onstage by having the mother take care of two huge stage children who perch precariously on her lap, threatening to engulf her.

But I wanted more than this evocative lyric. I wanted a complete, naturalistic story. However, neither Thom nor I could find one continuous action to run through the disparate episodes— dance passages I had already constructed before he came aboard. The basic problem was that the piece never found a theatrical metaphor. I was asking the stage to resolve problems that belong in a bigger world.

Yet for all my dissatisfactions, *When We Were Very Young* managed to be a qualified success at its 1980 premiere—an accomplishment, considering that I both choreographed and directed it and that the company (meaning my office) produced it. The decision to risk this challenge came from my growing frustration with our seasons at the Brooklyn Academy of Music. While my company had a long association with BAM, going back to our first performance there in 1969, and its audience is one of the most intelligent and receptive in the country, I felt we were never going to get the critical attention and public recognition, playing three blocks from Atlantic Avenue, that we could receive on the Great White Way. More importantly, BAM was still part of the not-for-profit world, where trying to survive had begun to feel like Russian roulette. My company generated about seventy percent of its revenue from earned income sources, but all performing arts organizations depend on philanthropy to make up the difference. Applications are filed annually, and each time I went through the process I felt demeaned, like a child asking for an allowance.

Entrepreneurial independence seemed to offer a possible alternative, a future where dance could run as a business with income and budgets responsibly projected into the future, free from the skin-of-our-teeth insecurity of not knowing what gifts to hope for. So I told Babs—Barbara Hauptman, our executive director since Rhoda had gone to the National Endowment as program director—that I wanted to produce our next season, and presto! we were into a Broadway engagement and a seventy-five-thousand-dollar debt to the Shubert organization.

You have to love show business. On opening night a subway strike accompanied by a blizzard left the city paralyzed. We would be finished, down the tubes. However, Anna Kisselgoff—who usually liked only my abstract works—raved about *When We Were Very Young* and the box office boomed. The piece struck a responsive chord. Women in the audience wept in sympathy for the stage mom's determination, endurance, and enterprise. Nonetheless, the somewhat melodramatic ending—I simply stepped over the footlights and fell into the pit—bespoke my true condition.

As a child I had wondered what it meant to be a grownup. In my thirties I wondered if I would ever know. Now, entering my forties,

When We Were Very Young: Rawe, Tharp, Katie Glasner, Kurshals, 1980

TWYLA THARP

I began to struggle against the loss I saw inherent in adulthood and beyond. Dropping into the pit, I was jumping the gun on what I saw coming—the double and triple whammy of forced retirement from the stage, menopause, and approaching death. All indicators showed me cosmically out of control, and I marveled when I saw on NBC News that people were braving the subway strike and snow, bicycling across the Brooklyn Bridge, to see Twyla on Broadway.

When We Were Very Young pulled off the impossible. We paid back the Shuberts—Babs had wanted to send them seventy-five thousand dollars in quarters—and after all the bills were paid, the final tally showed us five thousand dollars in the black. What's more, we had gained tremendous, invaluable national exposure. I felt completely vindicated: a Broadway attraction *was* taken more seriously than a modern dance company in Brooklyn.

We continued our experiment in self-producing, this time promoting ourselves on the road. This was unheard-of among small, not-for-profit modern dance groups. Even the larger ones, such as the Ailey or the Graham company, worked with presenters: the producers fronted the costs and if the tour was successful, reaped the windfall; the company received only its guaranteed fee. Our company had already successfully self-produced on Broadway, participating in the gate. Why couldn't we on the road?

The decision added to my feeling that I was doing too much—wearing, or trying to wear, too many hats. I directed the company, made the dances, performed, did all the rehearsing with no assistant, worked with the office staff. Focusing on producing, I was newly aware of exactly how many dollars each rehearsal hour was costing: the dancers' payroll, space rental, amortized staff, stamps. These concerns in the front of the brain make ambitious creative thinking an imposition. In the past I had always enjoyed doing interviews, being in the spotlight; I was genuinely interested in the reporters' perspective. Now each interview became a tension-filled situation, a make-or-break opportunity for a well-sold box office and next week's payroll. On the one hand you wanted to make everyone rush to buy tickets; on the other, you could not toot your horn too loudly or resentments in the dance community would evolve. Publicity became one more arena in which I saw myself out of control, my destiny linked to an anonymous reporter who maybe didn't like my haircut. Paranoia replaced curiosity.

As we started out toward my dream of fiscal independence, I had the good fortune to meet the master promoter Bill Graham. Unattached romantically since *Hair* and feeling lonely with all my responsibilities for the company, I was ready to be swept away.

Bill was legendary in the Sixties as the man who had turned the Filmore East and West into rock-and-roll shrines, and as the mastermind behind the Rolling Stones tours. He had sponsored and loved Janis Joplin and Jim Morrison with a passion only the inveterate rebel could muster. He turned his company into his family—just as I had—and was a complete workaholic.

He also loved giving parties. To celebrate our engagement at the Warfield, one of his theatres in San Francisco, he sent a trolley car to the stage door, packed us all off to his Marin County estate, and treated us to an afternoon of volleyball and tall tales. That evening I stayed over.

It was easy to be infatuated with Bill—a dashing bachelor who sped back and forth over the Golden Gate Bridge in a trademark silver vintage Jaguar. However, I was also attracted to him because I had begun to feel I had joined an imaginary club to which he belonged. I saw myself taking up membership in a society that knows the opposite sex as "a certain kind of stranger." Since leaving Bob, my relationships had all been transitory, and all had been with my collaborators. It's not that I had become promiscuous; I wasn't interested in flimsy one-night stands. However, no relationship had outlasted a given mutual project. I wondered if this behavior was an attempt to address the conflict implied by Bob's remark, "You love your work more than me," since now my men *were* my work, or whether this behavior came out of seeds planted much before.

Several years earlier I had returned to California. Finding my first love, I had had the opportunity to complete what we had started so many years before in the model A Ford. I refused because by then the possibility of a real relationship had become too mundane and too specific. My first love had become generic, purely and simply "male." As it turned out, I had acquired a taste and a use for the frustration, and like other club members I felt myself to be something of a Dracula, returning to my coffin's soil in the studio after a night of drinking anonymous blood.

Men belonging to the Society of Strangers are often highly accomplished, very successful, very powerful, usually very wealthy, charming, often spoiled, driven. All feel themselves bereft of mothering. Several of them, Bill included, had actually lost their mothers as young boys, and I often felt that their seemingly never-ending search meant they could not remain long with an individual woman because then she would become too much herself, no longer generically female. I had not lost my mother, but early on I had internalized her overbearing ambition, which constantly yelled, "Feed me." Like my stranger brethren, I knew at an early age I was going to have to work unstintingly to please her and that in fact pleasing her probably would never be possible any more than it was for the men whose mothers had died.

Bill had survived an extremely difficult childhood, and he remained on top in a highly competitive world where, on occasion, the word *excess* meant nothing. Through him I saw a bit of backstage rock-and-roll, its massive power, easy sex, and drugs flowing in amounts that could never be enough. Ultimately it was wanting to dance that afforded me a buffer amid all this seduction. My experiment with drugs, for example, had been limited to three puffs of marijuana in my entire life because I knew I could not be around the stuff for long and still show up in the studio the next day. Dancing has kept me honest. For Bill's part, this was not the first time he had seen unstable females seeking answers to their lives in his, and he helped keep things in perspective. Our flirtation stayed hot for only a brief moment, and his contribution to my life proved to be not himself but my next collaborator. One morning, I asked Bill who he thought was the most talented of the young, not-quite-discovered groups. He told me about an avant-garde band formed at the Rhode Island School of Design; over the last five years they had produced several albums, attracting a hard core of middle-class fans. They were called The Talking Heads.

I hadn't heard Talking Heads' left-of-mainstream music when David Byrne and I met at Magoo's, a restaurant not too far from the Franklin Street studio. I thought it a strange association, to name a group after the TV jargon for a static tight shot—when the camera cuts the figure at the throat—but I trusted Bill's judgment. I wanted a mega-hit with my next collaboration.

Usually a little early, I was already seated when David arrived exactly on time. I was struck by his youth—he was not quite thirty —and his straight, preppy look: black tight-fitting jeans, open-at-the-throat white shirt, book bag, pitch-black hair slicked flat to his head. Our match seemed dubious. He ordered tea in a soft voice. Not my idea of Elvis, but then I was still in my macho phase and probably had a beer with a shot. David was likewise completely unfamiliar with my work: he was sitting there simply because of my company's reputation as the right place to be (and maybe he'd been a bit strong-armed by Bill).

In the beginning neither of us had any idea what this collaboration should be. But we both knew, however unfamiliar we were with each other's work, however secretly arrogant—in fact, both thinking the other probably didn't matter all that much—we were unified in our ambition to succeed. We just had to find the right subject. Both of us had felt detached in our childhoods, David's family relocating from Ireland and mine from the Midwest, so for the moment we decided that the American nuclear family with its 3.29 members was in trouble. That was where we would start.

We didn't have a lot of time, so we decided to go ahead with the music and dancing and let the narrative develop—the unfortunate equivalent of directors deciding to take care of story points in the editing room. I bought some of David's old records and began to work to them in my studio, entering the edgy, tense, shrill world of his music. David then watched the videotapes I gave him, turning off the sound and absorbing whatever of the dancing he saw that made sense. Part of his desire to make music comes from his own wiry body's need to bob around. His angular, jerky style was already heavily influenced by early east L.A. break dance.

When we began in recording studios—cheap facilities over Chinese restaurants or Korean groceries—I found David to be an incredibly thorough worker, economical and well prepared. He always had his book bag stuffed with meticulously drafted notes and ideas. David's passion was a new sound, and I loved the adventuresomeness his enthusiasm promoted. He would try anything, and he never let himself be intimidated by his own innocence. Sometimes I thought he kept from going crazy in his electronic world, full of its infinite possibilities, by preserving a link to primitive things, such as the kitchen pots and pans he banged in one session. Often he would start with a tune on the ukulele, a specialty of his Baltimore childhood. David was self-taught on all instruments, but the highly unlikely, humble ukulele was one of his favorites. There is a great tension in the tiny instrument that was well suited to David's energy, which he liked to conserve, pulling it inward as tautly as possible then letting it explode with incredible speed. David's normal rhythm was quadruple time, and the ukulele worked well in that small, bright range.

Once in the studio, having put down a line, he would experiment, feeding it into synthesizers and through stacks of units for reverbs and feedbacks. David chose the collaborators at these sessions carefully. He had particular theories about engineers and often chose women, believing that females feel lower vibrations with greater sensitivity than men because of the difference in the structure of their guts. Sometimes he called in highly specialized musicians for just a single line, although as conscientious producers we both watched the clock.

Soon David and I were together most of the time, though neither of us would have called it living together. He was afraid of women invading his privacy, and I sympathized. Our conversations were animated by concerns about the work, mutual respect for each other's progress, or aesthetics in general. We shared some of the same fascinations, but we saw quite different things in our obsessions. We were both taken by the spiritual element in primitive art and read Frazer's *The Golden Bough* together, responding quite differently. Both of us understood the search for first principles that create universality in art, but we guided our researches in different directions—mine being to locate the timeless, to find those things that are never-changing, while his seemed to be to find the residue of ancient thoughts in the most up-to-date aspects of society.

David had a restless streak and would plunge unhesitatingly into the new. He had his finger directly on the pulse of the violence and anger in pop culture, and his ability to thrive in this zone frightened me. Calculated in his exploitation of excess, cold and methodical, he seemed a scientist of the bizarre. Songs like "Psychokiller" from 1977 cleverly spoke of dark currents, and a substantial portion of his following looked to him for the Devil's work. Aware of

The Catherine Wheel, BBC taping, 1982

The Catherine Wheel, Winter Garden production, 1981

this neurotic element in his audience, he changed his phone number frequently. For him, chaos was real, and sometimes I felt he substituted ambiguity for artistry. *Stop Making Sense*, he called the Talking Heads' concert film. He found a base in the absurd. I did not.

Inevitably our differences surfaced in the work. Once again—as with *When We Were Very Young*—the narrative became the problem. I was still insisting on seeing theatre as literal, demanding real answers to real questions in my real life. I couldn't acknowledge that narrative is fiction, working within its own logic and having its own demands. In dance, I understood this. I allowed myself to go into the studio and be swept up with the possibilities of the moment, losing track of real time and letting the preplanned go. But with narrative, I demanded truth. "Don't story me," my Grandma Cora used to admonish: storytelling was synonymous with lying, and fiction took you straight to Hell. David and I spent months trying to find a common ground between the rich mysteries of his investigations and my own sturdier, pragmatic, and highly judgmental Midwestern biases.

During June, the company had an engagement at Sadler's Wells. David traveled with me to London. He slept while I rehearsed the company, and we worked together at night in sound studios. We had started the finale, called "The Golden Section." Working with the dancers, I experienced a tremendous rush and release of energy. The group working with me at this time was one of the most powerful in modern dance—strong, articulate, quick. Through the touring we had done since *Hair*, they had performed all my repertory from *The Fugue* on, had become grounded firmly in my style and technique as it had evolved from my beginnings. As an ensem-

ble—because of our fifty-two-week employment policy—they were unmatched. There were thirteen dancers and there was one impulse. Some of the partnering we developed was possible only because the women had strength in their bodies usually reserved for tennis players and swimmers, the men an ability to function with assembly-line precision and complete responsibility for their partners. Each dancer was of principal quality, and all worked with a commitment to the dancing that overrode individual ego. The cast was essentially the *Baker's Dozen* group, although there was a big shift. Rose had decided to retire and became my rehearsal director. Katie Glasner took her roles, Mary Ann Kellogg replaced

"The Golden Section" from *The Catherine Wheel*; clockwise from lower left: Carrafa, Whitener, Uchida, Washington; Whitener, Uchida; left to right, John Malashock, Shelley Freydont, Glasner, Whitener; Young, Carrafa, Way

France Mayotte, John Malashock replaced Tony Ferro, and Keith Young was added to the men. After a spring spent wrestling with story, I made duets, trios, quartets, double duets, double trios, sextets, octets, women's sections, men's sections, solos, any combination of dancers that I could get hold of after our regular repertory rehearsals. All I intended was that each short section—none longer than a minute—should top the previous.

The sections were made quickly, usually in an hour-long rehearsal for each one. Often these rehearsals were directly backed into the next one (I neither peed nor ate in those days), and as each rehearsal group came in and watched the new section completed by the previous one, my reward was in seeing their genuine amazement, pride, and respect for what had been accomplished in that hour. No matter how many thousands of people might applaud us later, this first applause by those who really knew—both what it was and what it cost—always meant the most to me. Because I was ahead of David at this point I worked to baroque music, pulling from the build and climb of Bach concerti to show David the high-energy plateaus I needed. Everything kept modulating upward. After about fourteen sections he asked me to stop, saying he was afraid he couldn't keep up and have the piece—all the lyrics and his own performance—completed in time. Eventually this last section settled into three songs and became the one overpoweringly successful element of the whole collaboration.

The rest remained vague: a full-length spectacle of the disintegration of family—prototypes borrowed from *When We Were Very Young*—commented on by a chorus. A shadow play portrayed a pineapple—the traditional symbol of housewarming—turning into a nuclear bomb. Mom and Pop battled onstage, Daughter was sold into slavery, and the chorus leader was transformed from a goddess of innocence and sensuality into a hag surrounded by insane dancers, incapable of controlling their own bodies. This was a role I made for myself, but when I had to sit out front, watching the whole production, Sara came back (after eye surgery) to take the part. As with *Baker's Dozen*, a pattern was emerging. I couldn't do it all, and in the long run I was replacing the dancer, the part of me I could least afford to let go.

The Catherine Wheel lacked coherence and cohesion—David and I were at such fundamental loggerheads that we even called sections by different names—his "Blue Flame," my "Family Loop"; his "Big Business," my "The Leader Repents." I turned to production elements for the unity and order that the story failed to provide. Indeed, Santo Loquasto, who did the set, almost managed to redeem the narrative section. Made of iron, the set consisted of sixteen poles, evenly spaced onstage throughout the first two-thirds of the piece. Into this maze other huge and very beautiful steel elements flew, including a several-ton torture rack that descended to within a few inches of Sara's prone body, and sliding gates which threatened to decapitate any dancer on the floor who strayed from his or her exact grid spot by more than an inch. Then, as the first chords of "The Golden Section" began, the set vanished and the dancers stormed the stage with a new, positive energy; the narrative gobbledygook disappeared into a harmonious wash of light, costumes, music, and movement. Finally, in the abstract arena of pure energy, David and I melded.

Notwithstanding a devastating *New York Times* review in September 1981, word of mouth on *The Catherine Wheel* was excellent, and the weekly publications were extremely favorable. By the fourth week we were playing to capacity houses. Even so, the heavy set had put us approximately one hundred and seventy-five thousand dollars over budget, and we started working feverishly toward an extension of the run: one week at capacity could gross two hundred and fifty thousand. However, a road company of *Camelot* was booked in tight, our general management could not get a delay, and a move to another theatre on a limited engagement made no sense at all. So, closing an extremely successful Broadway run, we were left with the company's first real deficit. Five members of the company board and I all signed promissory notes to guarantee a bank loan covering the company payroll.

. . .

Soon after the show closed, David and I agreed to split up. Talking Heads had just returned from Japan, my company from Mexico, but it was our temperaments, not our travel schedules, that did us in. The truth was we only loved being close to the mystical and the out-of-control; deep down, each of us felt a need to be in charge—a conflict that became clear over the *Catherine Wheel* video. I raised the money for the project and I was going to direct. David felt differently, and after a brief meeting in my kitchen, we parted.

Although neither of us had really committed to this relationship, each sensing and valuing the restlessness in the other, still we both were sorry. David wondered aloud if he could ever settle down long enough to cement a relationship. Tina Weymouth, a band member, had just had a baby, and David, envious of all experiences, wanted to know about that. I, meanwhile, was sorry that David and our bright conversations would be out of my life and that my child was still fatherless. I was beginning to wonder if I would ever see a relationship outlive a project: David marked three in a row. Jesse still wanted a baby brother, but he had never counted on David to provide this. He had found David very strange—totally quiet around the house, always listening to music, and then crazy on-stage. Jesse was no more surprised by the breakup than I was, but now there could be no pretense whatsoever about a family life, not even the communication of noncommunication that had been part of our life with David. Jesse remembered that once when he and I had argued over what TV channel we would watch, David's solution had been a threat to smash the TV. Now we were back in the vacuum of the single-parent household.

Jesse had valid gripes. He was eleven and without a home. He had outgrown the ten-by-ten-foot dining room in our one-bedroom apartment and felt bandied about between two parents who had long ago and for separate reasons abandoned their responsibilities of parenting. Bob was part of a liberal generation that did not want

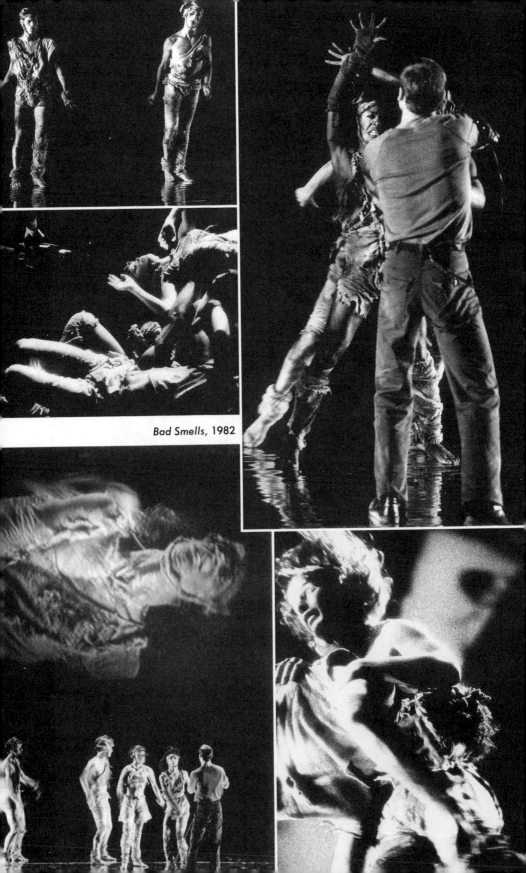

Bad Smells, 1982

Sinatra Suite rehearsal: Tharp and Baryshnikov, 1984

to tell their children what to do, while I did not want my son's life to be dominated by me, the way I felt mine was by my mother. To Jesse, both parents must have seemed more committed to their arts and professions than to him, and our patterns of acting out surely embarrassed him. He had seen one too many men pass through my life to kid himself that the current one might become his father. I continued to drink Scotch evenings, and was often too shaky to hold a saucer in one hand. Apart from Zoe, Jesse got little parenting except from the families of school friends he would sometimes adopt, and both Zoe and I worried that Jesse lacked male role models in his life at a critical age. So, soon after *The Catherine Wheel*, when Jesse came into the kitchen and smartly announced, "Mom, I love you very much, but you're weird. I want to go to boarding school. Here are three choices," my reaction was relief and sadness and a sense of deep failure. For the next five years Jesse went to boarding schools. I paid the bills.

Many years before, I had made two dances at once, isolating different impulses in *Jam* and *One Two Three*, and the work I did following *Baker's Dozen* was also a pair, playing different parts of myself against one another rather than even attempting to reconcile them. *Brahms' Paganini*, in 1980, was a very technical, rigorous, difficult, formal work, *Short Stories* a tale of rape, mayhem, and blasé destruction. Following David's departure, I began another pair, going into the studio with another broken relationship and ever more anger. The anger made a dance, quite an ugly dance called *Bad Smells* (1982), in which the same girl as the one featured in *Short Stories* is destroyed before our eyes. The last moment of the dance was inspired by an image planted in my mind during the Mexican trip. Somewhere I had heard, read, or seen that in the fourteenth century Aztec priests stood on one of the flat-topped pyramids and, when the sun was at just the right angle, sliced the skin of a human offering so that the body would roll out of it, down the monument's many steps, leaving the skin intact in the priest's hand as though a huge zipper had been undone. The victim's heart would somehow still be beating until the split second he or she hit the bottom. This image resonated with a feeling of victimization I had started to identify in my work with Dr. Stern, and I determined the "priest" was not only the men in my life, he was also my mother.

In my Quaker family we never said, "Look at me." That was immodest. We said, "Look at what I've done." At my center was a hole demanding either constant work or the presence of another being—a man perhaps—because I had nothing to put there of myself. This is probably why I could sustain so much pain in obviously damaging relationships with men too young, too old, too wealthy, too gay, too married. It would be a long while before I could accumulate enough person to wrap my life around, and when the time came I would do battle with my mother for the right to sit at the center of my own life. Now, with David's absence opening the vacuum once again, I decided to take revenge on Mother as she moved back in. I would design a long string of gorgeous, romantic duets, and I would set this to the music of Frank Sinatra, the perfect crooner for romantic adventure. Mother hated Sinatra's music because, she said, he "always sang flat."

I did not come easily to the duet form. My first attempt had been in 1976 when I set a work on myself and Baryshnikov. This duet was a very small piece, made for a television special I was directing; I had wanted to keep the dance small and intimate in order to hold the dancing in a very tight frame. However, because Misha's salary and the rehearsal space were being covered by ABT, the piece was also danced at a flashy, star-studded gala at the Metropolitan Opera House—to disastrous results. Everyone expected Misha to turn, whirl, and soar more than ever, but after the success of *Push*, he was intent on being avant-garde so we agreed to eliminate all virtuosics from this venture, pledging he would not leave the ground even once. Of course, we were roundly booed by the five-hundred-dollar-a-ticket crowd. Misha, who had never been booed in his life, was delighted. However, I had, and I was miserable and humiliated as he kept dragging me out for more calls. This response to my first duet opened an old wound.

As a kid, I had a wardrobe full of formals but I never went to a single school dance. I sat out those forbidden proms, the soft nights and beach parties. Later I would joke that I only danced if I was paid, refusing ever to step onto a ballroom floor with a man. Not only was I embarrassed at being touched in public, I was also terrified that I did not know what came next, because, of course, *he* was leading. I was in the dark about ballroom dancing until Milos asked me to choreograph *Ragtime*.

Researching the film project, I asked United Artists to arrange screenings of every scrap of footage and frame of film that showed dancing on ballroom floors, stages, or streets—anything that might reveal how society allowed male and female bodies to move together publicly until 1922. The footage was fascinating—there were rare moments of a touring company cavorting on a beach, bits of early vaudeville and revues (the limbs of the hopelessly plump chorines tapered to pointed satin slippers), classic routines of the great clowns caught on the dance floor in inimitable pieces of business. Tucked away in backgrounds on these snippets I could also see poorer folks locked in face-to-face embraces, doing their best to grind away in their heavy clothes and shoes, performing movements in vogue named for beasts—the Grizzly Bear, the Turkey Trot. Shown in a very few newsreel clips were low-class dives where the century's social dance was defining itself, as one- and two-steps spread like wildfire, promoted by the development of ragtime's syncopated rhythms.

There was also a two-reeler called *The Whirl of Life*, made in 1917, featuring Irene Castle and her husband, Vernon. Irene fascinated me—a notable feminist, a very elegant, extremely clever, scrambling lower-class girl whose audacity and style revolutionized a century of women. Castle, not Isadora Duncan, first got rid of corsets and cut her waist-length hair, turned fashion into business, and made a great deal of money promoting the infinitely inventive forms of ballroom dance, somehow adapting the humor and warmth of the raw sources to a singular aristocratic mode. Along with Vernon—a dapper British gentleman with elegant bearing and impeccable tailoring, the role model for an astute young Fred Astaire—Irene led society in the current trends and upcoming vogues, from the one-step to the two-step to the maxixe and even the tango, introduced by the Castles around 1914. Watching Irene, I felt I could finally master ballroom dance.

Afternoons, working with Sara and John Malashock, I reconstructed the steps of the Castles for *Ragtime;* mornings I worked with the same pair to see how we could update the possibilities of

Nine Sinatra Songs gala foldout by Avedon, 1982

men and women moving together. I realized, and surely Sara sensed, that the key was in the woman's role. Seventy years after Irene Castle, women seemed different creatures altogether: freed from corsets and high heels, our weight, our center of gravity, was set lower than our forebears', and we were certainly stronger, both in terms of overall endurance and upper-body strength. Except, of course, for our pioneer farm ancestors, the Sarah Margarets who had harnessed the horses, tended the fields, borne their children, and often buried their men.

These changes had to be reflected in our new version of classical ballroom dancing. We still wanted the beauty of the ballroom form, the shared participation, but the yin and yang of it, the balance of it, had to be different for the Eighties. The man's role still made sense—strong, supporting. But the woman's was demeaning—"strain city," Sara called it, because of the effort required to rein herself in and hold her weight higher; her calves cramped as she created a body light enough for the man to steer easily through the Castle partnering. No, our ballroom dancing had to be different from the Castles' up-and-down bobbing, one- and two-step straight paths, the pelvis held so rigidly in place. We needed to create a

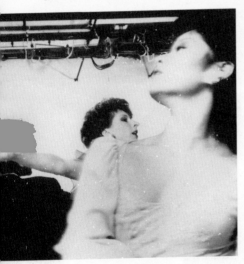

partnering in which the woman did her share of the work and it was sometimes she, not the man, who knew what came next. Mostly we found that after two decades of egocentric dancing, masses of individuals narcissistically moving to their own beat, no one knew how to partner.

At the time, our *Ragtime* research went into the second half of *Short Stories*, but it wasn't until three years later that it really paid off in *Nine Sinatra Songs*. As I began to work with Sinatra's music, I chose songs only in arrangements from the Fifties, when my parents were together, when all parents were together, the last time we assumed as a culture that of course men and women lived together and loved for a lifetime, a condition I was still craving but was beginning to see as against all odds. In *Nine Sinatra Songs* there are seven couples, and their individual duets combine to play out the stages of any relationship—at least as far as I'd heard about. First, Shelley Washington and Keith Young show us the innocence and infallibility of infatuation. It didn't hurt that Shelley is one of the warmest dancers of all time, with a jump that seems without top so that she could fly through space and Keith, an unusually strong partner, arrive under her—at the very last, breathtaking moment. As they wrapped into one another's arms with

great and juicy abandon, huge applause. Guaranteed. Actually, the audience had been goners since Shelley first stepped onstage, somehow managing to suggest shyness as she entered the ballroom the stage had become, its twirling mirror ball throwing bits of light out into the house, and at the same time, through that great smile none could resist, taking command of the house. Mary Ann Kellogg and John Malashock followed with seduction, a bastardized tango in which each used the other as a reflection of their own irresistibility. Next came the duet I was supposed to dance but, for the third time, Sara stepped into my part as I stayed out front, the producer and director taking all the company's rehearsals, attending all the fittings. Oscar de la Renta created marvelous stage versions of dancing gowns from the Fifties era and correct evening clothes for the men. Sara's duet with John Carrafa, set to "One More for the Road," was not based on any ballroom form, but pictured a pair who knew one another so well that, coming in late —three in the morning—they played their games so close to the bone as to be incestuous. They knew how to get to one another. And they were hot, very hot, Sara's slightly older woman playing with John's perennial babyface.

The fourth song is for the three couples, the music "My Way." In it I suggest that for a couple to work it needs to be a successful joining of two individual "my ways." As the arrangement builds so does the dancing, and by the end of this first half all three couples are performing aerial work, finally, simultaneously, charging the space, pitching the women high.

We come to the fourth couple, comic relief. They are shy—she awkward, he cadetlike in his formality. He discovers that she likes to turn. And turn. Faster and faster. They almost lose one another at the end and then come together as only children can, play-acting that they'd never really lost track. The next couple gets by on sheer glamour. The blue dress that Oscar designed is for Cyd Charisse alone and is always worn by a gorgeous girl. Performed to "All the Way," this is also one of the most difficult duets because it is more about acting than dancing. This couple presents us with no stunts, only a deep maturity that suggests the dream of an ongoing relationship whose partners reach their forties together. They are followed by the only couple who dance directly for the audience as though on display in a ballroom dancing competition. Billy Whitener was made for this role, which shows off the man, his strength, his speed, his clarity. Jenny Way, in a shocking-pink dress with ruffles forever, was his steadfast support: "Forget Domani," because dancing is for now and forever.

Then comes "That's Life." Tom Rawe had been having trouble with one of the company women, Shelley Freydont—they just didn't get along. "Throw them onstage together," I said. "That'll fix it. In an apache," I said. This dance from the seaport of Marseilles, where the guy wears a bandanna around his throat and a beret on his head and hurls his partner about, comes disturbingly close to cruelty. She, meanwhile, loves it, taking anything he can give out and more. (I have received protest letters on this dance.) Their partnering is split-second audacious. The audience always loves them best, poised so joyously on the cusp of disaster as they tease, torment, and endlessly connect, suggesting the best relationships survive the battles. Then comes a second "My Way," for all seven couples, to a later live performance at Madison Square Garden. Sinatra's voice is much more mature, his passion deeper and stronger, his commitment absolutely secure, as is the dancers'. The last cross finally puts all seven couples onstage together for one brief second of fulfilled fantasy as Sinatra peaks. Then the music dips and the couples exit one by one, leaving Shelley Freydont to gracefully promenade Tom. As the curtain drops, they too reach for the exit.

Nine Sinatra Songs: Carrafa, Rudner

Nine Sinatra Songs became an instant classic, one of the puzzling sort made of pop cultural materials that the academicians love to label "post-modern." All I knew was that finally, after the confusion of *When We Were Very Young* and *The Catherine Wheel,* the audience could follow my story from beginning to end. I did have to wonder, though, if the silent story of enduring relationships I told was not, just like the nineteenth-century ballets, a fairy tale.

When *Nine Sinatra Songs* premiered in Vancouver, I commuted from London where I was editing the television production of *The Catherine Wheel* at the BBC, and when the *Sinatra* went on in Tokyo, I flew over from Prague where I was preparing *Amadeus*— not only the film's choreography but also the opera segments, which I cast and directed. In between and around this were other dances: *Uncle Edgar Dyed His Hair Red* in 1981; *Fait Accompli* and *Telemann*, 1983; *The Hollywood Kiss, Bach Partita*, and *The Little Ballet* in 1984; other premieres, other tapes, other tours, other projects. Then another movie—*White Nights*, in 1985, with Misha and Gregory Hines. All told, from 1982 through '85 I flew the equivalent of around the world slightly more than five times. My internal clock was so screwed up I had begun to feel that nowhere in the world was it night.

By 1985, my company had become big business—on the road almost six months of every year. But we were caught in the classic Catch-22: the more we toured, the more it cost, so the more money we had to raise. I could see no way off this merry-go-round of success and frustration at home or on the road. My work distracted me from my personal problems while exacerbating them; my lack of a home life urged me to keep working while making my labor increasingly unsatisfying. My life pitched madly, from glamorous highs—dinner with Frank Sinatra at Jilly's after he took a surprise call with the *Nine Sinatra Songs* cast performing on Broadway or my company providing the evening's entertainment at the White House after a state dinner—to the low of coming home after any one of these events. It didn't really matter because twenty-four hours later I'd be gone again. As Dr. Stern liked to observe, I was totally out of control. There was no steady-as-you-go—except with the few friends who could tolerate my all-or-nothing cycles.

I have known Andre Gregory a very long time. He is of the rare breed of friend I can go for a year without seeing, and then suddenly over lunch it's as though we've never been apart. Andre and I have worked together twice—once when his Manhattan Theatre group performed with my company in a Town Hall lecture demonstration and then again when I acted with him in 1982 in *Bone Songs*, a two-character play he wrote. After the premiere he gave me an enameled Fabergé ivory dance card, with emeralds and diamonds on the front, that Diaghilev had ordered as an opening-night gift for one of his ballerinas.

It was also Andre who introduced me to Richard Avedon one spring morning in 1973, as we stood on the corner of Sixth Avenue and Fifty-sixth Street, down the block from City Center. Later, after my first big popular success, with *Deuce Coupe*, *Vogue* had asked Dick to do a center spread of me and my dancers. I agreed to have breakfast with him on Sunday because he liked to spend some time with his subjects before shooting.

Avedon portrait, 1982

Breakfast turned into the whole day, including tea at the Palm Court and a trip to see the two tulip trees at the Frick, a ritual continued every spring that Dick and I are both in New York. I was ecstatic, certain I was next in line for discovery—like Audrey Hepburn in *Funny Face*, a film based on Dick's career.

Of all the men who love women, none has made his obsession into more of an art than Dick. He doesn't simply adore women; he identifies their fantasies and desires and articulates them through their portraits. An early photo he took of his sister locates her in Central Park at the perfect knoll where, seen from just the right angle, the Belvedere Castle looms just to the left of her shoulder: in his lens she becomes a princess. His sense of the romantic is so unique that his photographs have defined feminine allure for over thirty years—from his Dovima in her Dior with elephant, to Brooke Shields in nothing but her Calvins. No woman can sit in front of his camera without hoping she'll enter the pantheon of beauties.

But even though I wanted to be beautiful, and I wanted *Vogue* and the world to love me, and I knew this was a very big deal indeed, I could not make my image over to suit anyone: I clung to my O.K.-shoot-when-ready-but-I'm-not-giving-anything-away, finest, stoniest Buster Keaton stare. Dick had to work hard to get beyond it and create something with life. Telling my dancers to pile on top of me then collapse slowly, he shot as fast as you can without jamming the shutter while the group tumbled down, and before I could react he got the shot. There I am, determined to look coolly in control as the world falls in all around me.

Real control abounded in Dick's studio. Disciplined but with the ease of Astaire, plus the absolute assurance that comes from self-knowledge and preparation, he has utter control when he shoots, and that allows you to feel safe. You want to be with him and this grace extends to his life as well as his work.

Dick is one of the very few people I know who still practices

First Avedon session; clockwise: Tharp, Rawe, Way, Wright, Rinker

social graces, insisting on being amusing and thoughtful with friends. He prevails upon you to dine with him every night when you're in trouble so deep no one else will even speak to you, hires a limousine with driver and caviar to take you through traffic between a tiresome matinee and an evening performance, plans a special trip to London for just one performance of *My Dinner with Andre,* and is always the first to call the next morning to analyze a review.

Dick is also a marketing genius. He commands enormous fees as a commercial photographer because his ability to read the passing scene is so intensely acute—and has been for over thirty years,

BAM 1984 poster: photos by Avedon; design by Israel/Cuomo

Rainbow Room gala, 1982: Avedon and Tharp

an unparalleled record. He can market anything, creating whole campaigns and narrative concepts to make you glad you bought whatever he's selling. Through him I've been given very special guidance. He's helped me sell my company on Broadway and at BAM and created special events for several of our galas.

One of the most sparkling of these was our 1982 fund-raiser held at Rockefeller Center's Rainbow Room, the perfect setting for *Nine Sinatra Songs*. The evening glittered from the very beginning. The audience turned out in elegant abundance, everyone in sparkling dresses and formally correct evening clothes. The setting was romantic—the round starburst parquet floor surrounded by the dinner tables, and beyond that the sky, kept out only by the thinnest glass—and impeccable. Each table setting was complete with a gift package and the beautiful foldout piece Dick had shot—photos tumbling and rushing off one page onto the next, the company caught in gorgeous disarray. Dick and Jesse—borrowed from boarding school for the evening—were my escorts, and *Nine Sina-*

tra Songs was the evening's pièce de résistance. Then, giving the audience something extra to talk about, Misha and I came out to do our version of Fifties dirty dancing—mine via *Rebel Without a Cause* and *The Wild One*, and his via Leningrad. Mother had flown in for the evening. Seated with Zoe, parked in the corner only she could make of a round room, my mother witnessed her daughter's triumph, viewing the scene with a dowager's stare. Like the rest of the world she chose to ignore that the fur was rented, the jewels borrowed, the penthouse I took Jesse home to leaky and lonely. No one mentioned that by the end of the evening and a lot of champagne I was wobbling pretty badly in those high-heeled slippers.

Rainbow Room gala: Left, Tharp, Baryshnikov; top right, with Paul Simon, Jesse, Richard Avedon, Baryshnikov; bottom, my mother; to her left, Zoe Rygh

12

I wake from a dream of
endlessly tumbling,
tangled masses yelling,
"Double time, asshole." No
doubt I'm lost in the
middle. Working in the
studio, I take an old
three-quarter gigue phrase
and kick it up a notch.
This gives me a six-eight
fling. Juxtaposing the
two frees me to drive for
the end.

GREGORY HINES AND TWYLA THARP, 1985

Jerry Robbins has a rule for commercial projects: "Never take a job someone else can do." I was about to learn why when I accepted the offer to direct a Broadway revival. In taking the project, all I could see was that this time, after several film projects, I would have complete control. Best of all, it seemed the show couldn't fail.

A revival of *Singin' in the Rain* had been running for years in London to capacity crowds, and its New York cousin looked like a shoo-in. With any luck I would be able to park my company in the show for several seasons, providing not only an alternative to our frantic touring but also, once the show was running smoothly, the opportunity to rehearse new dances during the afternoons. We could start a school to develop understudies and road companies. In my quixotic world, Broadway would subsidize art. More immediately, we would be free from long-term financial worries, and the opening-night benefit would clear out our *Catherine Wheel* deficit. That was the plan.

There were also lots of things that would get in the way. First, apart from my two months of work in *Bone Songs* with Andre, I had no experience in the theatre. While I had worked with actors inside production numbers on the four films I had choreographed, I had done no actual scene work. Second, the show could not be cast. There was no American equivalent to Tommy Steele, a national hero for the Brits, a kind of Danny Kaye and Danny Thomas rolled into one. Anyone who might have been able to carry the show— John Travolta, Greg Hines, Christopher Walken, Treat Williams— refused because they all realized they'd be compared to Gene Kelly. Moreover, the film's book scenes did not play onstage; the film characters were stereotypical and one-dimensional. But this was the larger-than-life style that the authors—Betty Comden and Adolph Green—had helped develop at MGM in the Fifties and which had brought them to prominence, and they were not changing it now. I also wasn't changing the dance numbers, not only because they were classics but also because the show's producers had negotiated a clause giving them ownership of all original choreographic materials. I have always insisted on retaining the right to my own work.

So our stage version was to become only a word-for-word, step-for-step staging of the old film. In the past, revivals were the only way the general public could get a look at old musical comedies, but television and VCRs had changed the nature of nostalgia. Everyone can hum "Singin' in the Rain" and everyone can have Kelly, Donald O'Connor, and Debbie Reynolds tapping and splashing in their living rooms. That was just one more thing I overlooked.

At a time like this, the only thing to do is call Jerry. Jerome Robbins and I had met fifteen years before. One day I had simply phoned him. "It's been long enough that I haven't met you. Come to dinner," I said—an act of chutzpah for which I've always been grateful. That night at dinner, in talking about his new ballet, *The Goldberg Variations*, my tough-guy persona was out in force. I suggested to Jerry that he should have given me every third variation; this would have given *him* the theme but *me* the last word.

With Jerome Robbins, 1987

Jerry, who had been seeing my work since *Medley* in 1969, took that in stride, saying he really didn't want to do the ballet over again, but maybe I would work with him on some other set of variations, That called my bluff, and instantly I got cold feet. A moment of horseplay at the door, when he waltzed me to the right and I switched roles and took him to the left, suggested potential confusion in such a collaboration. I promised to think about it, but then the reality hit home. How could I create with the Broadway legend who had made the focused violence of the knife fight in *West Side Story*, the Uncle Tom's Cabin sequence in *The King and I*, to say nothing of his many classic ballets at the New York City Ballet, from *Afternoon of a Faun* and *The Cage* to *Dances at a Gathering*? I said no. But Jerry is relentless. A befriender of strays, he prefers mutts with mostly terrier in them. Finally I gave in. We decided to use Brahms' Variations and Fugue on a Theme by Handel, and Jerry submitted the proposal to Balanchine. Jerry's talent is prodigious and his reputation awesome, but this was something else. When Balanchine approved the project, this was God speaking.

For all my adoration, or precisely because of my adoration, I saw Balanchine only three times over the years. For a long time I had steadfastly refused to take advantage of offers to be introduced, fearing I would simply burst instantly into tears. However, when I was in Nashville with Misha for the taping of *The Prodigal Son*, it had happened. I had watched as Balanchine demonstrated to the dancer performing the father's role how he wanted the very last moment of the ballet done for the camera—the moment when the father takes the repentant son into his arms. As Balanchine reached for Misha, the whole set tensed because Balanchine was not a large man and he was just recovering from a bypass operation. But Balanchine had insisted, and finally Misha pulled up his feet. Balanchine literally held all his weight.

Later that day, at lunch, Misha ate quickly and left to rest for the afternoon; I was alone and went back for seconds. The assistant director, Emile Ardolino, was standing by me and suddenly called my name. I turned around and there was Balanchine. I had no time to think; I simply bowed and Emile introduced us. Then Balanchine bowed, saying he was a great admirer, and I bowed, saying, No I was a great admirer . . . and back and forth it went a couple of stammering seconds for me until Balanchine asked if I would like to go back onto the floor because he needed to think a moment.

We went into the darkened studio and he talked about how much easier it was, how much quicker, to move dancers, altering formations if necessary, than to move cameras. Then he took a large velvet-bound book from a leather case. Inside were several

Portrait of Balanchine given to me in 1968

Russian icons enameled with semiprecious stones. He told me that the makeup people could not get the effect right on the Siren in *Prodigal Son*. He wanted her to have the richness of these saints' golden inlays.

In truth, that is all I remember of the meeting, except his appearance, which was, as always, perfect—black slacks, white shirt, his Western string tie. However, I was left with the feeling that all along I had been right: Balanchine was responsible for every detail.

Several years later, Balanchine was in the hospital. I went twice, wearing stockings with seams and being sure they were absolutely straight, and putting on a perfume that I hoped would please him. (On premiere nights, Balanchine always gave his principals fragrance, different for each girl.) The first time I went, his assistant, Barbara Horgan, brought me in. Balanchine nodded but did not speak. I showed him a Japanese cutout template I had brought as a gift. It puzzled him, but when I taped it to the window, causing the light passing through to cast patterns about the room, he smiled. The second time, he was very sick, and frightened, too, because a stranger had come into the room and the attendant was making quite a fuss getting him out. So I just left what I had brought for him—a Walkman with a favorite cassette of mine, one of Mozart's last works, the Adagio and Rondo in C for Glass Harmonica. After that, I got together with a friend and we made sure that every day from then on there would be a small, but different, flower brought to his room.

I read of Balanchine's death when I was flying back from a film location, in a *New York Times* that had been left on an empty plane seat. For the next year, every morning I went into the studio to work, I could not keep myself from crying. I missed Balanchine terribly—the thought that he would not be making any more dances, that he would not be springing into an incredible late blossoming as Matisse had, that I was now completely alone in the studio. I imagined making a dance to his memory, but the thought was ludicrous. He was embedded in every step I did.

By the time Jerry and I finally began to work on our ballet, Balanchine was gone. The New York City Ballet was struggling valiantly to go on, determined to keep his legacy alive. Jerry all along had worked in tandem with Balanchine, the two of them making their work with the company about dancing, not careers. When Balanchine was incapacitated, Jerry kept things going with *Dances at a Gathering*. We both knew the ballet we were beginning could not just be about respecting the past; it would also have to provide a challenge in order to keep things going. The New York City Ballet dancers had always been a part of my standard, the living evidence of Balanchine's discipline. Now I would be working with his dancers in his studio, even having the key to his dressing room, which Jerry and I shared. I wondered what it must have been like for Jerry to live in the shadow of Balanchine at the City Ballet for so many years, the intimidation Jerry must have felt as he contributed his own talents to this great company, helping to develop the very best in dancing. I had a dream in which Jerry and I ran into each other in a rickety old bus—the one that has chickens on top, is packed with natives who don't bathe, and has tires whose patches blow out regularly—sightseeing down in the Yucatán. When there was a stop for everyone to get out and visit the Loch Ness monster, Jerry and I declined, staying on the bus. But we knew the monster, a huge, dinosaurlike snake, lived in a filthy sewage-ridden murk partially covered by some of the oldest floorboards in theatrical history. You stood on these to visit with him. After I told this dream to Jerry over dinner one night, I asked him if he knew who the monster was. "Sure," Jerry said. "George."

Standing in Balanchine's traditional down-right corner of the stage at the State Theatre—the spot where he always stood to watch the performances—I felt woefully inadequate. However, Maria Calegari and Bart Cook, my principal couple, worked unstintingly to make both simple and complex material crystal clear. Rosemary Dunleavy, Balanchine's ballet mistress, entered each day asking if I would want to change anything and then set about doing it, never once suggesting in her attitude that tomorrow this too might be gone. The entire company was still committed, with a deep faith, to dancing, not to product. One day, when I'd come up with a good idea (one of the few Balanchine had not already had), asking Merrill Ashley to jump down into catches rather than up, and then used that momentum to propel huge tosses in the chorus, everyone in the room caught their breath because invention was what this institution had been bred for.

While Jerry and Balanchine had worked together on several occasions, I began without any idea of how to collaborate on a ballet. Jerry had the notion of dividing the company into two camps, the blues and the greens. He wanted the blues. "Of course, Jerry, you know green is a lousy color," I said. We began by alternating variations, although each of us could add anything or bring our group through the other's sections at any time so no one would know for sure who had done what. We worked off one another; sometimes we'd choreograph simultaneously in the studio, sometimes I'd take a theme of his and elaborate on it in a later variation. Sometimes I would see opportunities for a choral background in a figure he'd put down. He'd see a bit of movement he liked and he'd extend it—a swoop reversed, dipped, and lifted. We'd do a little partner-swapping, remating our principal couples (he'd taken Merrill Ashley and Ib Andersen), or I'd make a variation for Ib and he'd borrow Maria for a gloss on one of my sections, a brief satire. There actually never were any harsh moments between us. Jerry went out of his way to be encouraging as he passed through a rehearsal, and he remembers that one day, when he was boggled, I came into our dressing room and told him to take a big bite out of whatever was bothering him the most. We each tried to watch videotape to keep up with all the rehearsals and be as organized as possible, but the opportunities in this kind of situation are endless, and we were running out of time. One day Jerry and I both decided we could not have the ballet ready for its premiere—one of the problems with collaborations is that there is someone to bitch to—and Jerry went off to tell Lincoln Kirstein. Who sent him right back with: "George never cared what the critics would say on opening night. Just get it up." And we did. Best of all, Jerry and I remained friends.

Jerry has a reputation for being difficult. He drives himself crazy with his work, questioning everything over and over, trying this and that until everyone else is ready to go crazy too—but only because he believes there is a right way and a wrong way, not just a possible way. Jerry is one of the most complex people I have ever known, capable of every human response in the book: wise, generous, pragmatic, accepting, unreasonable are just a few. It has been watching Jerry work that I have best felt some of the possibilities of dance—whether listening to him extolling his dancers in rehearsal to forget they are dancers and "just start to move," or standing at the back of the orchestra with him during a revival of *The King and I*, waiting in that suspended, breathless pause just before the king sweeps off to the thunderous downbeat of "Shall We Dance?" or joining with him and a synagogue congregation in midtown Manhattan as everyone clasped hands and went dancing out into the streets, a scene in real life right out of *Fiddler*.

But even Jerry—always generous to me creatively, and financially through his foundation—couldn't help me now. "What the hell are you doing that for?" he said when I told him about *Singin' in the Rain*.

Jerry's instinct was right. *Singin' in the Rain* was about to become my worst nightmare. Everything needed salvaging. Dick did a sitting at cost for the entire production, designing the advertising campaign free of charge to gain me a point or two with the producers. Jerry tried to help, sharing his secrets about how to sell a story —difficult for him because his knowledge is so intuitive. He also instructed me in his laws of Broadway productions, the basic one being that the chances of disaster increase geometrically with the number of people involved. The whole production—designed by the best of my team, Jennifer Tipton, Santo Loquasto, and Ann Roth, the costume designer I knew from *Hair*—was topheavy, too literal: in the famous Kelly solo, real water fell onstage. In my naiveté I had figured the acting would take care of itself and put

Promotional
shoots for *Singin' in
the Rain*, 1985

dramatic scenes at the bottom of my rehearsal list. Too many of the company, cast for their singing and dancing ability, were weak actors. To help us along, I hired an acting coach for the show, Larry Moss, who started doing work on fundamentals. I reacted ambivalently to his contributions. While his presence was threatening to me as a fledgling director, I also realized I too was learning from his work. Still, it was too late; our biggest problems—the script and the cast—were beyond remedy. So far in my career, every project or dance I'd been involved with had squeaked by. This time I knew I was about to be bashed. Every producer, director, even every little starlet in town, came in to watch previews and conclude, No way, José.

Although *Singin' in the Rain* ran more than a year, keeping my dancers employed and making up the foundation's deficit with the opening gala, as hoped, for me the show was a catastrophe. Psychologically, I was humiliated by the horrible reviews. "Twyla Tharp Under Water," "Damp Diversion," "Singin' Down the Drain" read the headlines over devastating reviews. Physically I was in the worst shape of my life. I was sleeping only three hours a night and spent the rest of my time in nonstop meetings, talking to anyone who might have a save-it-all scheme. Managing somehow to keep my drinking in check, I would have only a glass of wine with dinner and a Scotch before bed to calm down from the twenty-nine cups of caffeine I'd consumed during the day. But these sedatives didn't work. I couldn't walk down the street for the humiliation. I began to feel extremely paranoid, sure everyone hated me. Voices yelled and screamed in my head. There was nothing to do then but run away.

I got on a plane to Los Angeles and moved to the Magique Hotel, well-known to show-biz gypsies. This is a place where you can get a suite for seventy-five a week complete with roaches, and for the first several weeks I simply spent a lot of time sitting in the sun. I tried to convince myself that I had not actually died, but the best I came up with was the hope that maybe there could be life after death.

For so long I had been on a trampoline, ricocheting from project to project and relationship to relationship, with no solid foundation, no clean beginnings, only rebounds. But the *Singin' in the Rain* disaster stopped everything. I began to find the bottom. I have always been romantically inclined to the train-hopping hobo, a part of American mythology like the Old West cowboy—not only to his restlessness, but also his freedom: he answers to no one. Like the artist at his most creative, the hobo seems to wake to unstructured time, taking both everything and nothing for granted. Free of the company, free—as I saw it—of my reputation, free of all schedules and barely taking care of myself, I wondered, Who was I?

Walking two blocks over from the Magique on Hollywood Boulevard, I felt right at home, seeing that the old Avenue of Dreams was in the same sorry shape as I. It had declined horribly since the summer I spent living at the top of Ivar Boulevard in the late Sixties. Everything in this particular part of town reminded me of *Singin' in the Rain*, only now it was all decrepit. Grauman's Chinese Theatre, where in the heyday of the Hollywood musical Louella Parsons had interviewed all the big stars arriving in limousines—just as we'd tried so faithfully to depict onstage—now showed horror films and pornography. The "Hollywoodland" sign in the hills that had been part of the set in our overture now had the "land" taken off because it was dangerously accessible—too many suicides had happened off it. Only the souvenir dealers who set up on corners seemed to be thriving, but then they were selling the past.

Yet *Singin' in the Rain* had given me something positive too, in the full awareness of how little I knew about theatre. Larry Moss was teaching a workshop in Hollywood, and in order to address my shortcomings with actors and acting, I had decided to take the class. Working in it challenged some of my biases. I started with illusion. I had always shunned the idea of pretend: pretending was what made me not pursue a career with Martha Graham. Dance to me was always literal—beauty coming from doing, not pretending.

But in my scene workshop with Larry, I began to understand both the magic and the work of pretending. I began trying to learn monologues from a departure point other than repetition, asking myself what did this character want, what did this character need. Then I tried to connect with that. Standing in front of Larry's class, my pages for Roberto Athayde's *Miss Margarida's Way* well out of reach, I was terror-stricken—sure my voice would fail, my mind would fail, in a cold sweat at the thought of the audience's expectations. As I worked up to begin, tears flowed profusely because I feared I would have to relinquish myself in order to become Miss Margarida. To the contrary, I had to anchor deeply in myself, learning to believe in the power of my imagination and finding its creations absolutely real, even though intangible, just like words, or like movement when it is still in the mind's eye. In my dancing my fear was limited because I could count on my technique and see my accomplishments, almost as an athlete can. No one can argue against the meters that measure truth. Dances were real because the body, as Martha Graham's father, a physician, noted, could not lie. Reality and honesty were deeply connected for me. If I could feel my character's desire tangibly, then it was truthful, and then I could generate actions that would make my character real. So I said, over and over. And began to believe. Not only for Miss Margarida but for Twyla.

I sat in the sunshine, asking myself, "Who am I now?" The answer began to come back: "Whoever you want."

Suddenly I realized I was no longer a victim of anything—men, Mom, the company, my dual life as artist and money earner. And, no longer a victim, I stopped requiring punishment. I had read there is a tendency in victims, as in children, to believe it is their own fault when evil befalls them and therefore they *should* be punished. No longer a victim, I could begin to feel what it would be like to change.

I got down to business. I told myself to forget this recent failure, forgive myself, and do what dancers always do: get back to work. My body would hear of nothing else. *Singin' in the Rain* went up

July 1. It was now near the end of August, and I started a high-carbohydrate diet, eliminating sugar and salt, drinking a lot of water, to lose twenty-eight pounds. For the first time since *Hair*, I also stopped drinking. I sacked the Scotch and the wine at night, and that meant eliminating caffeine during the day, an even harder thing for me to do. But I did it because finally, there in downtown Hollywood, I wanted to. I began yoga. I found a church that rented space and gradually started dancing again. It felt strange—nothing to start from and nowhere to go—but as I got into shape, doing barres and hours of improvising, bopping around, I began to see the possibility of returning to my life through the movement. As always, the chemical optimism kicked in. My body began to tone, getting back to its own bottom lines, and this encouraged me to stop harboring the omnipotent sense that lets bad directors feel anything is within their reach. I dropped some of my fantasies. I wasn't perfect but maybe not everybody thought I had to be. I picked up the phone and called Dick. We planned dinner the next week. A few people in my life could know that the ex-scum of the earth was returning, with the beginning of a new dance.

Always in the past, starting a new piece meant starting over, an innocent. This time was different. *Singin' in the Rain* had killed off the innocent in me. Never again would I work in theatre without a certain shrewdness which survival—through success or failure—brings. Sitting in the Magique Hotel, I had asked myself what work I was most proud of. The answer came back *The Fugue*, a simple three-part dance with no costumes, no music, no lights, just committed and extraordinary souls doing a day's hard work with intelligence and love. *The Fugue* had also marked my debut as a choreographer after five years of experimenting: in it, I used contrapuntal techniques to hold the dancing together. Now I wanted to use these rules again, but building on them and moving on.

So whereas *The Fugue* was essentially canonic—investigating a single voice in multiparts—the new piece would be truly fugal, a refined and developed form of canon. It would be buttressed throughout by the counterpoising of dual elements, whether in space, time, or personnel: left, right; linear, geometric; base-line, melodic figure; backward, forward; contrapuntal, harmonic; static, traveling; male, female. It would gain a fullness, as do all fugues, by examining several facets of every issue simultaneously. I wanted to build on all the dichotomies. This time everything would pay off. Nothing would just be stated. Everything would have to come around again, wiser, more mature, more developed.

The new work would alternate sections, just as Jerry and I had greens and blues, but here they would be two very different kinds of dancers. One part would be made for the "stompers," those

The Fugue: Sara Rudner, 1974

down-home, plain-spun folks who move within a vocabulary of parallel movement, driving through space with nothing other than the technique developed through determination. The other would be for ballet-trained dancers, their sections on pointe, lighter and more elegant, making up for a lack of raw force with the sophisticated technique that has developed over the last three hundred and fifty years. The stompers were not truly starting from scratch because two of the men (John Carrafa and Kevin O'Day) and two of the women (Shelley Washington and Chris Uchida) were holdovers from my old company. All were great dancers, all in their prime.

Then I began auditioning. I am often asked what I look for in dancers, and the answer is a strong technique, showing the willingness to work, in combination with a strong imagination, showing the willingness to drop anything the dancer may already know in order to try new ways. The truth is, the moment a dancer enters the studio and drops his or her dance bag and street clothes, I know if I can fall in love. It is just that unfair. This time around I took two dancers. Jamie Bishton had been a gymnast and had worked on the West Coast with Bella Lewitzky; Erzsebet Foldi

Yoga with Jonathan Watts, 1986

had studied at the School of American Ballet where Bob Fosse had discovered her to play his daughter in *All That Jazz*. Both these dancers had not only developed strong techniques, they were also great natural movers, with reservoirs of intelligence, desire, and the fire to dance.

For these three couples, there already existed a wealth of materials. There were over fifty hours of improvisational sessions I had recorded on my new lightweight video decks in Hollywood and in studios across the world, working on *White Nights* in Finland, London, Portugal, New York, Hollywood. All this had good thoughts in it, like a sketchbook. There were also some phrases that could be lifted whole, and these I set Chris and Shelley to reading off the tape, by themselves in another studio, while I worked with other dancers. (Predictably, they were no happier about this than Rose and Sara had been working with tape in the attic eighteen years before.) And there was one more feel, one more flavor, that got mixed into the brew: a developing knowledge of yoga, and its isometric strength, coming from Jonathan Watts, the ballet master I had hired to act as rehearsal director with this group.

Then I went for breakfast at Phil Glass's house to ask for a new score. In the past we had talked several times about a new work, once for a requiem, but something always got in the way. Now, too, Phil said he was very busy, in the middle of several projects. Maybe it was the early hour, but anything seemed possible to me. I suggested all I would need was for him to take a half hour after breakfast every day for a month. That would be enough. He had to do it. I already felt his music so clearly. I had been using it in the studio to fuel my morning sessions intermittently for many years, and I could sense a new kind of transition from move to move in the way his music progressed. Almost every dance I had made since *Sue's Leg* had some steps begun to his music. Finally Phil agreed, and we decided to use the title *In the Upper Room*.

These were the sources for my new work, these and the china dogs. In picturing the great ferocious and brave porcelain dragon

Fait Accompli, 1984; right, *Uncle Edgar Dyed His Hair Red,* 1981

dogs that guard Zen temples, I was also seeing a family of small black-and-white china bulldogs that were kept in the front parlor of my Gram Bertha's farmhouse. These had been passed down from Sarah Margaret Cherry Confer, my small Quaker great-grand-mother who held her world together through all adversity. As I cast Shelley and Chris in this role, to guard and organize the stage, I realized we had been building the strength for them to take on this work for more than a decade. These two women had become the ultimate in what I think of as my power women. This is a strain that developed through my own body, beginning with *The Fugue,* a work conceived through the notion that it would be so powerful, women could only perform it as prototypes, although after many male casts, everyone saw that no cast had the power of Sara, Rose, and myself. The strain continued to evolve in a very fast and diffi-cult quartet in *Mud* (1977), on into *Uncle Edgar Dyed His Hair Red* (1981) and through *Fait Accompli* (1983), its movements derived from the sessions I put in with Teddy Atlas, a boxing trainer who had worked with Cus d'Amato in training the young Mike Tyson.

This then was the lineage we had built to support Shelley and Chris as they stood downstage. Hit by blinding light, they each strike the stage with one foot, then lift one shin into a back attitude, holding the leg with the opposite arm, drawing the bone ever closer to their bottoms, then finally releasing the leg, the power driving them back into the space and opening an area for the dance. Suddenly three men appear directly upstage before our eyes. All I said to Jenny and Santo was, "I don't care how you do it, they must just appear out of nowhere." And shaped as a phalanx, the three men pierce the space, moving vertically toward us. The china dogs are joined by two couples, the women working in red pointe shoes, the first color we've seen so far in Norma Kamali's bold black-and-white costumes. All the movement is fierce, driving, and relentless. These two women, dubbed the Bomb Squad, sweep across the stage in a unison passage so fast it burns the retina. A quartet then begins as three men and one woman walk toward us out of nowhere. The tension within the quartet's cast and between the quartet and the Bomb Squad sustains the section until the end, when the dancers are unified and exist as three couples. Then the stompers work, the men's line playing against the women's line. Once in a while, the men lift the women, but the women's arms are linked around one another so that they are picked up only as a mass. As the men hoist high, I see communities building barns.

Each of the china dogs has a duet, then the three stomping men rip the space open, charging the stage from the back, impacting on the eye with a huge jump on the downstage lip of the stage, a karate kick forward. What follows is a display of athletic prowess based on endurance, power, speed, and timing. As they exit, the ballet cadre features the men partnering first one woman, now costumed all in red, then two, then finally four, until it feels the men are awash in a sea of blood. One china dog introduces the finale as the entire ballet is presented in its *Reader's Digest* form. Each synopsis is reversed from its original form, right now shown left, and condensed, passing so quickly it seems only distantly familiar. Interrupting this action is the second china dog with more new material. Then for the first time the entire cast is on, the women on pointe going high overhead as the two china dogs are cross-partnered downstage, all their new movement integrated within this last quartet. As the chorus splits the stage right and left, exiting, the two stomping men back out, punching the air once in their "black fist" victory gesture and falling backward into the void. Then the two china dogs cut behind the exiting chorus, reclaim the space, jumping high in the air. And as they land they pull down an imaginary old-style roll-up blind—to close the picture. Like the men's socking the air, this yank has great power but it is inward. The power women have the last word. Blackout.

In the Upper Room is the only piece that I've done, including those I wrote for Misha, that generates a standing ovation at almost every performance. No matter how large the house, the piece car-

In the Upper Room poster: photographs by Richard Avedon, design by Yolanda Cuomo, 1986

ries to the very back. Jerry had a rule for this too: we always do our best work after our worst disasters.

In the Upper Room premiered during a tour with some of the old repertory, assembled during a teaching residency at Skidmore College in Saratoga Springs, kicking off in Artpark. And then we were back in the rat race. Once again the routine was running me and the company—pay the bills, present the product, support the organization. Each dancer territorially defended his or her parts. Each staff member zealously proved how hard he or she was working. Booking scheduled the company three years ahead; fund-raising planned galas a year in advance; publicity lined up interviews into the next season. I felt I was working to support the machine rather than its being there to help me create.

I was now several corporate structures. First was the Twyla Tharp Dance Foundation, a not-for-profit corporation with a 1988 budget of two and a half million dollars. The fees and contributions it received went toward the expenses of new productions and the payroll of the company itself—seventeen dancers plus staff—overhead, rent, and miscellany, fifty-two weeks a year. Then there was my personal company, Tharp Enterprises, into which I tried to funnel all monies from my commercial ventures—before the company or the foundation could get their hands on it—to provide for Jesse's ongoing tuition and my personal costs.

The foundation's pay scale had become increasingly Byzantine. Complex schemes were developed to pay the dancers by seniority, in combination with the amount of performing each did. In 1988, my senior dancers were receiving nine hundred dollars a week with a good health plan and deferred annuity opportunities, putting them well ahead of AGMA scale, which was five hundred fifty-five dollars a week for a principal dancer. Nonetheless, an administrator qualified to be my foundation's executive director could not be found for less than seventy-five thousand dollars. This meant Sara was being paid less than a newcomer whom we had just hired. The

One of several collages assembled by Richard Avedon to benefit *In the Upper Room:*
above, Tharp with Isabella Rosselini; below, Avedon; 1986

market, it seemed, could use a good administrator more than a superb dancer. All of this went against the egalitarian principles I had fought so hard to establish for the company. But even within the company the egalitarian principles were eroding quickly.

As our tours started playing to bigger audiences and bigger houses, it was clear that the audiences had to have their stage reality focused for them: they wanted to see heroes. The problem was, I had a group of dancers nearly all of whom saw themselves as the hero. And they were. Down the list in seniority, Sara guesting, Rose teaching and consulting, Tom Rawe, Jenny Way, Shelley Washington, Richard Colton, Billy Whitener, John Carrafa—all of

In the Upper Room rehearsal, 1986

them had been dancing with me for more than ten years with no break, through tours that went worldwide several times, through Broadway seasons, through annual summer residencies, through films and other projects that took them into the gypsy dog-eat-dog world and then back into immensely long development periods in which they were asked to identify closely with new material, to become their roles and then selflessly give them back when the dance began to gel and parts were edited. They were asked to become actors, not simply dancers; they were asked to get out there and hold the audience and then remember how to pull back into unity with the group. They were asked to be master and student simultaneously, as a way of life, but they were beginning to ask what would be in it for them, once they could not deliver as the great athletes they all were. Everyone was approaching thirty-five, old for a dancer, and, like the one-hoss shay, it seemed things would all break down at once. Where were the character roles, where was the teaching, where was the school, where was the retirement policy that could allow them to become the nurturing generation for our youngsters? I could offer none of this, because while I knew how critical it was and longed to provide it for them all, dance in this country did not work like that. My bottom line still had to be what it had been for the last twenty-three years: the next new piece.

Our younger dancers had a different problem. Coming from

other professional experiences, they felt no loyalty or special connection to the company. Since now I could use only sophisticated dancers capable of immediately going into performances on the road, I could no longer afford the luxury of a marvelous green talent: if I'd been a kid in an audition, I couldn't have been hired by me. Most of them knew nothing about *Re-Moves* or *Dancing in the Streets* or what "the attic" was. They were professional dancers: they wanted their paychecks, their rehearsal breaks, their fringe benefits, their per diems. They didn't know how to demand the ultimate of themselves, and I no longer had time to show them. Their limitations became mine—I can work only as hard, and as well, as the bodies that work with me—and it rankled when they did not push themselves to the limit, or at the very least to the limits I had already experienced as a dancer.

I was willing to help subsidize my company as long as we were the best. I'd always felt good return on my money each time I'd walked into rehearsals and seen dancers working and thought, "Wow, do they love to dance. Boy, are they good"—dancers standing at the absolute edge of what was physically possible. But now the group was more and more becoming just another professional company bringing home the bacon. And that bacon was becoming less all the time.

With state and federal funding dwindling by the moment, fundraising was becoming harder pitched and slicker. Arts organizations everywhere were beginning to hire commercial publicity firms at substantial prices to woo corporate sponsors. Meanwhile, competition for audiences was increasingly fierce. Now touring large theatres, we were after the same audiences that went to Broadway shows, yet their promotional budgets dwarfed ours. We were in the black each season, but barely. My foundation had tried every possible way of gaining financial stability. Nothing worked very well.

I was slipping back. All my new resolves, so painfully formed in Hollywood after *Singin' in the Rain*, meant nothing. I blamed the company, seeing myself as the victim of this group and its miseries. After fifteen years of talking to Dr. Stern regularly, I could no longer avoid the obvious: my company was not my family. It had become a habit with me, a horrible codependency—we needed each other but we often hated each other. I felt trapped in a Sisyphean treadmill, a smaller and smaller person making better and better product. My bottom line was dance; the realest, truest me was a small creature yelling, "Feed me! Feed me!" I was the company, the company was me, and until we separated there was no private me for anyone, including my son, to be with.

Even if it meant I could no longer be creative, might never make another dance, I had to combat this neurosis. I could not go on like this. But how to stop my machine? We were a tradition in the dance world. Twenty-three years of successful management, an unparalleled record of sixteen dancers on year-round employment. The pledge I had made to my dancers with Rhoda in Minneapolis had been honored for thirteen years without interruption—even if it meant my apartment went up as collateral against bank notes. We were booked solid for the next year and a half of touring. While no one is independent, I felt at the mercy of so many factors in the dance system that there was very little of me to send into the studio to make dances, and I was not finding much reason to try. Still looking for my Kirstein, someone to help support not just the burden but the dreams too, I gave up hope. Rehearsing in a borrowed gymnasium space at Barnard College during the fall of 1987, it all began to seem foolish. I told the dancers they could count on paychecks during the upcoming year and that the foundation would find a counselor to work with them making adjustments, but the year after that, 1988, the company would not exist.

As we continued to make the last new piece I would do for the company, ultimately to become *Bum's Rush*, we began to work on dismantling the whole operation. Over the course of the next year, we declined engagements and tours while fulfilling contracts already signed and letting funders know that the not-for-profit burden had become insupportable. In June 1988, I called everyone into the office (whose lease we had been trying to squirm out of for the last six months) and said the company was finished. We were in the black. No tears were shed. It was a formality: the wake was over. Disbanding this family was probably the single most difficult decision I ever had to make. I met with the dancers in three groups to say good-bye and to give them severance pay based on longevity. The first group had worked with me less than five years, the second at least ten, Tom Rawe having been with me since 1973. The third group, whose meeting I held back for last, drawing energy from it to get through the first two, was going to hear good news. Shelley Washington, Richard Colton, Kevin O'Day, Jamie Bishton, Elaine Kudo, Danny Sanchez, and Gil Boggs would be going on with me. I had found us a new home, a larger context where I hoped we could escape the inbreeding of our small modern dance world. I was folding into American Ballet Theatre.

13

Whether *Brief Fling* is
a fast gigue, a short ballet,
a career of twenty-five
years spent in dance, or a
lifetime in the cosmos,
I don't know. But the
roustabout in me knows it's
time to move on.

I joined ABT intent upon utilizing its full resources. I believed my interests in dance would be well housed in a company with such broad interests, for I wanted to pursue not only the pure dance element in the ballet tradition but its dramatic side as well. The company's title, American Ballet Theatre, summed it up nicely. For "American" I would create a narrative ballet, *Everlast*, using the music of Jerome Kern, set in turn-of-the-century Boston, about an Irish boxer in love with the wrong girl, an immigrant making good in his own way—American as apple pie. For "Ballet" I would make *Quartet*, a strict formal work, featuring and dedicated to Cynthia Gregory, my inspiration as a student with Richard Thomas and prima ballerina at ABT for more than twenty years. Set to "G Song" by Terry Riley, this piece would be of the airless sort—abstract, pristine, rigorous—that Balanchine had trained audiences to see as nouvelle classique. My ongoing concern with realizing "Theatre" in dance would be a surrealistic caper, addressing my perennial theme of death in a vaudevillian mode: "Thhhhhat's all, folks," de de yum dum dum de dum. The first season, we would also remount *In the Upper Room* at ABT, where we could assemble an excellent cast. The seven dancers who came into ABT with me would be blended with ABT principals, soloists, and chorus to cast the ballets.

Misha and I had been talking about merging our two groups since Lucia Chase had given ABT over to him in 1980. In the past I had always left our discussions feeling a little flat because I was afraid I could lose my independence in the establishment. However, as my twenty-fifth anniversary of dancemaking approached I decided I already was an institution so there was no more threat and I became, along with Sir Kenneth McMillan, an Artistic Associate. As such, I gained a number of excellent dancers, proficient in several different styles. No longer would I have to oversee fundraising or management—my only job would be to create and rehearse. ABT would gain a prolific resident choreographer who had already proven adept with its dancers. *Push Comes to Shove*, writ-

Bach Partita: Robert LaFosse, Magali Messac, 1984

ten for ABT in 1976, had become a signature piece. *The Little Ballet* (1984), made for Misha, became a useful addition to the repertory, and *The Bach Partita* (1984), a full company work, was a solid critical success.

Work started up at ABT in the fall. The company was also committed to mounting Misha's *Swan Lake* and it was clear rehearsal time would be very tight. *Quartet* rehearsals usually ended up late in the day when the cast was tired. Nonetheless, everyone worked hard, led by Cynthia's determination, experience, musicality, and her willingness to be open. Meanwhile, at other times of the day with another cast, the "American" rehearsals were developing a drama more interesting than the scripted one. This ballet featured Susan Jaffe, a favorite of mine, an elegant and very gifted ballerina Misha had been fostering for years, along with Anne Adair, a chorus dancer I had spotted during company class. Trained with the Royal Danish Ballet, Anne's acting skills made her into a wonderfully fresh young ingenue, the perfect foil for Suzie's bad girl. Their swain would be Kevin O'Day, coming from my old company, as the boxer.

All dancers dream of having a ballet pinned on them, and many of the ABT dancers resented Kevin and Anne for having this opportunity so early in their careers. But the couple were perfect casting for the story, so that was that. I easily dismissed the dressing room grievances, but I was genuinely concerned about Shelley Washington. Shelley was twenty when she joined my company, I was thirty-four, and this age difference had always made her seem like the first of my second generation. Unlike Sara and Rose, Ken

Shelley Washington, 1980

and Tom, who worked freely with me as peers during the first decade, Shelley was one of the first dancers to come in on salary. In 1975 she had been welcomed into the company with her very own small solo in *Give and Take*, a work not particularly memorable for any other reason. She flew about the stage, buoyant and light and radiant as no dancer before or since. Her great athleticism was all the more notable because she was not dependent on it to hold a stage. Having spent one year with the Graham company before coming to me, she also knew about dramatics and developed into a very strong actress. From the beginning it was clear that Shelley was a superstar, and this was acknowledged by the modern dance world in 1987 when she received the Bessie award, its highest honor. Going into ABT, however, would be hard on Shelley. While technically she was as strong as any woman dancing, her technique was like mine, hard-earned and eclectic. Neither of us was a ballerina, and Shelley was the only female dancing at ABT without a pair of pointe shoes parked in her locker. I didn't like the fact that such a supremely powerful woman was a bit of a fish out of water in these hallowed halls, and I worried that Shelley would feel betrayed by the move. She completely surprised me, however, by finding a way to move up beside me after thirteen years.

As the *Everlast* rehearsals proceeded, Shelley began to confront her performer's ego. Subjecting it day by day to a larger context, she began to transform herself into my assistant. I started to pull her out of the dancing, bringing her up front to sit with me, watching rehearsals. As I sent her in to give notes to part of the cast while I spoke to the others, I saw that all the dancers respected Shelley's intelligence, skill, and imagination, as well as her very sharp eye. I knew I could trust her with more responsibilities and help her grow beyond dancing.

My "Theatre" venture, *Bum's Rush*, was the extension of a work in progress with my own company when it disbanded. As I continued to develop its characters and situations on my crossover group, I augmented the cast with some of the better sports among ABT's classical dancers, Sandy Brown being a notable addition as the B. F. Goodrich tractor tire on pointe. Sandy's humor gave this abstract form character, her tire making good choices, full of emotion.

Having made a strong start on the three ABT pieces, I flew to Paris to begin a ballet for the Paris Opera. Since Nureyev became the company's director in 1984, he had been asking me to do a work but I could never quite find a way to connect. Recently, however, I had been smitten by Sylvie Guillem, the prize of the company, a redhead with an extension that challenged the Tour Eiffel. I, along with all Paris, was in her thrall.

The Paris Opera Ballet is the oldest dance company in the world and is synonymous with classicism. Entering backstage, I was hit by the smell. The smell of a living tradition, it is composed of the dank that comes from its most ancient parts, erected centuries ago, the smell of latrines, open holes with flush cords to pour the water out from the overhead tanks. It comes from wicker travel baskets, from tons of stored scenery and drapes, from the wardrobes of thousands of ballets. And it comes from food. The opera house is a self-contained community reminding you that theatre is a collective responsibility. Its shops within the house build the scenery and create the wardrobe, shoes, and wigs, and its canteen is the best deal in Paris bistros, providing good meals for pennies that feed hundreds of workers—from singers and dancers to stagehands and carpenters, administrators and publicists. There is an in-house bank. Union notices of meetings are tacked to the walls, weekend forays to the countryside are listed, contemporary art is exhibited in the halls, and a library provides international publications. Opera house life is a rich mix with no conflict between living and working.

Rules of the Game, a formal work set to Bach's Sonata Number 1 in G Minor for Solo Violin, was completed in four weeks. I finally, after all these years, allowed myself to let the dancing figures I saw in my mind play directly with the music I heard, like surfers crest-

Rules of the Game rehearsal: Lionel Delanoé, Isabelle Guérin, Manuel Legris, 1988

ing waves. The ballet was pinned to Sylvie, the only dancer in all four of the ballet's sections. But her partner, Manuel Legris, was such a beautifully finished dancer and so adept in partnering her that the two of them brought as much to the table as she offered alone. The ballet also featured another marvelous étoile, Isabelle Guérin partnered by Lionel Delanoé, an enormously talented chorus youngster with great charm and wit. After I finished *Rules of the Game,* there was a break before its premiere during which the company would continue rehearsing its new ballet, while I flew back to get *Quartet* up in Miami, where ABT was performing. Here, the local string quartet was finding that the Terry Riley music was hardly the "piece of cake" ABT's musical director had pronounced it; they really couldn't play it accurately. Still, the dancers got through the ballet and the audience was enthusiastic. *Quartet* did what I intended, presenting a standard of classical ballet that pushed some of the best dancers in the world to the maximum of their techniques.

After a party to celebrate the cast, in particular toasting Cynthia, who would retire a year later, we flew to Chicago and the *Bum's Rush* premiere. Nothing could be further from the pristine black-and-white abstract world of *Quartet* than this moldy, off-

Quartet: Ricardo Bustamente, Guillaume Graffin, Cynthia Gregory, Cynthia Harvey, 1989

color ballet featuring a bill of short acts in burlesque mode—nurses on pointe, duets featuring carefully calculated mishaps complete with hysterical laughter and comics spewing preverbal sound, their baggy pants around their ankles more often than otherwise, and the B. F. Goodrich tractor tire rolling to place, screeching to a halt, bouncing impatiently as it waited to get back into the fray. The ballet's final image featured a hobo walking on the upstage diagonal left to right, scratching his rear and muttering unintelligibly as he proceeded toward a fiercely blowing blood-red curtain. The dance included other wind images, for I had remembered reading that many cadavers still, hours after death, emit one last rude fart, breaking wind one last time, making this our final act. In my mind *Bum's Rush*—a colloquialism from the Twenties meaning a "forcible or sudden ejection, rude or abrupt dismissal"—seemed a good accounting for the way we all go out. Needless to say, this "ballet," with its burlesque score punctuating story points from the pit with strippers' va-va-vooms, received a mixed response from the ABT audience. Because the ballet still had a number of technical problems—short on rehearsal time, the piece had gone on without even one full run for all its sound and light cues—I saw its premiere as a final dress. Following the performance I had a list of changes the length of my arm, and after meeting with the technical staff, these were put into the works. I went to the hotel to pack because I had to be back in Paris the next day. I was only too aware, however, that I was leaving Shelley—now my official rehearsal director—with a group of disgruntled dancers. Insecurities were starting up, even my stalwarts becoming vulnerable to the proponents of the status quo, always a force to be reckoned with in any institution.

Things were not much better in Paris. *Rules of the Game* was missing its ballerina. Sylvie Guillem had left the Paris Opera. I was not surprised. My contract stipulated the ballet could not premiere without Sylvie, who I'd heard could be quixotic. But I did not want to cancel the piece for by now I had come to love the whole difficult company. I sat down with the dancers and spoke in my fractured French. I told them that, as they knew from the ballet's structure, my infatuation with Sylvie had brought me to Paris, but that their commitment to me and the beauty and precision of their work made me very proud to be with them and I wanted us all to hold on. *Tutoyer*-ing—using the familiar family pronouns allowed once you break bread (or sweat more than ten hours) with a person—I said that I was willing, if they were, to work round the clock to completely rebuild the ballet in less than a week. It was true that

Rules of the Game rehearsal, Paris Opera Ballet, 1988

Sylvie was very special, and obviously some of them—mostly the great ballerina Isabelle Guérin—had been good about looking the other way while I made Sylvie "more equal than others" in this ballet. But all of the Opera dancers are very special. In five weeks I had learned their strengths and knew we could pull off the impossible if the dancers' union would waive some of its requirements. The French union is the strongest in the world governing all aspects of the dancers' work. Apocryphally, there are areas of the stage that cannot be stepped on by anyone but the étoiles.

To boost morale, I built a new opening called "les petits morceaus"—the little bits—in silence. There was one for each of the dancers in the ballet, either individually or in small groupings, showing them democratically—even though some were obviously younger and less experienced than others—before they were cast in the ballet according to their company ranks of principal, soloist, and chorus. I made a trio of Sylvie's moves in the first section for my other three principals, Isabelle, Manuel, and Lionel. I brought Carole Arbo out of the chorus to complete a quartet, which would usually be out of the question according to the union—only principals dance with principals. Isabelle went into Sylvie's duet in the Third Movement; Carole went into Sylvie's part in the Fourth Movement. But then Isabelle's part had to be enlarged because, true to form, Sylvie's role had been slightly more than equal, but Carole's should not be. After a week of work on time-and-a-half, everyone's nerves were on edge when it was time to move the ballet out of the studio and onto the stage.

The French add elements slowly and scientifically in their stage rehearsals. Because they are the resident company in the theatre, they have the time to mount new productions accurately. The first element is the spacing rehearsal needed to adjust the ballet from the smaller studio onto the stage. Now there is the additional element of offstage crossovers—no longer can the dancers simply walk behind the dancing—and the additional energy spent in covering backstage distances usually causes some grumbling. Next

day was the orchestra rehearsal. Tempers were terrible and dancers missed cues because the live instruments sounded very different from the rehearsal tapes. Tears followed the embarrassment of
having lost counts. The third stage rehearsal added wardrobe. The
dye ran, and soon the dancers had red legs and armpits. Guérin's
costume was not right. It had been in the fitting room, but that was
before she saw it next to Carole's higher-cut, more Degas-y skirt.
The men couldn't move their shoulders without their belts riding
up. On and on. The fourth day, the lighting rehearsal was the worst
of all. Dancers flew into rages when pirouettes went off as they
stumbled in darkness or were hit in the eye by spots that were too
bright. The disasters increased their sense of insecurity just at the
moment when the audience was about to be added. But the rehearsal staff, the teachers and the administration people, everyone
assured me the technical rehearsals were always a nightmare and
predicted nothing about opening night. Better that the dancers let
off steam in rehearsals, vent their nerves as part of the regular,
run-of-the-mill work process, take out their insecurities on a costume, or yell *"merde"* at the lighting designer than hold the tension
inside them and risk an injury. Still, nothing was going smoothly,
and I covered for my dancers during the publicity interviews.
When reporters asked me about *"le désastre,"* the defection of
Sylvie—who, it would seem, all of Paris was mourning—I replied,
"No, the Paris Opera is stronger than any one element and the
company will go on." I praised Legris and Guérin as truly great
dancers, Carole and Lionel as wonderful talents, and the chorus as
the world's best—easy to do. "Classicism is bigger than all of us,
any of us. Classicism is tradition and it survives and unifies."

The interviewers believed me, I believed myself, and on opening
night it all came true.

The dancers pulled the ballet together and the applause was that
great deafening roar—the one with no bottom to it—that we all
love. The dancers brought me a huge bunch of red roses from them
all, and an Opera T-shirt, which they had gotten together to sign

and which, given the difficulty of getting the French to agree on style—what color pen, which shirt, how large, who signed where —was an achievement in itself.

Nureyev was there too. I had seen little of him, since he was often out performing with his own group, although we had spoken on the phone, agonizing over Sylvie's intent and the replacements forced by her absence. I was sorry I had not been able to see more of him because I have always adored him. The first summer I was in Spoleto under my towel in *Scudorama*, he had just defected. He was the Festival's sensation, dancing with Margot Fonteyn, and I watched him taking class in the Spoleto opera house's rehearsal hall, my blood surging with the excitement of his movement. Much wilder than Misha, more virtuosic than Paul, Rudi had a physicality and a drive to dance that overcame his late start in the ballet world. Like myself, he was grounded in folk dance, and it was here that he had learned about raw movement. In Spoleto I was just making the transition from the strict confines of student rigor into the liberties of the professional dancer and I could not believe his seeming lack of discipline, bending the barre to his own requirements and leaving the center any time he seemed to please, wearing a wool cap to drive up his body temperature. I was both shocked and seduced by his flamboyance. Never one for the niceties of movement, he was definitely into passion; Rudi simply loved to dance.

After the premiere of *Rules of the Game*, Rudi was grateful for the way I had handled what could have become a scandalous situation for his company. He arranged a small dinner party at Les Halles and it was impeccable. On the matter of oysters, like so many others of connoisseurship, Rudi is master. I was completely exhausted by the excitement and apprehensions of the evening, still jet-lagged, and apprehensive about ABT in Chicago. In my mind I was already back at the grindstone. But Rudi kept ordering oysters and more champagne, going far beyond the boundaries of reason into excess to finally reach his comfort zone. Rudi has never learned to hold anything back from his audiences and he has never learned to hold anything back from himself. By the end of the evening, fairly drunk, he confided that he liked me very much, and by way of affirmation bit my arm very hard, hard enough to leave teeth marks for a day. Stunned, angry at the pain, I almost slugged him. Instead I chalked it up to animal passion.

Back at the hotel, I found a huge arrangement of purple tulips, beautifully packed bud to bud, from the Minister of Culture, Jack Lang. He thanked me, *la République* thanked me. It was late enough to see that the reviews were good and as I packed, deciding to stay up the four hours before it was time to leave for the airport and rehearsals with ABT, I had the rare feeling of a job well done.

The next day I was in San Francisco to start technical rehearsals for *Everlast*. *Rules of the Game*, a straightforward dance with one costume per dancer, fewer than ten light cues, and a resident orchestra playing Bach, had used up every second of its four allocated rehearsal afternoons. *Everlast* would have two afternoons. This ballet had a large number of moving scenic elements, all of which had to be clocked and coordinated with a very elaborate light plot. Several of the dancers had fast costume changes, the miking was a nightmare with onstage vocalists choreographed into

Bum's Rush: Washington, Colton, 1989

the action, and we were working with a full pit orchestra of pickup musicians. The ballet, having only been in small studios, would be hard to space, particularly since one of the cues involved shadows which I had tried to prepare for in special rehearsals still in New York. I also needed to steal a little time for the *Bum's Rush* repairs. All this had to be done in eight hours. Then it went into overtime, and there were no funds for that. None of us knew if all this could be done, but we certainly knew it couldn't be done right. However, there was no choice. Starting to work in the afternoon, I had gained eight hours between Paris and San Francisco and it seemed that was all that was going in my favor. By now there were serious rumblings inside the company, particularly from those who wanted to protect art for the elite and who preferred princes to hoboes for heroes. As the scenic elements for *Everlast* began to load in, the heavy set, as well as the special ensemble of vocalists on tour with the company for the Kern songs, became more cause for concern about my priorities. There were many who felt money should be going into payroll, not production. I understood that feeling well. I also knew that what I was doing with *Everlast* was to mount a full-scale original production in one act that could prepare me to create an original full-length, which, if it were successful, would be a financial godsend for the company several seasons from now.

Dancers most often do not see a larger picture. Even more than actors, they function in the short term, constantly judging time by their own bodies. The fact that *Everlast* was a big hit on opening night, promoting euphoric reviews, improved my stock for the moment. Next stop was Los Angeles and finally assembling an all-Tharp evening. No choreographer, other than Antony Tudor, has been so honored by ABT. However, everyone also knew that I could get the cover of the *Los Angeles Times'* Sunday magazine for the company and that the all-Tharp evenings would sell much better than repertory evenings usually do, pushing into the ninetieth percentile of capacity. Ordinarily only the full-length ballets, *Swan Lake, Giselle, Romeo and Juliet,* do this well. After *Everlast* opened, followed by *Quartet, Bum's Rush,* and then *In the Upper Room,* the curtain rang down on a solid ovation; reviews boded well for my ongoing presence in ABT. Following Washington and more supportive press, we finally reached New York's Metropolitan Opera House.

Everyone was beat. After eight weeks on the road, the production crew had loaded and unloaded thousands of tons of scenery. Dealing with both elaborate fly and sound cues—for both *Everlast* and *Bum's Rush*—in four different cities, the all-Tharp evening still had its technical glitches. Rehearsing a new string quartet in every city for *Quartet* but never finding one that could play the work, I was insisting it be done to tape in New York—an insult and near impossibility according to the union—at the Met. Of course, in New York a qualified quartet could have been engaged but now it was too late. The dancers had no rehearsal time nor energy. They were all fatigued, either injured or working overtime to prepare replacements for all the repertory.

Following the eight-week tour—actually a short one for ABT—I began to feel that without a school to nurture a unifying standard and without a home theatre to house a loyal audience and develop new productions, we were hopelessly handicapped. Having worked in the same season with the Paris Opera, it was clear to me that ABT was a road show, not a company. At the Paris Opera, protocol and dignity matter, from the principals' dressing rooms—each door's brass plaque engraved with all the names of their predecessors—to the company's regard for new work. The choreographer is the supreme being in the dance hierarchy, and his or her job is to deliver new work, "la création." At the Opera, all repertory is carefully rehearsed and preserved, but nothing is as important as "la création." Time will always be taken from repertory rehearsals if "la création" requires. The French public, as well as its artists, know that art, though a constant in life, must invite change. They understand this contradiction with ease. Where we attempt to go literally by all the rules to reach respectability, the French, be-

cause they are secure within the rules, do not have to cling to them. Past and present exist in a dynamic relationship.

Three days after the all-Tharp evening at the Met, Misha announced his decision to leave ABT. I sympathized with his dilemma; I suspected most of his problems were the same ones I had experienced with my company but on a bigger scale. We did not speak in detail, but he was exhausted by the commercial work he took for support (his deal with ABT paid him one dollar a year because he could not afford to lose his independence). Depressed by the vicious reviews of his *Swan Lake* (one critic had been overheard saying, "He's Russian, he doesn't understand that's part of our job"), annoyed at dancers' bitching about his absences, and feeling guilty all the same, he quit.

Taken off guard by the politics of the situation, I stayed six more months to parlay what was supposed to be a summer workshop into a rehearsal period, generate one more ballet, and figure out how and where I should be working next. The ballet became *Brief Fling*, incorporating lessons learned in *Rules of the Game*. It was a success but it offers no discoveries. Everything happened the way it was supposed to, just as in commercial work, because that's what the company required. I did not know where to turn, but ABT was no longer an alternative.

Things were really not so different now than in 1969 when I'd lent everything to the New York Public Library and gone to live on a farm. Twenty-two years later I gave my foundation's archives to Ohio State University, setting the groundwork for a long-term relationship and at least metaphorically finding a home in farmland. Then I went off to a screenwriters' workshop at Robert Redford's Sundance Film Institute. For the first time in a long while, I was free from schedules, not rushing from one project to another, outside the studio's isolation. I had been a silent child and I had

Brief Fling: left, Isabella Padovani, Robert Wallace; right, chorus; T-shirt logo and costume designs by Isaac Mizrahi, 1990

entered a silent profession and now I took advantage of my current situation to practice talking with people, not just serious film conversation but also small talk, about simple things like the weather and the Super Bowl, ways of expressing normal neighborly concern for other people. I thought of my mother's sardonic comment a few summers back. Reminded that I couldn't be trusted to drive to the store for a quart of milk because I still don't drive and can't always remember the difference between a quart and a pint, Mother had confidently retorted, "Well, she can always go normal."

I was not so sure but I was determined to try. Over his Christmas break, Jesse drove out to visit. Sitting around evenings in the kitchen, he ran down his Rules for Dating as they applied to his mother. He began, "Never sleep with a guy on the first date," and continued more seriously with, "Don't date guys you work with." This rule came from Jesse's observation that with my piecemeal life, I seemed doomed to a pattern of breakups as projects ended. This had happened yet once again recently, when a writer and I who had been working together on the *Everlast* scenario had parted ways. Jesse was the only man surviving my life. Almost twenty-one, his struggles to become a man were giving me a new connection to his gender, a sort of tender angst as I'd see him begin to do something just like a guy. I'd want to yell out, "Oh God, not that." And then I'd just smile and ask myself, "What better way did I know?"

Once Jesse left for school and I was alone again, practicing small talk with Hollywood screenwriters doing Robert Redford a favor began to seem not much training in normalcy. After struggling with five script beginnings in as many weeks, learning that the rusted-out '47 Ford pickup truck (just like the one at my mother's drive-in) that I wanted to learn to drive on wouldn't get up the mountain, and being pretty much reduced to frozen dinners, I had no problem deciding to pay a local kid to shop, asking Sundance to take out all the furniture in the large living room, and starting to dance again. I didn't know it then, quite, but as I took my body out of the deep freeze I was preparing to perform again. I had not danced at all in

With Sean Kelleher, New York, 1987

seven years. I had not danced well since *Sue's Leg*, fifteen years before. In dancer's time this is a lifetime, and feeling a little foolish, I wondered if it could be done. As I moved around in the living-room space, I felt different than I did working in an arid studio. I began to see the missing furniture in my mind, and I peopled the chairs and sofa with invisible extras who radiated adoring glances. Dancing in this arena felt like being in a scene from a Hollywood musical. It was perfectly normal for me and Astaire to fly over furniture in such a room.

Back in New York, I discovered John Lake in the gym where I worked out almost daily. Pumping iron with my trainer, Sean Kelleher (Sean does 530 pounds on the bench and is working toward 600), I had seen John over my shoulder. Everyone in this gym who is serious, including myself, can at least press his or her own weight ten times on the bench, and John was no exception; however, he also had his weight higher in his legs than most of the other power lifters and was faster on his feet. I could see that this very large and muscular man could also dance—if he wanted. I learned that he had had several semesters of modern dance training in college and was entertaining the idea of applying for a scholarship to work with Paul Taylor's company. I asked him if he would like to come to work with me in a studio on an exchange basis, my time for his time, and he agreed.

John and I talked in the gym and when we worked in the studio it was easy to continue our conversations as we danced. I turned the music down and discussed topics like how he felt about his mother and how these feelings affected his personal relationships with women, all the time throwing so many different movements at him that his mind was kept too busy relaying commands to his muscles for him to have time to think. My theory was that this would give John no time for either becoming self-conscious or concocting rationales. I fantasized about hanging out a shingle and franchising my new analyst/analysand concept, but rather than inventing a new therapy, I was really finding an incredibly convoluted way to talk to John about issues that were very troubling to me.

For several years I had realized that my rage toward my mother was causing me to make foolish choices as I tried to use gentlemen easily at hand to force her out of my emotional center. In spite of Jesse's warning about my becoming personally involved with my work mates, I seemed headed that way all over again. The fact was I didn't want only a dancer in my studio. I also wanted a man. I wondered if instead of inviting John to dinner and easing into an acquaintanceship with him, I had asked him to work in the studio as an equivalent to inviting him up to see my etchings. As with my weight training and drinking with the boys, my hunting and shooting and taking men almost anonymously as the other members of my Society of Strangers took women, wasn't I just continuing the fraternity's stereotypical behavior, mirroring the ways of womanizing men who look for mothers in their lovers? I thought about my past, and I realized my affairs fell alphabetically by occupation: athlete, artist, acrobat, banker, butcher, baker, candlestick maker. Like primitive peoples eating the hearts of lions to consume bravery, I seemed to mate to acquire talents. John was very strong. Poor John.

As we horsed around, trying to teach each other to waltz and fox-trot, which neither of us did very well, we were really jockeying around the leader's position: who was pushing, who was pulling. It became ridiculous, this tiny one trying to weigh ten thousand tons, bossing around a very much larger though still light-footed and good-natured overgrown boy. What was I competing for in this studio where I was master? Suddenly the obvious could not be avoided. John was young enough to be my son. As I took his wrist between my fingers, running the rhythm from my feet directly through my fingertips into his veins, the way my early tap teachers had done with me, I sensed a new motivation, a fresh reason to be working with John. At that moment I broke a habit that had been ruling and ruining my life for some while. I beat the *re*'s.

Twenty-five years ago, with *Re-Moves* at the Judson Church, I had tried to cleanse myself of my first abortion. Ever since, I had been in the habit of drawing the energy to work from a drive to revenge and repair the past, fueling myself with resentment, rebellion, through reaction, by rebounding, in reclaiming, from regret. My work had begun to feel like dirty water recycling. Up until now, as John and I worked in the studio, the duets we'd been making still came from competition, victimization, seduction, and fantasy, and although our duets looked very different, they actually were not very far from those in *Nine Sinatra Songs:* men and women on the ballroom floor dancing metaphors for the games that pass for love much of the time. Now, however, with John's wrist between my fingers, love was of a totally different order. In my mind, John became Jesse. I was definitely the mom.

I was ready. I had acquired the confidence, not the least of it through three years of power training, to be my own net. I didn't need John to be strong for me; I could do that for myself. Weight training proceeds by small intervals, adding two-and-a-half-pound plates, which look like paperweights, and amassing to fifty-pound monsters. Adding weight patiently for my curls, presses, and jerks, I was learning to become consistent and to appreciate stability. I began to think of a phrase that derived from a book Jesse had been reading in Sundance: *Zen and the Art of Motorcycle Maintenance.* For me it became the art of constant maintenance, and the commitment to continue became the best definition of love I knew.

In the studio, as John and I continued to pursue our roles, I would sometimes become a caricature of moms, a demanding, shrill creature (I pictured her in khaki fatigues) for whom nothing could be good enough, but even then John's good-natured presence made this game into fun. Through his behavior, I gradually began to know John Lake, specific person, previously "guy." This made me no longer a "guy" either, and I canceled my membership in the Society of Strangers.

As the work came closer to performance, I moved onto a stage. John had little experience with audiences and so I asked Kevin O'Day to work as my partner. We were able to rehearse at City Center, which was dark over the summer months. Exchanging small talk with Brenda, the backstage guard, I began to feel more at home daily. As I opened the door from the corridor onto the bare stage, all I could see was the single raw bulb, head-high on a plain stand, that is kept illuminated to mark the lip of the stage, the drop into the pit just beyond. Every theatre has one. It is called the ghost light, and it was the only visible presence in the empty 3,000-seat house.

Fumbling for the work-light switches stage right, I thought of Sheila Raj damaging her metatarsal on the concrete mezzanine in 1969, of *Deuce Coupe* and *As Time Goes By* premiering onstage in 1973; I remembered there had not been this stage-right extension then, or when Balanchine had worked here in the Forties and Fifties. As I walked to bring the ghost light over to the stage-right corner, I took care to stay away from "his" floorboards, those center-stage boards where Melissa Hayden was first tossed from partner to partner in the *Agon* premiere in 1957. The audacity of that move, I figured, bought Balanchine these boards forever. Then I turned round and there Graham sat; her photo had been Scotch-taped to the inside of one of the stagehands' doors, a crudely assembled bunch of letters cut from various papers and magazines spelling out WE MISS YOU MARTHA, indicating the universality of Martha's dance.

For by now Martha, too, had died, closing the history of American modern dance. With Graham's and Balanchine's passing, the American dance world had lost the two poles that anchored it for more than fifty years. Modern dance—the dance associated with Martha and the work of her progeny—was new, rebellious, and most important, utterly self-contained. On the other side, ballet represented tradition, a sense of history and continuity. Take the difference between Balanchine's and Graham's use of the flexed foot. When in a Balanchine piece, a dancer flexed a foot, breaking the line at the ankle, the movement was posed in relation to something else. Everyone knew the movement stated an option; the foot was "not pointed." Because Balanchine had such a strong sense of classical ballet, he could absorb this "wrong," this bent foot, into the larger vocabulary of dance; indeed, his often superficially unseemly innovations finally enriched the classical ballet's tradition. But when one of Graham's dancers flexed the foot, the movement wasn't contrary or perverse; it was a statement of primitive force and power, a movement not defined by what it wasn't, but by what it was, intact, whole, self-sufficient—a movement that came from Martha herself: gnarled ancient legs and grotesquely deformed feet planted flat on the earth, energy bearing straight down.

At the time, Martha's insistence on creating from scratch was a source of originality and energy. But this impulse to do something simply for itself, in defiance of the wider world, has shrunk in, become increasingly self-referential and hermetic. The two attitudes, represented by Graham and Balanchine, like the two techniques, are no longer either / or, no longer a "modern" dance separate from a "classical" dance. Now there is just one dance in our past. How to protect and extend the lessons and beauty of that past without burying our own energies and imagination is the challenge for every artist.

All these feelings rush about me at City Center as I thank the ghosts for their abundance and decide to let them go. This happens as I work, always beginning the day alone, stretching, warming, strengthening to begin taking possession of the stage. It happens as I focus on my material and on how I want it to reach out to those empty seats. The new work now has a name. Plays are often called "pieces," and because I think of the work Kevin and I are doing more as theatre than as dance, it is called *The Men's Piece*. About my attempt to know men individually, not generically, it evolved along with my developing relationship with Jesse. It is a dance with language, a series of duets whose arc spans the beginning, which is a canon—Kevin's part simply reflecting and echoing my own—through a duet reminiscent of Astaire and Rogers, in which both roles are romantically idealistic (she often supported by him), to a final duet in which the two partners support one another through equal force. An isometric duet, it is left loose, improvised from day to day, allowing things to breathe. I had sketched this before, in the very first partnering I ever did, with the very first lift, in the Haydn quartet of *The Bix Pieces*. However, only the placement of that lift had been flexible—where it would happen in the quartet; the lift itself was always the same. In the last duet of *The Men's Piece*, very little had to be set because I knew that if my partner dropped me, I could catch myself.

The piece was finished but only days old when I asked Jerry Robbins to a rehearsal. Afterward he told me I was pushing and reminded me of the Stanislavsky circle, that small area you find about yourself and into which you quietly bring your audience.

Brahms/Handel: Maria Calegari, Jock Soto, 1988

"And remember," he said, grinning on his way out, "they want to like you."

I began to work with this in mind. I asked myself, Where was this circle, other than on this bare stage? That was too vague, the circle had to be more specific. The answer was easy: the circle was my Sundance living room, a place where I could entertain. Working to extend the circle just a little, I put one empty folding chair on the front of the stage facing back at me. Then I needed someone in that chair. Suddenly there she sat. In fact there she sat, Moms, in every one of the house's three thousand seats. But as I worked I found I was no longer asking her permission or needing her approval. Dancing and speaking to that empty chair, I was calm, for now I was simply sharing this new work with her. Afterward I could thank her truthfully for taking the time to listen, thank that vast sea of Mom faces out there and almost feel a decent stage bow taking form because I was no longer beholden. I felt intact.

The Men's Piece premiered at Ohio State University in October

The Men's Piece: with Jamie Bishton, 1991

1991, the Wexner Center sponsoring a residency that made its production possible. In New York, at City Center, the season began selling out early, and I finally felt like a commercial-world grown-up when scalpers started getting two to three times the box-office price for orchestra seats. We managed, however, to keep the second-balcony tickets popularly priced at fifteen dollars. This was only possible because the overall venture got additional funding from several very special friends. While the foundation received a fee, I worked, as so often in the past, with no salary at all for eight months. This once, however, I did not mind so very much, because audiences were rooting for us and we all loved being able to deliver. As always, my ultimate payback was the lessons I learned.

The Men's Piece is dedicated to Jesse turning twenty-one. He's suffered the various adolescent traumas, I with him. But unlike me at his age, he has been in the world. I know he is angry with me, somewhat justifiably and somewhat not, just as I am with my mother. But I have turned a corner, letting her get far enough away for me to say thank you. There is great energy as I close a chapter, thanking her for my children, both the one by my side, whom I love dearly, and that earlier one, the one who first showed up in Quail Canyon, daring to take on a stunned snake to perform the ancient rites. Finally I can feel that my attempts to discover truth through objective distance have linked up with my gut, bringing my feelings into focus, allowing my own passion to flow into my classical forms. Letting the anger unify with the gratitude, I have made one dance, not two. I will continue to learn, but the apprenticeship is over. Finally I can feel I have caught up with myself.

Very special thanks to
Laura Shapiro,
Charles Michener,
Lewis Cole,
Nena Couch,
and Beverly Lewis.

TWYLA THARP
DANCE CHRONOLOGY

1965:

TWYLA THARP, MARGARET JENKINS

TANK DIVE
Premiere: *April 29, Room 1604, Hunter College Art Department, New York City.*
Costumes: *Robert Huot.*
Lighting: *Jennifer Tipton.*

STAGE SHOW
Performed: *June and July, Alaskan Pavilion, New York World's Fair, Queens, New York.*

STRIDE
Choreographed: *August and September.*
Costumes: *Robert Huot.*
Cameraman: *Robert Barry.*

CEDE BLUE LAKE
Premiere: *December 1, Room 1604, Hunter College Art Department, New York City.*
Costumes: *Robert Huot.*
Lighting: *Jennifer Tipton.*

UNPROCESSED
Premiere: *December 1, Room 1604, Hunter College Art Department, New York City.*
Costumes: *Robert Huot.*
Lighting: *Jennifer Tipton.*

TWYLA THARP DANCE CHRONOLOGY

1966:

TWYLA THARP, MARGARET JENKINS, SARA RUDNER

RE-MOVES
Premiere: *October 29, Judson Memorial Church, New York City.*
Costumes: *Robert Huot.*
Lighting: *Jennifer Tipton.*

YANCEY DANCE
Premiere: *October 29, Judson Memorial Church, New York City.*
Costumes: *Robert Huot.*
Lighting: *Jennifer Tipton.*

1967:

TWYLA THARP, MARGARET JENKINS, SARA RUDNER, THERESA DICKINSON, MARGERY
TUPLING, CAROL LAUDENSLAGER

ONE TWO THREE
Premiere: *February 18, Kunstverein Museum, Stuttgart, Germany.*

JAM
Premiere: *February 23, Stedelijk Museum, Amsterdam, Holland.*
Costumes: *Robert Huot.*

DISPERSE
Premiere: *April 27, Richmond Professional Institute, Richmond,*
  Virginia.
Costumes: *Robert Huot.*
Lighting: *Jennifer Tipton.*

THREE PAGE SONATA FOR FOUR
Premiere: *July 6, State University of New York, Potsdam, New York.*
Costumes: *Robert Huot.*
Lighting: *Jennifer Tipton.*

FOREVERMORE
Premiere: *August 27, Midsummer Inc., Southampton, New York.*
Costumes: *Robert Huot.*
Lighting: *Jennifer Tipton.*

1968:

TWYLA THARP, SARA RUDNER, THERESA DICKINSON, MARGERY TUPLING, CAROL
LAUDENSLAGER, SHEILA RAJ, GRACIELA FIGUEROA, ROSE MARIE WRIGHT

GENERATION

Premiere: *February 9, Wagner College Gymnasium, Staten Island, New
York.*
Costumes: *Robert Huot.*
Lighting: *Jennifer Tipton.*

ONE WAY

Premiere: *February 9, Wagner College Gymnasium, Staten Island, New
York.*
Costumes: *Robert Huot.*
Lighting: *Jennifer Tipton.*

EXCESS, IDLE, SURPLUS

Premiere: *April 29, Notre Dame University, South Bend, Indiana.*
Costumes: *Robert Huot.*
Lighting: *Jennifer Tipton.*

1969:

TWYLA THARP, SARA RUDNER, THERESA DICKINSON, MARGERY TUPLING, SHEILA RAJ,
GRACIELA FIGUEROA, ROSE MARIE WRIGHT

AFTER "SUITE"

Premiere: *February 3, Billy Rose Theatre, New York City.*
Costumes: *Robert Huot.*
Lighting: *Jennifer Tipton.*

GROUP ACTIVITIES

Premiere: *February 24, Opera House, Brooklyn Academy of Music, New
York.*
Costumes: *Robert Huot.*
Lighting: *Jennifer Tipton.*

MEDLEY

Premiere: *July 19, The American Dance Festival, Connecticut College,
New London, Connecticut.*

TWYLA THARP DANCE CHRONOLOGY

DANCING IN THE STREETS OF LONDON AND PARIS, CONTINUED IN STOCKHOLM AND SOMETIMES MADRID
Premiere: *November 11, Wadsworth Atheneum, Hartford, Connecticut.*

1970:

TWYLA THARP, SARA RUDNER, GRACIELA FIGUEROA, ROSE MARIE WRIGHT, STEPHANIE SIMMONS, ISABEL GARCIA-LORCA, BETTY FAIN, DANA REITZ, SYBILLE HAYN

PYMFFYPPMFYNM YPF
Premiere: *March 8, Sullins College, Bristol, Virginia.*

THE FUGUE
Premiere: *August, University of Massachusetts, Amherst.*

ROSE'S CROSS COUNTRY
Premiere: *August, University of Massachusetts, Amherst*

THE ONE HUNDREDS
Premiere: *August, University of Massachusetts, Amherst*

1971:

TWYLA THARP, SARA RUDNER, ROSE MARIE WRIGHT, ISABEL GARCIA-LORCA, BETTY FAIN, DANA REITZ, SYBILLE HAYN, CHRISTINA HAMM, KENNETH RINKER, MARY CURRY, NAOMI COHN

THE HISTORY OF UP AND DOWN, I AND II
Premiere: *January 22, Oberlin College, Oberlin, Ohio.*

EIGHT JELLY ROLLS
Premiere: *January 22, Oberlin College, Oberlin, Ohio.*
Revised: *September, New York Shakespeare Dance Festival.*
Costumes: *Kermit Love.*
Lighting: *Jennifer Tipton.*
Music: *Jelly Roll Morton and The Red Hot Peppers.*

THE WILLIE SMITH SERIES   *Seventeen hours of videotape made throughout the nine months of Ms. Tharp's pregnancy.*

MOZART SONATA, K.545
Premiere: *August, The Mall, Washington, D.C.*

TORELLI
Premiere: *May 28, Sunrise, Fort Tryon Park, New York City.*
Music: *Giuseppe Torelli*, Concerto in D Minor.

THE BIX PIECES
Premiere: *November 2, at the IX International Festival of Dance, Paris, France.*
Costumes: *Kermit Love.*
Lighting: *Jennifer Tipton.*
Music: *Bix Beiderbecke, performed by Paul Whiteman's Orchestra; "Abide with Me" by Thelonious Monk.*

1972:

TWYLA THARP, SARA RUDNER, ROSE MARIE WRIGHT, ISABEL GARCIA-LORCA, KENNETH RINKER, MARY CURRY, NAOMI COHN, NINA WEINER

THE RAGGEDY DANCES
Premiere: *October 26, ANTA Theatre, New York City.*
Costumes: *Kermit Love.*
Lighting: *Jennifer Tipton.*
Music: *Scott Joplin; Wolfgang Amadeus Mozart.*

1973:

TWYLA THARP, SARA RUDNER, ROSE MARIE WRIGHT, ISABEL GARCIA-LORCA, KENNETH RINKER, NINA WEINER, TOM RAWE, CAM LORENDO

DEUCE COUPE
Premiere: *February 8, The Joffrey Ballet, Chicago, Illinois.*
Costumes: *Scott Barrie.*
Lighting: *Jennifer Tipton.*
Music: *The Beach Boys.*

TWYLA THARP DANCE CHRONOLOGY

THE BIX PIECES   *A television production of the stage piece for CBS's* Camera Three.

AS TIME GOES BY
Premiere: *October 10, City Center, New York City.*
Costumes: *Chester Weinberg.*
Lighting: *Jennifer Tipton.*
Music: *Franz Joseph Haydn.*

1974:

TWYLA THARP, SARA RUDNER, ROSE MARIE WRIGHT, ISABEL GARCIA-LORCA, KENNETH RINKER, NINA WEINER, TOM RAWE

IN THE BEGINNINGS
Premiere: *January 26, Tyrone Guthrie Theatre, Minneapolis, Minnesota.*
Costumes: *Kermit Love.*
Lighting: *Jennifer Tipton.*

TWYLA THARP AND "EIGHT JELLY ROLLS"
First Airing: *May 12, London Weekend Television.*

ALL ABOUT EGGS   *A television work commissioned by station WGBH, Boston, Massachusetts.*
Costumes: *Kermit Love.*
Music: *Johann Sebastian Bach's* Cantata BWV 78.

THE BACH DUET
Premiere: *September 5, New York Shakespeare Dance Festival, New York City.*
Costumes: *Kermit Love; revised by Santo Loquasto in 1975.*
Lighting: *Jennifer Tipton.*

1975:

TWYLA THARP, ROSE MARIE WRIGHT, KENNETH RINKER, TOM RAWE, JENNIFER WAY,
NANNA WILSON, SHELLEY WASHINGTON

DEUCE COUPE II   *Remodeled version of* Deuce Coupe, *first
  choreographed with The Joffrey Ballet.*
Premiere: *February 1, St. Louis, Missouri.*
Set: *James Rosenquist.*
Costumes: *Scott Barrie.*
Lighting: *Jennifer Tipton.*
Music: *The Beach Boys.*

SUE'S LEG
Premiere: *February 21, the St. Paul Civic Center Theatre, St. Paul,
  Minnesota.*
Costumes: *Santo Loquasto.*
Lighting: *Jennifer Tipton.*

THE DOUBLE CROSS
Premiere: *February 21, the St. Paul Civic Center Theatre, St. Paul,
  Minnesota.*
Set and Costumes: *Santo Loquasto.*
Lighting: *Jennifer Tipton.*

OCEAN'S MOTION
Premiere: *June 21, Teatro Nuovo, Spoleto Festival, Spoleto, Italy.*
Costumes: *Santo Loquasto.*
Lighting: *Jennifer Tipton.*
Music: *Chuck Berry.*

THE RAGS SUITE FROM "THE RAGGEDY DANCES"
Costumes: *Santo Loquasto.*
Lighting: *Jennifer Tipton.*
Music: *Scott Joplin: "Fig Leaf Rag"; "The Ragtime Dance";
  Wolfgang Amadeus Mozart's* Variations in C Major, KV 265.

TWYLA THARP DANCE CHRONOLOGY

1976:

TWYLA THARP, ROSE MARIE WRIGHT, KENNETH RINKER, TOM RAWE, JENNIFER WAY, SHELLEY WASHINGTON, LARRY GRENIER, CHRISTINE UCHIDA

PUSH COMES TO SHOVE
Premiere: *January 9, The Uris Theatre, New York City.*
Costumes: *Santo Loquasto.*
Lighting: *Jennifer Tipton.*
Music: *Franz Joseph Haydn and Joseph Lamb.*

SUE'S LEG, REMEMBERING THE THIRTIES
First airing: *March 24, Public Broadcasting System, Dance in America series.*

GIVE AND TAKE
Premiere: *March 26, Opera House, Brooklyn Academy of Music, New York.*
Costumes: *Santo Loquasto.*
Lighting: *Jennifer Tipton.*
Music: *Gregor Werner, John Philip Sousa, Edwin Franko, Frank Meacham and Ann Ronell.*

ONCE MORE, FRANK
Premiere: *July 12, New York State Theatre, New York.*
Costumes: *Santo Loquasto.*
Lighting: *Jennifer Tipton.*
Music: *Recordings by Frank Sinatra.*

COUNTRY DANCES
Premiere: *September 4, Edinburgh Festival, Scotland.*
Costumes: *Santo Loquasto.*
Lighting: *Jennifer Tipton.*
Music: *Adapted by Richard Peaslee from traditional American country music.*

HAPPILY EVER AFTER
Premiere: *November 3, City Center, New York City.*
Costumes: *Santo Loquasto.*
Lighting: *Jennifer Tipton.*
Music: *Adapted by Richard Peaslee from traditional American country music.*

AFTER ALL   *Choreographed for gold-medal figure skater John Curry, commissioned by the New York State Olympic Committee.*
Premiere: *November 15, Madison Square Garden, New York City.*
Costumes: *Santo Loquasto.*
Lighting: *Jennifer Tipton.*
Music: *Tomaso Albinoni,* Concerto for Trumpet in B Flat.

1977:

TWYLA THARP, ROSE MARIE WRIGHT, TOM RAWE, JENNIFER WAY, SHELLEY WASHINGTON, CHRISTINE UCHIDA, RAYMOND KURSHALS, RICHARD COLTON, KIMMARY WILLIAMS, JOSEPH LENNON, ANTHONY FERRO, and SARA RUDNER. SPECIAL GUEST ARTISTS: GARY CHRYST,* KENNETH RINKER

MUD
Premiere: *May 12, Opera House, Brooklyn Academy of Music, New York.*
Costumes: *Santo Loquasto.*
Lighting: *Jennifer Tipton.*
Music: *Wolfgang Amadeus Mozart.*

SIMON MEDLEY
Premiere: *May 12, Opera House, Brooklyn Academy of Music, New York.*
Costumes: *Santo Loquasto.*
Lighting: *Jennifer Tipton.*
Music: *Paul Simon.*

MAKING TELEVISION DANCE, A VIDEOTAPE BY TWYLA THARP
First airing: *October 4, nationally over the Public Broadcasting System.*
Costumes: *Santo Loquasto.*
Music: *"Snuffy" Jenkins, "Pappy" Sherill, and The Hired Hands.*

CACKLIN' HEN
Premiere: *May 12, Opera House, Brooklyn Academy of Music, New York.*
Costumes: *Santo Loquasto.*
Lighting: *Jennifer Tipton.*
Music: *Adapted by Richard Peaslee from traditional American country music.*

* Appearing courtesy of The Joffrey Ballet.

TWYLA THARP DANCE CHRONOLOGY

1978:

TWYLA THARP, ROSE MARIE WRIGHT, TOM RAWE, JENNIFER WAY, SHELLEY WASHINGTON, CHRISTINE UCHIDA, RAYMOND KURSHALS, RICHARD COLTON, KIMMARY WILLIAMS, JOSEPH LENNON, ANTHONY FERRO, WILLIAM WHITENER, FRANCE MAYOTTE, JOHN CARRAFA, and SARA RUDNER

HAIR   *Choreography by Twyla Tharp for the United Artists feature film directed by Milos Forman.*
Film Release date: March 12, 1979, Ziegfeld Theatre, New York City.

1979:

TWYLA THARP, ROSE MARIE WRIGHT, TOM RAWE, JENNIFER WAY, SHELLEY WASHINGTON, CHRISTINE UCHIDA, RAYMOND KURSHALS, RICHARD COLTON, ANTHONY FERRO, WILLIAM WHITENER, FRANCE MAYOTTE, JOHN CARRAFA, KATIE GLASNER, JOHN MALASHOCK, MARY ANN KELLOGG, SHELLEY FREYDONT, and SARA RUDNER

1903
Premiere: *February 15, Opera House, Brooklyn Academy of Music, New York.*
Costumes: *Santo Loquasto.*
Lighting: *Jennifer Tipton.*
Music: *Randy Newman.*

CHAPTERS & VERSES
Premiere: *February 15, Opera House, Brooklyn Academy of Music, New York.*
Costumes: *Santo Loquasto.*
Lighting: *Jennifer Tipton.*

BAKER'S DOZEN
Premiere: *February 15, Opera House, Brooklyn Academy of Music, New York.*
Costumes: *Santo Loquasto.*
Lighting: *Jennifer Tipton.*
Music: *Willie "The Lion" Smith.*

1980:

TWYLA THARP, ROSE MARIE WRIGHT, TOM RAWE, JENNIFER WAY, SHELLEY WASHINGTON, CHRISTINE UCHIDA, RAYMOND KURSHALS, RICHARD COLTON, ANTHONY FERRO, WILLIAM WHITENER, JOHN CARRAFA, KATIE GLASNER, JOHN MALASHOCK, MARY ANN KELLOGG, SHELLEY FREYDONT, KEITH YOUNG, and SARA RUDNER

THREE FANFARES   *A work commissioned by the Lake Placid Olympic Committee for the closing ceremonies of the 1980 Winter Olympics. Performed by: gold-medal figure skater John Curry.*

BRAHMS' PAGANINI
Premiere: *March 24, Winter Garden Theatre, New York City.*
Costumes: *Ralph Lauren.*
Lighting: *Jennifer Tipton.*
Music: *Johannes Brahms'* Paganini Variations.

WHEN WE WERE VERY YOUNG
Premiere: *March 26, Winter Garden Theatre, New York City.*
Sets and Costumes: *Santo Loquasto.*
Lighting: *Jennifer Tipton.*
Music: *John Simon.*

DANCE IS A MAN'S SPORT TOO   *Choreographed for NYCB's Peter Martins, Pittsburgh Steelers wide receiver Lynn Swann.*
First airing: *ABC's* Omnibus.

ASSORTED QUARTETS
Premiere: *July 29, Saratoga Performing Arts Center, Saratoga Springs, New York.*
Costumes: *Santo Loquasto.*
Lighting: *Jennifer Tipton.*
Music: *Traditional fiddle reels.*

SHORT STORIES
Premiere: *September 29, Opera House, Ghent, Belgium.*
Costumes: *Santo Loquasto.*
Lighting: *Jennifer Tipton.*
Music: *Supertramp; Bruce Springsteen.*

TWYLA THARP DANCE CHRONOLOGY

THIRD SUITE
Premiere: *October 6, Théâtre Champs-Elysées, Paris, France.*
Costumes: *Santo Loquasto.*
Lighting: *Jennifer Tipton.*
Music: *Johann Sebastian Bach*, Third Suite for Orchestra.

RAGTIME   *Reconstruction of period dancing for the Dino de Laurentiis film, directed by Milos Forman.*

1981:
TWYLA THARP, ROSE MARIE WRIGHT, TOM RAWE, JENNIFER WAY, SHELLEY WASHINGTON, CHRISTINE UCHIDA, RAYMOND KURSHALS, RICHARD COLTON, WILLIAM WHITENER, JOHN CARRAFA, KATIE GLASNER, JOHN MALASHOCK, MARY ANN KELLOGG, SHELLEY FREYDONT, KEITH YOUNG, AMY SPENCER, BARBARA HOON, and SARA RUDNER

UNCLE EDGAR DYED HIS HAIR RED
Premiere: *May 1, Elmira, New York.*
Costumes: *Santo Loquasto.*
Lighting: *Jennifer Tipton.*
Music: *Dick Sebouh.*

THE CATHERINE WHEEL
Premiere: *September 22, Winter Garden Theatre, New York City.*
Sets and Costumes: *Santo Loquasto.*
Lighting: *Jennifer Tipton.*
Music: *Commissioned score by David Byrne.*

CONFESSIONS OF A CORNERMAKER   *A videotape directed by Twyla Tharp featuring* Baker's Dozen, Short Stories, *and* Duet from the Third Suite
First airing: *October 13, CBS Cable.*

1982:

TWYLA THARP, ROSE MARIE WRIGHT, TOM RAWE, JENNIFER WAY, SHELLEY WASHINGTON, CHRISTINE UCHIDA, RAYMOND KURSHALS, RICHARD COLTON, WILLIAM WHITENER, JOHN CARRAFA, KATIE GLASNER, JOHN MALASHOCK, MARY ANN KELLOGG, SHELLEY FREYDONT, KEITH YOUNG, AMY SPENCER, BARBARA HOON, and SARA RUDNER

NINE SINATRA SONGS

Premiere: *October 14, Queen Elizabeth Theatre, Vancouver, British Columbia.*
Costumes: *Oscar de la Renta.*
Lighting: *Jennifer Tipton.*
Music: *Recordings by Frank Sinatra.*

BAD SMELLS

Premiere: *October 15, Queen Elizabeth Theatre, Vancouver, British Columbia.*
Costumes: *Santo Loquasto.*
Lighting: *Jennifer Tipton.*
Music: *Glenn Branca.*

SCRAPBOOK TAPE   *A video anthology of Twyla Tharp's works since 1965, directed by Twyla Tharp.*
First airing: *October 25, Public Broadcasting System.*

1983:

TWYLA THARP, TOM RAWE, JENNIFER WAY, SHELLEY WASHINGTON, CHRISTINE UCHIDA, RAYMOND KURSHALS, RICHARD COLTON, WILLIAM WHITENER, JOHN CARRAFA, KATIE GLASNER, JOHN MALASHOCK, MARY ANN KELLOGG, SHELLEY FREYDONT, KEITH YOUNG, AMY SPENCER, BARBARA HOON, ROBERT RADFORD, and SARA RUDNER

THE CATHERINE WHEEL   *A television special based on the original stage production.*
First airing: *March 1, British Broadcasting Company.*
First U.S. airing: *March 28, Public Broadcasting System for "Dance in America" series.*

FAIT ACCOMPLI

Premiere: *November 9, University of Texas Concert Hall, Austin, Texas.*
Costumes: *Santo Loquasto.*
Lighting: *Jennifer Tipton.*
Music: *Commissioned score by David Van Tieghem.*

THE GOLDEN SECTION   *The final section of the full-evening work*
   The Catherine Wheel.
Sets and Costumes: *Santo Loquasto.*
Lighting: *Jennifer Tipton.*
Music: *Commissioned score by David Byrne.*

TELEMANN
Premiere: *November 9, University of Texas Concert Hall, Austin, Texas.*
Costumes: *Santo Loquasto.*
Lighting: *Jennifer Tipton.*
Music: *Georg Philipp Telemann*, Concerto in E Major.

1984:

TWYLA THARP, TOM RAWE, JENNIFER WAY, SHELLEY WASHINGTON, RAYMOND
KURSHALS, RICHARD COLTON, WILLIAM WHITENER, JOHN CARRAFA, KATIE GLASNER,
JOHN MALASHOCK, MARY ANN KELLOGG, SHELLEY FREYDONT, KEITH YOUNG, AMY
SPENCER, BARBARA HOON, ROBERT RADFORD, KEVIN O'DAY, and SARA RUDNER

THE LITTLE BALLET
Premiere: *April 1, Northrup Auditorium, Minneapolis, Minnesota.*
Costumes: *Santo Loquasto.*
Lighting: *Jennifer Tipton.*
Music: *Alexander Glazunov*, Scenes de Ballet.

BRAHMS/HANDEL
Premiere: *June 7, New York State Theatre, New York City.*
Costumes: *Oscar de la Renta.*
Lighting: *Jennifer Tipton.*
Music: *Brahms*, Variation and Fugue on a Theme by Handel.

SORROW FLOATS
Premiere: *July 7, The American Dance Festival, Durham, North
   Carolina.*
Costumes and Stage Design: *Kermit Love.*
Lighting: *Jennifer Tipton.*
Music: *Georges Bizet*, Jeux d'Enfant.

AMADEUS
Choreographed: *May 1983, in Prague, Czechoslovakia.*
Film Release Date: *September 19, 1984.*

BARYSHNIKOV BY THARP   *An Emmy Award-winning television*
  special featuring Mikhail Baryshnikov in Push Comes to Shove,
  Sinatra Suite, *and* The Little Ballet.
First airing: *October 5, Public Broadcasting System.*
Directed by: *Twyla Tharp and Don Mischer.*
Produced by: *Don Mischer.*

BACH PARTITA
Premiere: *December 9, Kennedy Center for the Performing Arts,*
  Washington, D.C.
Costumes: *Santo Loquasto.*
Lighting: *Jennifer Tipton.*
Music: *Johann Sebastian Bach,* Partita No. 2 in D Minor.

SINATRA SUITE
Premiere: *December 9, Kennedy Center for the Performing Arts,*
  Washington, D.C.
Costumes: *Oscar de la Renta.*
Lighting: *Jennifer Tipton.*
Music: *Recordings by Frank Sinatra.*

1985:

TWYLA THARP, TOM RAWE, JENNIFER WAY, SHELLEY WASHINGTON, RAYMOND
KURSHALS, RICHARD COLTON, WILLIAM WHITENER, JOHN CARRAFA, KATIE GLASNER,
JOHN MALASHOCK, MARY ANN KELLOGG, SHELLEY FREYDONT, AMY SPENCER,
BARBARA HOON, ROBERT RADFORD, KEVIN O'DAY, and SARA RUDNER

SINGIN' IN THE RAIN   *Choreographed and directed by Twyla*
  Tharp: the Broadway musical based on the original screenplay.
Premiere: *July 2, 1985, Gershwin Theatre, New York City.*
Orchestrations: *Larry Wilcox.*
Screenplay adaptation: *Betty Comden and Adolph Green.*
Costumes: *Ann Roth.*
Lighting: *Jennifer Tipton.*

WHITE NIGHTS
Film Release Date: *December 6, 1985.*

TWYLA THARP DANCE CHRONOLOGY

1986:

TWYLA THARP, SHELLEY WASHINGTON, RICHARD COLTON, WILLIAM WHITENER, CHRISTINE UCHIDA, JOHN CARRAFA, KEVIN O'DAY, JAMIE BISHTON, ERZSEBET FOLDI, STEPHANIE FOSTER, JULIE NAKAGAWA, CATHY OPPENHEIMER, ELLEN TROY, KAREN STASICK, KEVIN SANTEE, CHERYL JONES, MICHAEL SCHUMACHER

IN THE UPPER ROOM
Premiere: *August 28, Ravinia Festival, Highland Park, Illinois.*
Costumes: *Norma Kamali.*
Lighting: *Jennifer Tipton.*
Music: *Philip Glass.*

BALLARE
Premiere: *August 30, Ravinia Festival, Highland Park, Illinois.*
Costumes: *William Ivey Long.*
Lighting: *Jennifer Tipton.*
Music: *Wolfgang Amadeus Mozart.*

1987:

TWYLA THARP, TOM RAWE, SHELLEY WASHINGTON, RICHARD COLTON, WILLIAM WHITENER, JOHN CARRAFA, AMY SPENCER, KEVIN O'DAY, JAMIE BISHTON, ERZSEBET FOLDI, STEPHANIE FOSTER, JULIE NAKAGAWA, CATHY OPPENHEIMER, ELLEN TROY, KAREN STASICK, KEVIN SANTEE, CHERYL JONES, MICHAEL SCHUMACHER, ELAINE KUDO, GIL BOGGS, DANNY SANCHEZ, KATE LANGAN, KRISTA SWENSON

1988:

TWYLA THARP, TOM RAWE, JENNIFER WAY, SHELLEY WASHINGTON, RICHARD COLTON, AMY SPENCER, KEVIN O'DAY, JAMIE BISHTON, STEPHANIE FOSTER, ELLEN TROY, ELAINE KUDO, GIL BOGGS, DANNY SANCHEZ, KATE LANGAN, KRISTA SWENSON, ROBERT MOSES, KEVIN SANTEE

1989:

TWYLA THARP with AMERICAN BALLET THEATRE: including SHELLEY WASHINGTON, RICHARD COLTON, KEVIN O'DAY, JAMIE BISHTON, ELAINE KUDO, GIL BOGGS, DANNY SANCHEZ

QUARTET
Premiere: *February 4, Theatre for the Performing Arts, Miami Beach, Florida.*
Costumes: *Santo Loquasto.*
Lighting: *Jennifer Tipton.*
Music: *Terry Riley,* G Song.

BUM'S RUSH
Premiere: *February 8, Civic Opera House, Chicago, Illinois.*
Set and Costumes: *Santo Loquasto.*
Lighting: *Jennifer Tipton.*
Music: *Dick Hyman.*

RULES OF THE GAME
Premiere: *February 17, L'Opéra de Paris, France.*
Sets and Costumes: *Gilles Dufour.*
Lighting: *Serge Peyrat.*
Music: *Johann Sebastian Bach*, Violin Sonata in G Minor BWV 1001.

EVERLAST
Premiere: *March 2, War Memorial Opera House, San Francisco, California.*
Set and Costumes: *Santo Loquasto.*
Lighting: *Jennifer Tipton.*
Music: *Jerome Kern.*
Arrangements and Continuity: *Michael Dansicker.*
Orchestration: *William Brohn.*
Scenario: *James Jones.*

1990:

TWYLA THARP with AMERICAN BALLET THEATRE: including SHELLEY
WASHINGTON, KEVIN O'DAY, JAMIE BISHTON, ELAINE KUDO, GIL BOGGS

BRIEF FLING
Premiere: *February 28, War Memorial Opera House, San Francisco, California.*
Costumes: *Isaac Mizrahi.*
Lighting: *Jennifer Tipton.*
Music: *Percy Grainger's "Country Gardens"; "Handel in the Strand."*

TWYLA THARP DANCE CHRONOLOGY

1991:

TWYLA THARP, HOMER AVILA, ROGER BELMAN, JAMIE BISHTON, ALLISON BROWN, STACY CADDELL, MAURI CRAMER, LIONEL DELANOE,* STEPHANE ELIZABE,* ISABELLE GUERIN,* ROBERT LAFOSSE,† PAUL LESTER, JODI MELNICK, DELPHINE MOUSSIN,* AMY O'BRIEN, KEVIN O'DAY, SHAWN STEVENS, MICHAEL WHAITES, KEITH YOUNG, AND SHELLEY WASHINGTON, Ballet Mistress

GRAND PAS: RHYTHM OF THE SAINTS
Premiere: *October, L'Opéra de Paris, France.*
Costumes: *Santo Loquasto.*
Lighting: *Jennifer Tipton.*
Music: *Paul Simon.*

THE MEN'S PIECE
Premiere: *October, The Wexner Center for the Arts, Ohio State University, Columbus, Ohio.*
Costumes: *Santo Loquasto.*
Lighting: *David Finn.*

OCTET
Premiere: *October, The Wexner Center for the Arts, Ohio State University, Columbus, Ohio.*
Costumes: *Santo Loquasto.*
Lighting: *David Finn.*
Music: *Commissioned score by Edgar Meyer.*

1992:

TWYLA THARP, JAMIE BISHTON, ALLISON BROWN, STACY CADDELL, MAURI CRAMER, LIONEL DELANOE,* STEPHANE ELIZABE,* ISABELLE GUERIN,* ROBERT LAFOSSE,† PAUL LESTER, JODI MELNICK, GORDON WHITE, DELPHINE MOUSSIN,* AMY O'BRIEN, KEVIN O'DAY, SHAWN STEVENS, MICHAEL WHAITES, KEITH YOUNG, AND SHELLEY WASHINGTON, Ballet Mistress
Special Guest Artists: PATRICK DUPOND* and SARA RUDNER

SEXTET
Premiere: *January 30, City Center, New York City.*
Costumes: *Santo Loquasto.*
Lighting: *David Finn.*
Music: *Commissioned score by Bob Telson.*

* Appearing courtesy The Paris Opera Ballet.
† Appearing courtesy New York City Ballet.

CREDITS FOR PHOTOGRAPHS AND ILLUSTRATIONS

CREDITS FOR PHOTOGRAPHS AND ILLUSTRATIONS

INDEX

Page numbers in boldface refer to photographs.